Praise for the 2016 Shotgun Players production of HAMLET

"*A mind-bending new production... The actors' ability to pull off this* Hamlet *is simply awe-inspiring. And the format makes you examine your preconceptions of both the play and the nature of theater: All lines of gender, age and race will be crossed at some point.*"
– SAN FRANCISCO CHRONICLE

"*Uplifting and weirdly affecting... You immediately notice that there isn't a conventional Hamlet in the cast. They are a wonderfully eclectic bunch: men and women, a smattering of ages and races, even different acting styles... We are plunged into a democracy of infinite possibilities... A unique and rich response to the play... We should be thankful to witness such a circus of daring.*"
– KQED.ORG

"*The work is raw, rough, and unsentimental. [The] audience is called upon both intellectually and imaginatively to extend the performance far beyond what is materially presented in front of them... This is not 'gift shop Shakespeare.' It is not pretty, celebrity studded, or made topical. Jackson and his cast are excavating the essential text from under a lot of accumulated baggage, and what emerges is often highly original and gut wrenching.*"
– SHAKESPEARESTRIBE.COM

"*Absolutely terrific... Director Mark Jackson took a huge risk here, and maybe the tightrope-like conceit added necessary excitement and unfamiliarity (not to mention a little panic, surely, in the actors). But the staging and clarity of this* Hamlet *transcend any theatrical stunt and polish Shakespeare's old yet ever-relevant chestnut anew... I left eager to see the play again.*"
– 48HILLS.ORG

"*It's a daunting premise, but one that the cast of director Mark Jackson's* Hamlet *pulled off with wild success... By opening up* Hamlet *to thousands of possible casting combinations, Jackson inevitably defies traditional assumptions about the gender, age and race of the play's well-known characters... This spontaneous diversity seizes upon the universality of Shakespeare's work in a way that many other productions fail to — fully revealing the kernels of common humanity within each character... An exhilarating journey, and one that manages to stoke the audience's appreciation for the very mechanics of theater while its powerhouse cast brings new vitality — and vigor — to a well-known play.*"
– EAST BAY EXPRESS

PLAYING HAMLET ROULETTE

Failure, Expectation, Possibility & Democracy

EDITED BY

Mark Jackson

EXIT PRESS
SAN FRANCISCO

Published by EXIT Press
First Edition: November 2017
Cover design by Kevin Clarke
Book design by Mark Jackson
Cover photos by Pak Han, used with permission, from the 2016 Shotgun
Players production of *Hamlet*. www.pakhan.com

For additional information about U.S. copyright laws go to:
www.copyright.gov

For additional information about The Shotgun Players go to:
www.shotgunplayers.org

For additional information about Mark Jackson go to:
www.markjackson-theatermaker.com

ISBN: 978-1-941704-14-1

EXIT Press
156 Eddy Street
San Francisco, CA 94102-2708
USA
www.exittheatre.org

for the seven Hamlets
five designers
two stage managers
our guest Laertes
the Shotgun Players staff
and those many audience members who came to see the show
anywhere from two to thirty-six times
(that's right I said thirty-six)

thine ever

Contents

Foreword:
Toward a Culture of Accountability
Patrick Dooley
Artistic Director

Pioneers of uncharted territories, survivors of trauma, and others who have achieved the unimaginable through sheer will and endurance capture the imagination because they challenge us to set higher expectations for ourselves. If someone can survive ten days buried under rubble, certainly I can keep my wits while changing a tire in a thunderstorm! The theatrical ventures that have always held the most allure for me are those where the complexity and potency of the material is matched only by the physical, intellectual, and emotional challenge of bringing the story to life. I like sweat with my truth.

In twenty-six years of running The Shotgun Players, I've had the privilege of helping create some of these rare pieces. Productions that catapult into the imagination and lodge in our consciousness, because they are a spectacular fusion of truth and human achievement. What's kept Shotgun going all these years is not that we've always succeeded in reaching this goal. We usually don't. It's that we never give up trying.

I remember where I was standing when Mark Jackson first laid out this fantastic idea of a *Hamlet* where a company of actors would learn the entire play and choose roles from a hat. The opportunity to produce something like this, where both audience and actor could explore the intricacies of this masterpiece through the shifting lenses of race, gender, age, and sexual orientation, was intoxicating. The depths of truth and layers of humanity that could be revealed seemed limitless. And the CHALLENGE! Stepping into the world of *Hamlet* is intimidating enough. Submitting oneself to the chaos of possibilities felt terrifying. How could we *not* do it?!?

Shotgun's mission has essentially been a call to create theatre that challenges us to re-examine our lives, our community, and the ever-changing world around us. But is that enough? The current confluence of social, political, and environmental tipping points emerging around the world is shining a light on fence sitters. For theatre to be relevant to this moment—for it to make a difference—it must propel us from examination to *action*. We'd always hoped the sheer audacity of this production would inspire audiences to step outside their own limitations. It also provoked us, as creators, to set higher expectations—and perhaps craft a new mission—for our work.

This book is an extension of that same impulse. Just as we hope our theatre will compel audiences to be a catalyst in the ever-changing world around them, we invite you, the reader of this book, to participate in the conversation it elicits. A culture of accountability is a cornerstone of a healthy society. A great play must be alive and responsive to the times. So too—we hope—will this book be, and, ultimately, one another.

Foreword:
The Impossible Is Possible
Carolyn Jones
Board Member

It has been said that there is nothing new under the sun. On the other hand, when seven actors learn an entire play and then each night, at show time, pick the characters they will perform out of a hat, well, maybe that's new. The *Hamlet* roulette was the inspired brainchild of Mark Jackson, a consummate theatre maker, who was given the basic idea by a fellow playwright, Clark Morgan, in conversation some years ago. Mark carried the idea around for a time and then over coffee mentioned it to Patrick Dooley, the artistic director of the Shotgun Players. I have been on the Shotgun board for about seven years, and Patrick and I have a long history of batting around our notions about plays and theatre and making things work and one day he happened to let slip this idea of the *Hamlet* roulette. It sounded impossible. And thrilling. As the idea continued to germinate it became clear there would be huge challenges in nearly every aspect of the endeavor. But the more we thought about it the more excited we got.

All of this is much simpler in the telling than in the actual process of bringing it about. You would need talented, intrepid actors who would also make the time commitment. You would surely need to perform longer than the usual six week run; After all they would be memorizing *Hamlet*. All of *Hamlet*. And since it was the Shotgun Players' twenty-fifth anniversary season we were already celebrating by doing something else big: a repertory year, five wonderful plays with the same actors appearing in two, three, even four at once. They had to be excellent, and willing. And we would definitely need the cooperation and support of our board of directors.

As a member of the board, I have seen extraordinary growth and extraordinary artistic success at Shotgun. We have taken on challenges that I'd never have expected, both financially and artistically, and the board itself has grown from the process of supporting and accommodating these challenges. However, the repertory season was an entirely different animal. We were going to have actors commit to an entire year—so now they were employees and not independent contractors. The unions were initially unwilling to make concessions in spite of the unusual circumstance and the fact that we have a very small house. The repertory would also impact our stage and house crews, lighting, set and sound designers. We highly value our artists and staff, and wanted to make sure they could survive this endeavor. I will tell you that not everyone on the board was immediately on board. It took some real convincing for some of them to be willing to take this financial and artistic leap. But one by one they acquiesced and then it became not if we would do it but how. We had a tremendously strong fundraiser among our board members who had great enthusiasm for the project and who led us on. It was a great experiment and absolutely everybody was "in."

There are lots of stories in this book about how the *Hamlet* roulette came together—the actors, the house staff, the ever-growing number of audience members who came back again and again. I was among them often. We began to recognize each other. We became friends. We were, and are, all Hamlet. The experiment worked, proving the impossible *is* possible. Not easy. But infinitely possible, when enough passionate individuals come together.

Foreword:
A Concept That Disappears Into Belief
John Wilkins
Critic

In the Shotgun Players' production of the *Hamlet* roulette, directed by Mark Jackson, we appear to have a concept, but what we really have is a set of beliefs: about people, the theatre, audiences, plays, and community. Like all true experiments, the concept is replicable but empty: take any play, have the cast memorize every part, line them up five minutes before the performance, and assign roles. It's a stunt and all you have to do is see it employed in less radical and meaningful ways—Brandon Jacobs-Jenkins' *Everybody*, for example—to realize how empty it is.

Shotgun's *Hamlet* roulette is not a concept at all, but in more daring fashion a series of aesthetic and social demands. The actor does not have ownership of the part, but is an extension of the production. The play is the source of all meaning, but that meaning is always unstable. The production is not meant for the ages, but only for the moment—that night, that audience, and that particular configuration of the cast. We're going to watch *Hamlet*, the most famous play in the Western canon, and we have no idea what's going to happen.

In contemporary American theatre we almost always know what's going to happen. Not because theatre is an ancient art that relies on ritual, but because our theatre has become a bland product of institutional edicts. For all the social aspects of the art, we seem to have forgotten that it is made by and for people. We talk about the cast and the audience, or maybe the playwright, the director, or a particular actor if any of them happen to be noteworthy stars, names that might sell a ticket. Yet they are all just place markers for an assembly line product.

So one fascinating aspect of the *Hamlet* roulette is the demand that we recognize people not as equals—that's too close to interchangeable parts—but as individuals. And you can feel it in every moment of the acting. This was never and could never be a settled production, where the actors slip into the repetitive rhythms that a long run brings. Instead, surprise becomes an aesthetic principle.

Each night every new scrambling of the cast forces a radical adjustment: I saw Nick Medina, a little doughy and youngish, and Cathleen Ridley, middle-aged and African-American, play Ophelia on successive nights. Each of them practically burst out of the role. They weren't becoming Shakespeare's suicidal waif, so much as taking her for a ride. How would Ophelia act if she had linebacker shoulders? Or if she had seen and felt our country's long history of racism? The production never attempts to answer those questions, which would have been ridiculous; rather, the production lets everything it touches run free.

What could have been a dry exercise becomes a celebration of each actor and their capacity for play and the vast resources they bring to a role. We often think of acting as a form of renunciation, a giving up of the self, a vanishing act. Here, there is no hiding who and what they are. They are the cast of *Hamlet*, but they are not Hamlet, Horatio, Claudius, Gertrude, Ophelia, Polonius, Laertes, or Rosencrantz and Guildenstern. Instead of actors—to borrow one of Hamlet's more theatrical pronouncements—they are the players.

And the players have to play for someone, so another tricky demand of the *Hamlet* roulette is that the audience is a creative force. At every moment we're negotiating at least three different productions. The one before us that chance has arranged for our benefit. All the other possibilities that we might have seen that night and didn't. And finally, the Platonic version of *Hamlet* that we carry with us, or the version we intuit from what's before us. So what we bring to the production is a kind of organizational imagination.

Jackson and his actors don't have to try to create the perfect *Hamlet*, where we all—artists and audiences—slink towards an ideal. Rather, they lead us to a provisional one that holds at bay the vast hordes of past and future productions that haunt Shakespeare's greatest tragedy. The casting roulette hints at the infinite, but each performance brings us a daring singularity. Here is the only version of *Hamlet* we will see tonight and it's a surprise to everyone involved.

The effect was electric. You could see the actors feeling their way through radically new variations of the play and production. At times, they actually seemed shocked by the events before them, as if they—like the characters they played—were experiencing these events for the first time. The casting might not be realistic, but the acting was brutally close to what it feels like to live in the chaos of the world.

What happens when you become Ophelia, or Gertrude, or Horatio, or, are thrown into any role in any version of a constantly changing cast? Or, most importantly, what happens when you suddenly become Hamlet? The answer that Jackson and his cast came up with appeared to be that you believe it no matter how ridiculous it seems. And that cuts to the heart of why this production was a triumph: it allowed us to imagine infinite possibilities, but to experience them as singular events. That all of it happened by chance made every single moment all the more real.

Foreword:
"Why, what an ass am I!"
Beth Wilmurt
Actor

I knew the task of learning all the roles in *Hamlet* was going to help me understand the play on a deeper level. It did that. But more so, in certain ways it forced me to understand myself. It made me confront my desire for control over my performance. My desire to be prepared. My desire to go deep. My desire to be present. In many respects the experience ended up being about getting by.

Going into it, on an intellectual level I understood that failure and accidents would be a part of it. But I didn't realize the extent to which we'd end up highlighting these things, and that there was no guarantee this emphasis meant audiences were going to think deeper about the play, its themes or its resonances. Despite the number of people who said they enjoyed it, there were still people who watched it and said *It's not good enough, not deep enough, the actors don't know their lines...* We couldn't escape that.

Thinking about all this in hindsight, and about why I find it difficult to write this foreword, I feel aware of my not wanting to portray my failure as a success by writing about why it all was good in the end. On some level I've even questioned the purpose of this book. Is it simply an attempt to save face in hindsight? But then I recognize how my question and my hesitations demonstrate that I'm still stuck in my own biased definition of failure, and still experiencing shame around it.

The successes of the *Hamlet* roulette for me personally were that I did get some Shakespeare in my mouth, something I've not done much of in my career. And over time some speeches did start to make sense to me on a much deeper level—not necessarily in performance but while walking around the streets of Berkeley and San Francisco repeating them over and over. Also, I lived to tell the tale. Had I never said "Yes" to the project, I'd never have done something that I was convinced I couldn't do.

The success of the production itself, I'd say, was that it was theatre that felt charged, every night. There was real adrenaline on stage. There wasn't a lot taken for granted. It was never on autopilot. It helped keep the audience in a more active place because there was actual risk taking place, as opposed to their being impressed by the effortlessness of a performance. As theatre makers we tell our audiences and ourselves that we're supposed to present dangerous and uncomfortable life situations on stage, to allow audiences to identify or to question what their own experience might be, or that of their neighbor. But when as artists we just portray these things with ease, the audience might be impressed by the acting, the set, a series of well executed choices, but not actually have to wrestle with the "messy" or "difficult" situations being presented, because nothing on stage is actually messy or difficult. So a success of our production is that it provided a real mess and real difficulties that kept the audience actually engaged.

During the run of the production I had an idea that we weren't really getting Hamlet's plight across, because to do that a group of actors need to be well rehearsed, slick, in the know, and "capable" in some unified, agreed-upon, prescribed way. One needs to be a star, or "a great actor," to properly present Hamlet's plight. But in performance I couldn't help but present my own actual plight, which was shame and dyslexia.

Hamlet's plight is of having been forced into a situation not of his choosing, and he behaves badly even as he's rigorously trying to get to the bottom of things. His father has been taken away from him, and he's been given a new father by his mother, and something about how this all came to pass seems conspiratorial. Something isn't right. Yet at the same time he doesn't fully take action to change anything, he repeatedly stops short, and he carries a lot of shame about his inability to see things through. He's very caught up in himself and his own perspective in the beginning of the play, and can't shake himself from his anger and frustration. But then toward the end of the play he comes to the insight to just let things be, that maybe he had perhaps been pushing too hard, forcing things. He realizes that ultimately he cannot control things:

> There's a special
> providence in the fall of a sparrow. If it be now,
> 'tis not to come. If it be not to come, it will be
> now. If it be not now, yet it will come. The
> readiness is all. Since no man has aught of what he
> leaves, what is't to leave betimes? Let be. *(Act 5 Scene 2)*

So in a certain way Hamlet's arc mirrored my own, or mine did his, in that my personal struggles—to learn the text, remember the staging, deliver the kind of detailed work I prefer to deliver—these struggles became the overwhelming concern of my experience. Did I myself ever get to the point of letting be? Am I still working through this? I'm not sure yet. I do think, though, a great personal outcome for me is having confronted my dyslexia in public, and understanding—accepting—that it's an undeniable part of who I am. This production shoved my dyslexia out of the closet. Instead of trying to hide it, I had no choice but to let it be a part of the show. I needed to be on book a lot and call for line in performance. Hearing the same lines out of a different face the next night was confusing. I didn't always know where to go or what costume to put on, and I had to ask for a lot of help. It was hard to ask for help, but I knew I had to. It was survival.

I connected most of all to the speech "O what a rogue and peasant slave am I." That soliloquy speaks to a deep frustration, the humiliation of not being able to do what you want to do. Hamlet is talking about an actor up on the stage. The actor can do things in a fake play, he says, so why can't I in real life? Like Hamlet I felt this gap in my abilities. Why couldn't I play Hamlet like an actor is supposed to play Hamlet? And I was an actor! A double shame!

> O, what a rogue and peasant slave am I!
> Is it not monstrous that a player, here,
> But in a fiction, in a dream of passion,
> Could force his soul so to his own conceit
> That from her working all his visage wann'd,
> Tears in his eyes, distraction in's aspect,
> A broken voice, and his whole function suiting
> With forms to his conceit? and all for nothing!
> What would he do,
> Had he the motive and the cue for passion
> That I have? He would drown the stage with tears
> And cleave the general ear with horrid speech,
> Make mad the guilty and appall the free,
> Confound the ignorant, and amaze indeed
> The very faculties of eyes and ears. Yet I,
> A dull and muddy-mettled rascal, do nothing.
> Am I a coward?
> Who calls me villain? breaks my pate across?
> Tweaks me by the nose? who does me this?
> Ha?
> 'Swounds, I should take it: for it cannot be,
> But I am pigeon-liver'd and lack gall,
> I should have fatted all the region kites
> With this slave's offal! Bloody, bawdy villain!
> Remorseless, treacherous, lecherous, kindless villain!
> O, vengeance!
> Why, what an ass am I! This is most brave,
> That I, the son of a dear father murder'd,
> Prompted to my revenge by heaven and hell,
> Must, like a whore, unpack my heart with words!
> Fie upon't! fie! *(Act 2 Scene 2)*

As actors we search for those moments when we meld with a character, when we feel that the character is coming through us or we're seeing through the character's eyes, and suddenly it no longer feels like a performance so much as a genuine engagement, not a portrayal but an authentic expression of something true. At times I felt this happen during this speech—not because I'd transformed myself into the character Hamlet but because I deeply believed what he and I were saying.

The main point I wish to make is that the audience actually needs to see artists struggle. They need that gap between reality and perfection so they can step in, empathize, understand the humanity of a play. *Hamlet* is a play populated by flawed individuals, yet the language can make one feel one must be an expert to do it or to understand it. So what does it mean to do Shakespeare when you simply can't be "expert" at it? This wasn't our own original insight. People have taken Shakespeare into prisons and done it with grammar schools, places where expertise is not the key for actors and audiences to connect with the play. These people and places demystify the sanctity of "expert" Shakespeare, and demonstrate its broad flexibility and accessibility. Yet even I, who believe this, went into the *Hamlet* roulette still holding tight to this other belief that I needed to be fluent, articulate in my speaking of the text, dynamic in my theatrical choices, in certain preconceived and acceptable ways. I didn't realize the degree to which I wasn't walking my own talk. I still thought I needed to be some particular kind of expert who does it "right."

There were times in the process when it was clear to me I was never going to remember all my lines, that I would continue to get confused, that we were all really going to have to lean on one another and in some ways that was really exciting. It's natural to always want to strive to do better. But sometimes it was exhilarating to go up on lines! I loved it and felt proud to call "Take it," which was our agreed upon signal to the prompter that you were so totally dry you needed them to take the text for a longer stretch and you would continue only with the movements until you got back on track with the words. The two times I did this were both in the moment of Hamlet's dying, and it actually made a weird, thrilling kind of theatrical sense for the poisoned, delirious, dying Hamlet's body to be in one place and her voice in another. Many people said they loved this. It was an accidental success that, had it been planned and staged, might have been a clever intellectual choice but not a real, visceral moment. But despite moments like that, at other times I felt ashamed. Maybe I feel most shameful when I allow my dyslexia to keep me from feeling alive and present. In those moments when I called "Take it," I was fully giving in to the given circumstances and was actually free, and it worked. Of couse, if I had really relaxed, I'd have forgotten lines constantly. So I never relaxed. Good thing, too, because in fact on closing night I pulled Hamlet again.

I'm one of many people who were involved in this production. It was the kind of task that anybody was going to have a memorable, sizable, potentially profound experience doing. And each of us on stage had different standards about what kind or extent of failure was okay and what wasn't. On a very basic level, the value of processing such an experience in the wake of it is hard to deny. To not take the time to do so would seem a greatly wasted opportunity. My own experience was so profound for me, and I know everyone else was confronted with innumerable personal and technical issues—every single one of us, from our stage managers, Nikita Kadam and Heather Kelly-Laws, to the actors, to Mark as director, the producers, everyone. Even the audience. To let that all disappear, remain packaged up in the past… It was so rich and challenging an experience that we owe it to ourselves and to the show to look at it, unpack it, question it, process it, and to attempt to put into words what we didn't have time or brain space to do while we were doing it. There was no time for reflection then. We had to just do it.

But I also want to say the book is not ultimately for those of us directly involved. The benefit, one of the most interesting things, is that the experience of the show speaks to a greater conversation about the question, Why theatre? And to the value of communal experiences in which failure and success so dramatically intermingle, how they are two sides of the same coin, not separate. As you'll read in this book, for audiences and artists alike the *Hamlet* roulette compelled an acceptance of our fellow humans, and of ourselves. That kind of acceptance, and the feelings and critical thinking that come of it, makes the world a better place.

Introduction
Mark Jackson

Books about specific theatre productions, usually Broadway musicals, are often written as a commemoration, a nostalgic souvenir recounting the chronology of a show's evolution and sold in the lobby. Then there are the production histories written about specific plays, tending toward the scholarly in their accounting of the given play's themes and how various productions over years and continents handled them and were received.

This book aspires to neither of these. Rather it uses the 2016 Shotgun Players production of *Hamlet*—an elaborate game of *Hamlet* roulette in which seven actors learned all the roles, each night drew from Yorick's skull which characters they would play, then had five minutes to get ready before BAM: show time!—to get at the four words in the book's subtitle: failure, expectation, possibility, and democracy. Considering these subjects within the context of this book, I offer the following starter-definitions:

> Failure—a problem, a creative opportunity, a crack in the plan offering the light or darkness needed for learning.

> Expectation—that ever-narrowing corral, that false hope and killer of creativity.

> Possibility—expectation's opposite, open to searching and to diversity.

> Democracy—that impossible ideal that in its full unfettered bloom is chaos, but of which societies nevertheless seek to exploit the merits by subjecting it to one control system or another.

These four subjects are what this book is ultimately about, with live theatre the venue for their consideration. The reason this particular production of *Hamlet* makes a worthy prompt for an exploration of these far-reaching themes will, I hope, be made clear over the course of the book's chapters, each of which focuses on a different aspect of the project. But in short, the production was such a monumental challenge for the artists involved, and their success at failing at it was such, that a remarkable number of audience members were compelled to return anywhere from two to thirty-six times while some left at intermission, and their varied and diverse responses begged many interesting questions.

The production's sixty performances were spread over the ten-month period of The Shotgun Player's 2016 repertory season, which also included productions of Penelope Skinner's *The Village Bike*, Heidi Schreck's *Grand Concourse*, Christopher Chen's *Caught* and Edward Albee's *Who's Afraid of Virginia Woolf?* So in addition to all the roles in *Hamlet*, the cast learned roles in those plays as well and by the season's final months were performing all five plays at once, complicating the task of *Hamlet* further. Audiences attending *Hamlet* were either gifted with or subject to—depending on who one asks—an experience of democracy that threw expectations of not only acting, Shakespeare, and theatre, but of gender, race, and age, into perpetual chaos, dislodging the world's most solidly famous play from its traditional effects and tossing it into the sociopolitical moment of the early twenty-first century, hyper-conscious as it is of the utter importance and vitality of difference.

To get at the questions this circumstance yields, the book—already well underway by this point with a full handful of introductory perspectives—first recounts the processes that went into creating the production. By describing various activities and points of view of the creative process, this initial chapter hopes not to provide a How-To report but rather to amass a productive mess that might compel creative reflection, and from which one might devise ideas for further creative processes that emphasize an awareness of the relationships between intent and impact. This chapter could be read in or out of order, by skipping ahead or circling back, and the reader is encouraged to take the path of their interest.

The subsequent chapter, on the other hand, is likely best read in the order written. Here the production itself is addressed, though not in the typical manner whereby the surface of things—plot, character interpretation, design, directorial choices—is journalistically relayed. It is instead a critical exploration of the *content of the experience*, its sociopolitical implications, and its place within recent international trends toward performance-making as an intervention that questions traditional modes of theatre-making with an eye toward change-making. This chapter also points toward other possible, non-rouletted aesthetic approaches to engaging audiences in critical thought.

The audience experience itself is then addressed directly in the third chapter, with commentary from multiple non-artist attendees. And finally, as a kind of elaborate appendix item, the script is included for reference and reflection—only because it was not possible to include sixty videos of the sixty *Hamlet* roulette performances, which together would have comprised the most accurate record of this production.

A single author would be entirely inappropriate for a book on all this. And so you will find my perspective as director of the show juxtaposed with the perspectives of actors, designers, critics, and audience members, and theirs with one another's. Commentary ranges from the anecdotal to the analytical, from casual and nostalgic to considered and critical. Some thoughts remain unfinished or inconclusive. Discrepancies of memory and of perception are left standing side by side, unresolved. There is a great deal of repetition throughout the book, but in the way *Rashomon* repeats— the same story told from different perspectives, and therefore ultimately different stories related by the central event but producing distinct impacts. This *Rashomon* effect speaks to a democracy of viewpoints in contrast to a capitalism of consensus. Its failure to achieve a singular coherence is its successful demonstration of truth's multiplicity.

Space is also made in the book for the reader to contribute. Specific questions are posed for consideration or written response. On nearly every page, there are footnotes with no note written and not yet given a footing within the main text, inviting your quick impressions should you choose to leave them, forever open to possibility if you don't. Likewise, entire pages are left blank in the event you or someone you lend the book to is compelled to add another point of view to the mix. Scribbling in the margins would also not be remiss. And the Conclusion(s) chapter is an open forum awaiting any reflections and arguments with which you might wish to punctuate the book. Hopefully these empty spaces allow the book to be a living, evolving document, echoing the sixty performances of the *Hamlet* roulette and their unrelenting openness to accident and surprise, ultimately making the book a unique account of each reader's reading of the events and ideas recounted herein. In these ways the reader is invited to help make the meaning(s) of the book.

Finally, I am very pleased that Clark Morgan has written the book's afterword, which bookends the four forewords and this introduction. The basic idea that a group of actors would learn all of *Hamlet* and at each performance draw their night's role from a hat was his. He shared it with me over drinks many years ago. We stirred this remote fantasy around in our beer and marveled at how difficult but surely exciting it would be, and I never forgot it. After I told Patrick Dooley about it and he was keen that we do it, I asked Clark for permission but Clark said he wanted to do it himself one day. Some years later, around 2014, Patrick pressed the issue again. I gave Clark an ultimatum: that if he did not produce the show within two years, dishonor among thieves would kick in and I would steal it. Clark agreed. Toward the end of the run he came to see the production twice, and, to my relief and delight, embraced it with great enthusiasm. That he now ends a book about this idea that began with him is perhaps incongruously neat and tidy, given the messy nature of the project that the book hopes to preserve. But I accept this minor bit of inconsistency alongside the rest, and with gratitude. Thank you Clark. And if you have any more outlandish ideas, the first drink is on me.

Okay.
Here we go.

Process(es)
Mark Jackson

With annotations and commentary by Heather Basarab,
El Beh, Kevin Clarke, Christine Crook, Cathleen Riddley,
David Sinaiko, Matt Stines, Megan Trout,
and Beth Wilmurt

This chapter attempts two things at once. Woven into an account of the basic stages of the process from auditions through closing night are commentaries and reflections on collaborative practices and their politics, as they relate to failure, expectation, possibility, and democracy. I wrote the body of the text, and members of the creative team annotated it with their perspectives. No solutions or advice regarding the problems of making theatre are offered here. Experiences are described and among these some interesting and useful questions can be found. Rather than an orderly chronicle or scholarly analysis, what is offered here is a shaggy tapestry of observations and points of view from which loose threads are left to dangle. Trace those threads back to the whole and then step back, and one hopefully gets a coherent sense of the experience of assembling and maintaining this particularly intensive project.

Auditions

Actors Kevin Clarke, Rami Margron, David Sinaiko, Megan Trout, and Beth

---

1

Wilmurt were cast in advance without an audition.[2/3] I had worked with each of them before and knew them to be flexible enough in their talent and skill sets, and also crazy enough as people, to be a good fit for the project.[4] I had originally intended to cast five more actors, for a total of ten. As the extensive and protracted audition process went on (and on...and on...) it became evident that the challenging combination of talent, skill, diversity, and availability necessary was not materializing. A further complicating factor was that actors in *Hamlet* needed to also fit roles in other plays featured in Shotgun's repertory season. Adding still further to this equation was the number of union versus non-union contracts available to us. Not wishing to sacrifice any one factor for another, when we had found two more actors who fit the bill—El Beh and Nick Medina—I looked at the character list again and determined we could do the project with seven actors. So we did.

Nobody likes auditions and I am no exception. I prefer to cast people based on past experiences with them, whether working with them or seeing their work, and otherwise try my best to devise an audition process that's as painless as possible, and, in the best scenarios, enjoyable enough that maybe for at least a few precious minutes the actors can forget it's an audition. That's hard to achieve and I suspect I've only rarely succeeded. For *Hamlet* I asked actors to select two pieces of their choosing: any soliloquy of Hamlet's and a scene between two characters, one of which they deemed to be very much

---

[2] Mark Jackson: "Rami Margron pulled out of the Shotgun Players repertory season in November 2015 to pursue another unique job opportunity. We were sad to see her go but excited for her opportunity. We were then very lucky to welcome Cathleen Riddley into the repertory company. Cathleen performed in *Hamlet* as well as Heidi Schreck's *Grand Concourse*."

[3] David Sinaiko: "I distinctly remember when Patrick Dooley told me about the possibility of the project and offered it to me, outside the back door of the Shotgun rehearsal space. I was thrilled just to hear about it, let alone be given a chance to be a part of it. It didn't take long for the terrifying reality to hit. But it was never less than a completely energizing terror."

[4] Mark Jackson: "While working on this chapter, in one of my old pocket notebooks I found this scribbled: 'Hamlet actors need confidence, curiosity, and fear. All three of those, and not in perfect or static balance.'"

5

not their "type."[6] We scheduled people in fifteen-minute slots. The actors would share their work. Then we'd chat about choices and they would try one or the other piece again. We'd finish by my acknowledging the unusual concept and asking if they had any questions about it. They always did. This was intended as an opportunity to invite them into a conversation about the project, for us to meet one another on the more casual level of chatting about something of mutual interest. It also became an unexpected opportunity for me to better understand what we were actually doing, given the number one question asked of me: "Why are you doing this?"[8]

_____

[6] El Beh: " I actually auditioned three times, learning a new character and monologue (or scene) each time. For my first callback I did a big chunk of Ophelia's mad scene, playing both Ophelia and Laertes. While I'm not sure it'll ever be possible for me as an actor to 'forget it's an audition,' this round was probably both the most stressful and enjoyable. The rapid shifts of intention and physicality, creating dynamic as well as doable staging for two characters in one body, and the demanding work ethic required to pull it all off, made me all the more excited and scared to be part of such a beautiful monster. And then immediately after doing that I was asked to come back again with Claudius. Ha!"

7

[8] Cathleen Riddley: " For the audition, Mark sent me these instructions: 'Choose a three-minute scene to work on that features two characters, at least one of which is very much NOT what you'd ever be cast as. A scene that gives you a chance to play into and against type, whether due to gender or age or temperament. Work out the staging of how you change from character to character in some simple, direct, effective way. It shouldn't be a parody. Take the characters and their drama seriously.' ...Here's where my second, third, and fourth thoughts of 'should I really audition for this?' came up. What a challenging audition, and unlike any I'd ever done before. I chose the closet scene with Gertrude (absolutely my type) and Hamlet (absolutely against type). I was horribly nervous when I went in, but Mark was very friendly, even with his serious face and thick eyebrows. I went through it once and he asked me to do it again and take my time to let the changes between characters happen. Don't rush through the moments. That's always a good instruction for me and I appreciated it. We then talked for a few minutes,

By this point in the process I had not yet put my gut reasoning for doing the *Hamlet* roulette into any organized words. This repeated question forced me to try, again and again. And the answer was: diversity and democracy. Eventually! At first I began with three references. One was the anecdotal comment—attributable to whom, I cannot recall—that Hamlet is the only character Shakespeare created that one can imagine wrote his own play and could perform all the roles himself. What might come of disrupting that singularity to unleash multiple points of view by having several Hamlets, each playing all the roles, go at it together?[9]

The second reference was Steven Berkoff, the British actor and director, who once suggested that no actor can be miscast as Hamlet given the character "touches the complete alphabet of human experience…"

> The bold extrovert will dazzle and play with the word power, the scenes of vengeance, and blast Ophelia and Gertrude off the stage. The introvert will see every line pointed at him, the outsider, the loner, the watcher, he, with his one trusting friend, and a quick answer for everything lest it be a barb. The wit will play for laughs and the lunatic for madness. The romantic for ideals.
> (Berkoff, 1989: vii)

The third reference was director Robert Wilson, who said of *Hamlet*, "I think that Shakespeare's text is this indestructible rock, that you can't really destroy it" (Kessel, 1995). Paradoxically this rock is an incredibly malleable one. There are so many ways to approach, interpret, and enjoy it. And if one doesn't

---

and I was one of those who asked 'Why are you doing this?' It was truly eye opening to hear him talk about democracy, diversity, about what had been learned from the workshops, and the belief that all of us are Hamlet. I left the room thinking 'I AM Hamlet.' The possibilities seemed endless, while still in my mind a Herculean task."

[9] El Beh: "This was one of the first things that appealed to me about this project and that I would reference when people I talked to about it didn't understand the interest. The idea of converging so many different points of view and experience, having so many ways in that I may never have thought of alone, the possible depth of investigation with that many minds on each matter and character, and the investment required from every single person in the ensemble in order to do so, was so sexy to me."

10

care for a given production, there will likely be another opening somewhere else in five minutes. So we are never short on opportunities to explore the possibilities of *Hamlet*. Why not multiply those possibilities within one production? Entire careers—of actors, directors, critics, scholars—and at least two industries—academia and mainstream theatrical production—have been built on the shaky notion that there is a way Shakespeare "should" be done. Many have staked their claim in one "should" or another. These people do a disservice to their audience and their art. The reason to engage with Shakespeare is not to lock down possibility, but rather the opposite: to open possibility up! This is one great offer of the classics. So, for example, if *Hamlet* is a universal meditation on ethics, action, loss, and death then it can also be a very kinesthetic, forward-footed one. The play lurches and hurls through stretches of philosophy and twists of plot like a great old rickety roller coaster, fun at least in part because one suspects things might go off the rails.[11] Why tie any of that down to one or another point of view?

As conversations with actors continued from audition to audition, and I watched a gay white man in his late sixties take on the lead role of all lead roles, followed by a straight black women in her twenties, a queer Asian man in his thirties, a full figured middle-aged straight white mom… gradually the full import of Wilson and Berkoff's comments began to hit me, and my thoughts moved on from merely quoting them to considering the potential impact of a chaos of diversity, a "circus of daring" as one critic eventually called it (Wilkins, 2016), that by closing night would never settle on one perspective. Perhaps the answer to the question *Why do this?* was: to practice a democratic utopia.

Script Workshop

In July 2015 we held a six-day workshop to collectively edit the text. Directors typically edit Shakespeare's plays themselves, sometimes with the help of a dramaturge. But for the *Hamlet* roulette it was much more appropriate to take up this task as a full group. A collective edit would better reflect multiple perspectives, a central mission of the production. It would also

---

[11] El Beh: "This phrasing reminds me of feedback I gave to Megan after she played Hamlet for the first preview. She was like a train going at such a high velocity and with such force, which made it all the more exciting because you didn't know if she was going to fly off the rails or not. She didn't, which is what made it awesome."
12

allow the actors to begin their research together, to invest themselves in the foundations of our particular telling of the story, and to better ensure our success as an ensemble united by our differences toward one aim. And, in theory, it might also give them a jump on memorizing the text—a daunting endeavor!—due to their being that much more familiar with it.

As this was the first gathering of the full cast, I articulated what at that point I anticipated to be our task with the project. I cited the anecdote, Berkoff, and Wilson references I'd been leaning on throughout auditions, noting in them a general intent to shake up audience expectations of this very familiar, often preciously protected play so people actually hear and see the play itself, rather than only their preconceptions of it. I noted what I thought we did not need to do: (1) put our individual stamps on each role; and (2) continue to edit and debate our cutting of the text once we were in formal rehearsals—there'd be too much else to do! And I noted what I thought we did need to do: (1) obsess over *Hamlet* with open eyes, ears, hands, hearts and minds; (2) learn from one another's attempts, successes and failures; (3) borrow each other's ideas; and (4) take a generous approach toward making a generous production, by which I meant our work needed to be about everyone other than ourselves. Each scene needed to be one's acting partner's scene. Each moment needed to be developed to impact the audience, not us.[14] (5) I further anticipated we would need to share a basic staging and allow for differences to come about organically and by necessity, as opposed to seeking differences out. Our staging would need to be bold and dynamic by way of very simple, striking means—strong images that imprint the dramatic moment on the mind's eye, not only so the actors could remember the staging but also to help the audience understand our particular telling of the story. (6) Finally, I believed we needed to make a production of *Hamlet* so kick-ass that within ten minutes the audience would forget about the roulette concept entirely and simply enjoy the play. Other than that I knew (7) we'd mime the swords, likely be on stage all the time

---

13

[14] El Beh: "Tasks (2) (3) and (4) were what excited me the most at this meeting, partially because I'm such an ensemble creature and love tapping into the wealth of knowledge and talent in any given room, and partially because—especially with (4)—I think this is what good acting is. The opportunity to lean into those tasks with this particular project was tenfold."

even when not in a scene, be the collective prompter,[15] and generally create an actor/text/tableaux-centric production whereby the design is a canvas on which the actors convey the story.

We got to work making our way through the text with our scissors. Actors would rotate roles every scene. One first order of business was to determine the seven character tracks, with doublings that might have dramatic resonance beyond the practicality of logistics.[16] A great deal of attention was given to Ophelia and Gertrude, the only female characters in the play and each in dire need of fortification to bring them into the twenty-first century.[17] The idea to double Ophelia and Horatio came up early on, providing an interesting overlap of Hamlet's steadfast friend and his estranged lover. This brought about the idea to cut the travelling players and have Ophelia and Hamlet perform *The Mousetrap* together. Some logistics

---

[15] El Beh: " By 'collective prompter' Mark means we'd all prompt one another in chorus when anyone forgot their lines on stage. Oh what a grand idea this was at the time! Once we were in formal rehearsals, it didn't take too long for us to realize what an impractical idea it was. To get the timing and cadence for a choral line prompt to actually make sense and serve its purpose would take a whole other rehearsal process on its own. Let alone the impossibility of collectively making the split second decisions of where to start a line from, how it should be given, etc., if an actor was jumping all over the page. In any case, we killed that baby right quick."

[16] Mark Jackson: " Laertes was the only track to include only one character, so we designated him the onstage line prompter between his scripted appearances. When Laertes was occupied on stage, the Ghost/Gravedigger track or the Priest (part of the Polonius/Priest/Osric track) took up prompting duty. Since the Priest had prompting duty during his scene (Act 5 Scene 1), he used the open script as his prop Bible, in order to mask the prompting task a bit."

[17] David Sinaiko: " We went round and round about these two, and trying to solve the problem of giving them more agency. It was always difficult for me to understand the actions with the love letters and how they fit into the nunnery scene and, subsequently, to the play within the play. Whether, and how, Ophelia was mad or faking madness was tough terrain for all of us, one way or the other. In the end I think we did well with it. It is a good example of a place where we all successfully found our own approach to it, while also sharing and stealing freely from each other. I am not sure we succeeded in giving Gertrude much more agency."

would need to be worked out, but it seemed this might further heighten the dramatic tension while also providing Ophelia with more substantial material and personal substance. We began to think of her as a younger Hamlet—not as privileged by birth and gender as him but equally talented, thoughtful, and conflicted. This led us to determine that her mad scene might actually be played sane, with Ophelia putting on her own closing act of skillfully crafted "antic" songs and monologues, tailor-made for an audience of people who had not stood by her in life.[18]

Our desire to similarly strengthen Gertrude led us to think of her as a variation on late twentieth-century American first ladies, more Nancy Reagan than Hillary Clinton—a quietly strong woman, listening to everything and saying only what matters, standing behind her man as his true chief advisor, actively complicit in all his crimes and successes.[19] At the start of the play, Gertrude and Claudius would relate to one another as equals, with Claudius always checking in with her, not with Polonius, for approval of decisions. As the play progressed, their bond would gradually strain and unravel, with Gertrude eventually regaining her buried conscience and Claudius charging deeper into blood.

When we reached the final scene, Rami Margron suggested that Horatio's famous summation speech ("so shall you hear / Of carnal, bloody, and unnatural acts…") not be delivered nobly or as a warning but very personally, from someone in shock after their friend has just been killed. From this idea

---

[18] Kevin Clarke: "While at this early stage we hadn't discussed it, over the long haul I came to think that having Ophelia 'perform' virtuosic multiple roles in the play within the play—her quick-shift double role in the dumb-show being a comic highlight for audiences and a great moment for individualized play for each actor—established our Ophelia as a skilled actor, setting up her 'performed' mad scene later on quite nicely."

[19] El Beh: "As we got the play on its feet when 'formal rehearsals' began, this ended up being an interesting divergence between actors, with each of us deciding how much we did or did not know as Gertrude. How differently our individual interpretations translated to our audiences, I couldn't say. I do hope our base remained stable though, and that, through a few subtle but key staging and action choices, it was clear that our Gertrude had much more silent power than is offered to her on the page alone."

20

eventually came the solution that Horatio deliver the speech to the dying Hamlet, that the last spoken line in the production be Hamlet's "The rest is silence," and the last moment of the production be that silence itself. Rather than Fortinbras barging in out of nowhere to muddle things with drums and flourishes, Horatio would be left alone with the dead body of his friend, surrounded by bloody evidence of accidental judgments, casual slaughters, deaths put on by cunning and forced cause, and purposes mistook fallen on the inventors' heads.

We ended this workshop with a very roughly hewn edit of the script. Over the next month I tidied it up and sent it out to the cast so they could start memorizing their two-hour-ten-minute monologue.[21]

Rehearsal Strategies Workshop

One has to remember that they must all be a bit nuts
to even consider this... makes it interesting doesn't it?
*–Carolyn Jones in a private email to a friend, November
2015*

The purpose of this second workshop was to address the daunting question, *How are we going to do this?* One unsurprising conclusion was that we needed more time than originally allotted. So we pushed opening night back by eleven days. This did not mean any additional rehearsal time but it allowed us fourteen previews, rather than Shotgun's usual five, prior to opening night.

Over the course of our five-day rehearsal strategies workshop we experimented with various approaches to rehearsing scenes and soliloquies. I took notes every day and emailed their summations to the cast and production team each night. A lot of what happened in those five days

---

[21] David Sinaiko: " A personal note about fellow actor Nick Medina and the text: Nick is such a passionate delver into the text that it was a really great part of the experience for me, during the early text workshops, and throughout the entirety of the months-long rehearsal and performance process, to have continual conversations with him about the text. The investigation of the text never stopped for Nick and I came away from each of our many conversations thinking more deeply about it. As it should be with that text. It was definitely a way we sustained ourselves along the way."
22

could be worth recounting. But as this book does not intend to be a proper chronicle, what follows is the final summation (amended slightly for the clarity of the reader who was not present) that I emailed everyone after the workshop had concluded:

Mark Jackson   Sent – October 20, 2015 at 6:02 PM
Subject: Highlights from Denmark
To: Kevin Clarke, Beth Wilmurt, Hanah Zahner-Izenberg, Megan Trout, Nick Medina, El Beh, Rami Margron, David Sinaiko.
Cc: Patrick Dooley, Joanie McBrien, Liz Lisle.

Danes,

As promised, here's a summation of the key discoveries of our October workshop. Certain ideas recur throughout. Perhaps this is telling. Of course there are many things not noted here. But given our various activities and discussions, these stood out to me as salient.

Keep this summation alongside the daily reports from October for reference between now and February as you work on memorizing the text and as we continue to wrap our brains around our extraordinary endeavor. Wouldn't be a bad idea to print this one out and keep it with your script, too.

Mantras & Philosophies

"Strict with ourselves, gentle with each other."

This phrase comes to us courtesy of David Sinaiko, and is right in line with our "generous process for a generous production" mantra named back in July. It's about being individuals who comprise a group, and, as such, taking individual responsibility to collectively maintain efficient use of the talking/doing balance; being ready and open to working and learning in a variety of ways; checking our own habits, needs, and communications while allowing for those of others and negotiating when these inevitably come in conflict.

23

"Discover, don't invent." [24/25]

We spent a lot of time pondering this one. It is at the foundation of how we do what we're doing on this project:

> It relates to Gandhi's observation that we have two ears and one mouth, meaning we're built to listen twice as much as we speak. Yet so often we reverse this, both on stage and off.

> It relates to what we call play and playing in rehearsal and on stage, which can mean so many different things. In our case, playing begins with listening and responding, in order to firmly establish our acting targets and triggers.[26] By front-loading this in our work, we lay a clear

---

[24] David Sinaiko: "'Discover, don't invent' is such a simple but profound approach. I found it incredibly useful in many ways. It provided a sort of a compass to follow when we were trying, under a very tangible time-based pressure, to crack open a scene. Not only did it guide our attention and intentions as characters interacting within a scene, but as actors within an unusual and difficult rehearsal process. It helped get us back to basics when the impulse to get clever was keeping us from getting to the heart of the play or the problem we'd set ourselves by attempting to do it in this crazy way."

[25] El Beh: "This was a core mantra that was extremely helpful to come back to, not only in the rehearsal process of this show but also the other shows we were later running simultaneously during the repertory. Not surprisingly, it ended up being integral in our discussions of show-maintenance over the course of the year. It is often the case as a show sinks more into itself and actors get more comfortable, that actions possibly get habitual and an actor can suddenly feel the need to 'do' something or 'make something happen.' Even without the comfort of sinking into a single role with this show, given the extended period over which we performed we certainly fell prey to this all too typical phenomenon, and 'discover, don't invent' was a very quick reminder that the integrity of what we had created would suffer from such invention. I can't say that we were all able to heed our own advice all the time, but it was certainly helpful."

[26] Mark Jackson: "As acting terms are often not uniformly used or understood, I'll note that by 'target' I'm referring to the person, object, thought or other thing that has a character's attention in a given moment. By 'trigger' I'm referring to something said or done that causes, compels, or incites a character's actions and responses."

foundation of intentions on which to layer those details—behavior, stage business, finessing language—we typically consider "playing" and "acting."[27]

And so *"Discover, don't invent"* emphasizes the roles attention and intention play in our playing. On the night we worked Act 1 Scene 2, for example, there was a lot of inventing going on, especially when an actor was playing a character removed from their own gender or age. The results were inevitably false, veering into caricature. When people stripped that stuff back and away, kept the vocal or physical adjustment much simpler and smaller, and made intention the larger and more prominent thing, suddenly they were more believable in the character. This tells us that big physical/vocal characterizations don't work in our context, though they may be perfect in another. We may find that slightly larger physicalizations might work, when layered in later in response to the initial target/trigger work. But anyway, attention and intention are our first guides.

---

[27] Mark Jackson: "The question of how to act in a given production is often conceived as a question of 'style,' itself often conceived as a matter of appearances. But as theatre scholar Nicholas Ridout notes, 'How shall I act?' is one succinct way of posing the question of ethics. It is also, as you will of course have noticed from the very beginning [of Ridout's book on the subject], a theatrical question. In both senses it is a difficult question...' (2009: 5-6) So, to suggest our acting approach for *Hamlet* should emphasize intentions, and that these intentions be shaped through a process of listening and responding, of discovering what's there rather than inventing (at the risk of imposing) what is not, underscores the impulse behind the production toward inclusiveness and against conclusiveness, and that the production be itself intention-centric more so than aesthetics-centric. Though the former cannot be discerned without the latter, this emphasis speaks to the hopes and aims of the *Hamlet* roulette: that it was intentionally aimed outward toward the audience and sought to respect their perspective, allow space for it, and in this way encourage their embrace of their own individual perspectives alongside those of others. This is political. And so we see how acting choices are political choices, how the staging question, 'Where do I stand?' like Ridout's question, 'How shall I act?' is both a practical and ethical question for actors and audience alike."

28

The scene is about how your character is trying to impact the other character(s), not about what your character feels. Make every scene about the other character. This keeps one listening and seeing, i.e. discovering rather than inventing or slipping into executing clever ideas. In the confrontation scene between Gertrude and Hamlet, for example, when Hamlet is forcing Gertrude to look at the two paintings of Claudius and his father, it's not about what Hamlet feels about those two men, how he hates the one and is grieving the other. It's about Hamlet really asking his mother the question: How could you possibly have left this man for that one?! Why did you do that?! How could you do it?![29]

"It's evident!"

If something is "evident," it means either everyone or most of us feel the given moment pull us toward it and we want to point to it excitedly. These are important moments for us to recognize. They are the moments we want to find and keep. Whether it's a gesture for a particular character, or a cross from stage left to right for a particular exchange between two characters, or a particular intention by which a character is driven. We will not always agree, and when at a stalemate I'll make the call based on "all things considered." But the best moments are those that create an evident

---

[29] Mark Jackson: "Defining the difference between discovery and invention was indeed a rolling collective endeavor. It could be a fuzzy fine line at times, and perhaps subjective. Sometimes it was clear, as when a choice appeared either merely or too clever, a distraction from the given moment rather than a revelation of it. And maybe that's a defining factor: that invention in this context is merely clever, attention-grabbing, and feels somehow cheap or easy compared to genuine, in-the-moment discovery and response, which requires a certain generous, outward, and open attentiveness."
30

Oh! of excitement in the room.[31]

As Théâtre du Soleil demonstrates,[33] this "evident" principle does not eliminate the possibility of heartbreak when ideas or points of view get discarded. We all need to be ready to let go of things as lightly as we must hold on to them tightly when trying them out.[34] "Evident" is a principle that values the whole over the individual bits. Sometimes our brain *really* wants an idea to work, but our gut recognizes that for _____ reason(s) it does not. Fine. Ideas are cheap. There are a million ideas. We'll always have others. We'll always have too many to know what to do with. So what are the ideas that suddenly, spontaneously become evident as exciting by their nature? That's what we want! Conversely, what are the ideas we can eliminate immediately because we see they do not fit into whatever rule structure we've established as "evident"? Etcetera.

---

[31] David Sinaiko: "'It's evident!' was harder for me. There is often a period in a creative process during which the endeavor seems to get less clear and more confusing, and for *Hamlet* this was especially true. Possibly my own anxieties about whether we would (or could) succeed made it difficult for me to really know when something was 'evident,' but it was rarely completely clear to me. It felt a little like a kind of mushy version of consensus. Once again, I think time pressures played a big role in this. There was (is) a great deal of reverence among the whole cast and creative team for the 'European' model of rehearsal, where companies tend to be better subsidized and there is less emphasis on meeting a deadline. Plays can be workshopped for many months before the decision is made that it is ready to open. We had no such luxury, though we often wished we did."
32

[33] Mark Jackson: "We had watched *Au Soleil même la nuit*, a film documenting Théâtre du Soleil's 1995 production of Moliere's *Tartuffe* from its first day of rehearsal through performances at the Avignon Festival." (Darmon & Vilpoux, 2011)

[34] Mark Jackson: "I'm paraphrasing Anne Bogart and Tina Landau here. In their words: 'Hold on tightly, let go lightly. Dive into any endeavor with strength, fortitude and intention, but at the same time be willing to adjust. Know what you want, and be completely unattached to getting it' (2005: 161)."

Creative Process

We have an out-of-the-box project that demands we each work out of our own boxes, that Shotgun Players as a producing organization works out of its box, and the audience work out of theirs. In line with that:

We must be open to new and unfamiliar ways of going about scene work, managing our time together and apart, defining what "prepared" means, what "developing a character" means. (Beth said she renounced "character" long ago, and I suspect that will serve her well in this process. Get a beer in her hand and ask her to talk about what she means by rejecting character. It will be a conversation that inevitably winds its way back to discovering rather than inventing.)

We are doing the play, not the characters in it.

We are all understudies. That means each other's work is an aspect of our script.[36]

Sunday night dinners after rehearsal! It struck El Beh that this might be a good outlet for the wandering, extended, more relaxed conversations we won't have the desired time for in rehearsal proper. And everyone's gotta eat, right? I don't imagine this to be a mandatory participation thing. But if we earmark Sundays after rehearsal as potential social time where we eat, drink, and talk together, without even realizing it we'll actually get a lot

---

35

[36] El Beh: " We got to learn a lot from watching each other. A concept that Mark introduced early on, and which I wish we had utilized even more during the run itself, was the power that imitation had in our particular process. If we witnessed someone having an interpretation of a particular line or moment that we found worked well, we could and should use it. This proved to be a double-edged sword because sometimes what worked on one body would not work on another—and we wouldn't know if it was translatable or not until someone else tried it. It was an interesting investigation, to continue to figure out what worked and what didn't in this regard throughout the repertory season. And it was yet another line of communication we had to figure out how to navigate."

of work done over those meals while rejuvenating at the same time. I am reminded of the German actors in an ill-fated Frankfurt production I was involved with in 2009, who said one factor in the demise of our show was that we didn't go out for drinks enough after rehearsals![37]

"Zip-Bop-Zap-Zing."[38] This game, which we played every day, worked as a

---

[37] El Beh: " In our initial meetings we all had excitement around how much we would be able to mine out of this story and its characters with the potential of our shared knowledge. We were titillated by the idea that we would have no secrets from each other, the way some actors might in a more traditional process when they are playing only one role and, to heighten the stakes between them and their acting partners, may not want to reveal all their cards. If one of us were to make a discovery about a character, a moment, an intention, it would become the property of the collective trust of knowledge for us all to share and benefit from. In the end, given all that we were taking on and perhaps because we didn't imbibe enough together, we still left a decent amount of stones unturned. Turns out a body can get pretty tired on a Sunday after 30+ hours of rehearsal on top of working close to full time day jobs and memorizing 2+ hours of Shakespeare. Nobody can say we didn't try!"

[38] Mark Jackson: "This is a game played in groups and used to exercise one's sense of rhythm in connecting words and gestures, requiring quick kinesthetic thinking. The group stands in a circle. The four one-syllable words—zip, bop, zap, and zing—each have a corresponding gesture associated with them. Each is used to pass the game on to the next player in some particular way. 'Zip,' said with a sideways clapping gesture, passes the game on in the direction it's already going. 'Zap,' said with a single arm aimed straight out toward a person, sends the game across the circle to anyone other than the person on the sender's immediate left or right. 'Zing,' said with a gesture of pointing to the feet of the next person and looking there too, actually skips that person and moves the game on to the next adjacent person. 'Bop,' said with a hands-up-at-gunpoint gesture, reverses the direction of a 'zip,' 'bop' or 'zing,' but cannot be used against a 'zap.' As the game progresses from person to person around the circle, the rhythm can always speed up but can never slow down. A player 'dies' if they break the rhythm, or if they misfire a gesture or word in some manner. It then becomes the responsibility of the 'dead' to continue to monitor the 'living' to help catch errors and verify what exactly went off if

practical metaphor for the values of our process and production.[39] Namely:

- Establishing a strict and limited set of rules that, by the limitations they impose, open up the possibility of exciting play.
- Layering difficulty in over time.
- Using the rules of the game to help fellow players whom we notice are struggling.

---

it's unclear to those still in play. This then becomes an opportunity to practice being an audience to the players."

[39] David Sinaiko: " Zip-Bop-Zap-Zing became one of the rituals that I found very important throughout the initial and rep runs of *Hamlet*. After individual warm-up time we'd all gather on stage and play two games before fight call: Zip-Bop-Zap-Zing, and a game whereby four objects were tossed among the circled cast, each object added in one by one and tossed from actor to actor in a pattern established spontaneously, then repeated for several minutes. These games became a centering place for us as a cast. It helped each of us find each other on a level place, regardless of what our day had been leading up to it. It calmed and focused us. And, while Zip-Bop-Zap-Zing had a competitive edge, it was always followed by the more collaborative object-tossing game, which required us to make strong eye contact, to make tacit agreements with each other, to pay acute attention to the whole group, to remember the patterns, and to work the inevitable mistakes and failures into the fabric of the game as seamlessly as possible. As each new object was introduced the environment became more chaotic. It was challenging, a lot of fun, and an ironically poetic analog to our whole endeavor.

" Another pre-show ritual that we adopted, in addition to the more familiar ' Break a leg' and 'Toi Toi Toi,' was to gather as a group in a tight circle, arms around each other, and take a few seconds in silence to look directly into each castmate's eyes, followed by three deep breaths in unison. This was a way for us to remind ourselves and each other that we were there together, that we would succeed and fail together. And though the tension of not knowing who you were going to play on each night never went away, this ritual was especially effective in the early part of the initial run when that anxiety was especially high. Looking into each other's eyes was especially important to me. It was a simple and powerful way to say: ' If we're out on stage together and things feel shaky, look here and I'll be right there with you.'"

- Matching the word to the deed, the deed to the word.
- Sharpening our conscious attention to rhythm and shifts of rhythm and responding to it with ease and sensitivity.
- Discovering, not inventing, and yet playing with strategy, sportsmanship, and showmanship.
- Joy fuels the engine.[40] Failure is often the most exciting and fun moment of the game, where we explode with laughter and get an energy jolt.

Staging...

As we found, working out staging in a fully horizontal collaborative way takes a lot of time, which we don't have. So, I will more often than not bring in starter templates for staging and impart these at the top of our work on a scene. The staging will naturally get fleshed out and improved by our then working on it. We'll discover what needs to change by putting the staging template into practice.

Some rehearsal strategies accommodate our splitting up into groups, and each group might create a staging template that we can then make decisions about when we come together and share. This is more time-consuming, but might work for soliloquies or shorter scenes with fewer characters.[42]

Our general shared approach to staging, in any case, is about identifying bold, clear, simple, dynamic images and movements. This is actually a great

---

[40] Cathleen Riddley: " I so looked forward to coming to the games and having El Beh smile and say ' hello, friends.' Zip-Bop-Zap-Zing became something that I would almost run over my grandmother to get to rehearsal or performance in time to play. We learned so many things about each other through this: who is most inclined to take the hit if rhythm is broken, who is most likely to dispute a decision, who giggles most easily, who is a true cutthroat game player ... But most importantly, we connected, unified, became the ensemble accountable to each other and there for each other."
41

[42] Mark Jackson: " As it turned out, time did not allow for much of this approach. Even with my bringing in starter templates and our then splitting off into groups, the clock spun very quickly. The actors had so much to juggle given all the rotating from role to role. Starter templates soon became the standard procedure."

challenge. Minimalism means finding the most potent, evocative minimum possible—the minimum that explodes with maximum impact. What is the one spatial relationship that says the most about the characters, their relationships and psychologies? What is the one gesture that can sustain an entire soliloquy? A good example of the latter is Beth's hands-off-this gesture for Hamlet's "O that this too too solid flesh" soliloquy. Nick then took up the gesture Beth had made and could play very fruitfully with it. On a subsequent day it was shown to new people with fresh eyes to it and was immediately recognized by them as a potent gesture for that soliloquy. It was evident![43/44]

Things to check at the door upon arrival:

- Our egos
- Our habits
- Our expectations
- Our preconceptions

Regarding habits. In the workshop we talked about individual actor habits

---

[43] Mark Jackson: "The evident success of this gesture proved less so once we got into rehearsals. The actors actually had great difficulty making it work, outside of Beth who had originated it. At some point early in the run, I suggested everyone free up from the strictness of it. This created new problems but also yielded much more organic and successful results, so we kept with that. By the end of the run the gesture had still never settled into a consistent place across the cast, nor did we find anything to replace it. Next time!"

[44] Kevin Clarke: "One of the great gifts in performing our *Hamlet* was watching/studying each other's discoveries. Backstage during the run during this soliloquy, I often wished I could watch other actors' handling of this gestural moment in performance. But this was a rare moment of Hamlet onstage by himself. (Even Horatio, racing around the building to make his next entrance, couldn't catch much more than the final few seconds of the 'Too too solid flesh' speech.) I would listen to it on the monitors backstage, but with the chance of more study I might have gotten closer to personally inhabiting this gesture, because, per Mark's footnote above, it remained elusive to me through the run."

45

very specifically. This seemed to work well. There were no eggshells or ego problems and it helped us identify how each person must handle things in particular.[46] With Kevin and Nick, for example, a little facial expression goes a long way. Whereas Beth tends not to put on much expression up front and so initially her characters feel indistinct. For El it was about clear diction and avoiding contemporary melodies of speech. For me, as director, it's about figuring out new patterns of when to offer notes or how much staging to bring in up front. By talking about these things openly we can help ourselves as a group arrive at our shared approach—both to the process and the performance.

Getting together periodically in Nov/Dec/Jan, whether to run lines or to review these notes with those who were and weren't there, wouldn't be a bad idea. Social time is good. Every bit of mental marinating on our task is good. It would be easy not to do this. But it might prove a quite effective boon to do it.

Rehearsal Strategies

More often than not we'll start work on a scene by reading it once through together to make sure the basic through-line of intentions are shared and understood, and to clarify any obscure language. Also this is when I would impart any staging templates.[48]

It's important that everyone look up obscure phrases and words on their

---

[46] El Beh: "Because of the specific challenges this particular project set forth, it was actually kind of a surprising and amazing gift to get to work on my personal actor habits in the midst of everything else. I hadn't originally imagined there would be much time for honing in on any one thing, but the opportunity to play such a variety of characters—and, in the case of rehearsals, in such quick succession—really made individual habits more 'evident.' This was one area in which I was able to track growth over the year, which I'm grateful for."
47

[48] Mark Jackson: "The first part of this got rearranged almost immediately. We'd jump straight to the staging template, then split off into different rooms (see 'Think Tanking' below) where actors started by reading the scene in their group before then getting up on their feet."

own, outside of rehearsal. We don't want to devote rehearsal time to that. Come memorized on our first day of rehearsal: February 9th. I know I know I know! But work toward that goal in earnest. It's okay if you don't succeed.[49/50]

"Round Robin"

A strategy by which a scene is run seven times. With each run, we rotate who plays whom. Notes are given within and between each run, more so initially and less so as things develop. Then we sit and talk about the scene and what we've discovered. (So the doing time and the discussion time are largely discreet.) Then we get up and run it seven times again, in rotation, with only minimal notes if any, to allow what's been discovered to set in. This strategy works well for scenes with lots of characters.[52]

---

[49] Cathleen Riddley: " I knew in my heart that being memorized at our first rehearsal, no matter how hard I tried, would be damn near impossible, so the specter of failure hung close for a while; possibly for the entire run of the show. I think that we often hear that not being successful is all right, but rarely have I really, as an actor, believed it. This caused me to realize, through the power of the community creating this piece, that success and failure mean different things in different contexts, and are rarely objectively measurable. The phrase 'From each, according to his ability, to each according to his need' became real for me in a practical sense. I had many needs, but I also had a lot to offer, and working on this piece gave me the opportunity to experience need and weakness and 'failure' as well as contribute love and support, wisdom and energy."

[50] El Beh: " Looking back, and especially in context of this book, it was probably a good and humbling lesson that most of us started rehearsal right off the bat with a failure here."

[51]

[52] David Sinaiko: " Keep in mind, this means we'd each run each character in a given scene twice in a night, and then move on from that scene. Repetition is a huge part of what actors crave to get comfortable and confident. Twice a night did not feel like enough."

"Think Tanking"

A strategy by which two or three groups of actors each work on the same scene in separate rooms, then come together to share the results. This works well for shorter scenes with fewer characters.

"Schizoiding"

Our derivative of the Théâtre du Soleil practice of "Godparenting," or "Twinning," by which one actor with a more developed, alternative or otherwise useful hit on a role works literally alongside an actor with a less strong grasp on that role and they play it together at once, switching off who takes the text but always moving alongside one another and feeding off each other. (Miller, 2007: 44 & 133. See also Darmon & Vilpoux, 2011.) In our spin on this collaborative practice, one actor handles the text of a character and the other handles the physicality. This allows each actor to focus fully on one aspect. Then the most intriguing results of the physical work are applied to the text. This proved fruitful in Nick and Beth's joint development of Hamlet's "O that this too too solid flesh" soliloquy. Nick handled the text and Beth moved. We identified a single gesture that seemed to have a particular chemistry with the text. Then Beth put that gesture and the text together. Nick then tried it. These trials revealed what worked and what didn't about the gesture, and helped us refine the rules of its game. Schizoiding combines efficiency with a collaborative approach to developing

---

53

the soliloquy.[54/55]

"Three-Night Stretch"

We work on three scenes over three nights. Each night, three groups each take one of the three scenes and work separately. At the end of the night, we come together and share, give notes, make collective decisions on what to take forward. On the second night, groups swap scenes and take the

---

[54] Megan Trout: " In the early days of rehearsal, I remember feeling a lot like Harry Potter. On one of our eight-hour weekend days, Mark was working with us to crack the soliloquy, 'O that this too, too solid flesh.' We had given ourselves some physical restrictions to play within. 1, let the horrifying image of your mom screwing your slimy uncle back you slowly upstage until you can't back up anymore. And 2, let your arms and hands get stuck above your head but be free enough to express all the feelings you might be having regarding the morally questionable choices of your family members. But back to Harry Potter for a second. You know the scene in the third book where Professor Lupin gives each student a chance to defeat the shape-shifting boggart as it impersonates their greatest fear? That is exactly how I felt that morning as I hopped onstage to grapple with that stunning bit of text: Terrified and brave. Fucking ALIVE! With each of our attempts to succeed in the face of almost certain failure, we gleaned a few more answers and scratched off a few more questions. In this way, the next Hamlet's attempt was a little more clear and focused. We were early in our process, working an early moment in a famously difficult play that we had made exponentially more difficult... But I was already in awe of my compatriots. We were slaying dragons and making real magic."
[55] El Beh: " This was a strategy I was particularly excited about and it ended up not being used as often in our formal rehearsal process as we had hoped. Perhaps if there was more time... But I actually think our other strategies served our purposes more in the long run. All the more practice in letting go! And I'm still interested in this strategy for other possible projects."

previous night's groups' work forward. And so on.[56/57]

"A Run-Through WEEK"

The idea we had for handling preview performances might be how we work on things after our initial pass at staging the full play, which is estimated to take four full weeks at least. So, in one Tuesday through Sunday period we would run the show seven times, guaranteeing each actor has a shot at each track. Then maybe we hit specific scenes that are most challenging for most people. Then do another week of run-throughs. And continue in this pattern throughout previews.[59]

Sword Fights

Working in pairs to develop moves, and then teaching them to the others, worked great. It was efficient, fun, and yielded really exciting, dangerous seeming sword fights—totally mimed![60] The principles by which the mime

---

[56] Mark Jackson: " We never ended up using this strategy in our formal rehearsal process. I can't recall why."
[57] El Beh: " Regarding Mark's footnote above, I think it was another time thing. 'Round Robin' ended up being the most efficient approach, both with collective note-giving and allowing each of us to actually touch all the roles in a given scene at least once before a Run-Through. 'Think Tanking' let us dig a little deeper, but there just wasn't much time left to employ the other strategies."
[58]

[59] Mark Jackson: " The first pass at staging the full play actually ended up taking five weeks, leaving one more week prior to tech rehearsals. During that week we ran the show seven times so that each actor could have a run in each character track."
[60] Cathleen Riddley: " To build the three sword fights we went in small groups to different rooms, and each group made a fight. I was with El Beh and Megan Trout. I was intimidated, assuming they had more stage combat experience than I had and I would have no idea where to even begin. Well, it turns out that none of us were sure. But, sure enough, we came up with a good fight, and a move that was borrowed and used by the other teams as well. This experience taught me—both for this situation

worked and didn't work are easier to discuss in person. But in short: physical stops become very important for the audience to follow the action, and actions often cannot be executed as they would be done in real life with real swords. When the object is absent it takes a different way of moving to help us see it and remain focused on the characters.

Characters

Regarding Gender

We concluded that Hamlet can be played according to the actor's own gender, and yet we need not be so literal about this. There's great flexibility with Hamlet.[62] Horatio can also be the gender of the given actor.[63] Whereas Claudius, Gertrude, Ophelia, and Polonius must be the gender of the character as written.[64]

Hamlet

He's in grief. He's caught between thinking and doing. We're watching a

---

and the scene work that we used the 'Think Tank' method to develop—to JUST DO IT!"
[61]

[62] El Beh: " It's interesting to me that, although I revolt against gender binaries and stereotypes in my daily life, throughout our entire process I referred to Hamlet with male pronouns when talking about them as a character, in anyone's body. There's more at play here, but: Hi, Systemic Patriarchy!"

[63] El Beh: " I actually don't remember this. Or maybe this was something that shifted later. But I thought we had decided Hamlet was the only one who was gender fluid. Thinking back I'm not sure why Horatio or even Ophelia (especially if Hamlet was not male identified) couldn't have also been fluid. In any case they all kind of ended up being some degree of genderqueer given the diversity of bodies we were putting these characters on."

[64] Beth Wilmurt: " At a certain point early in the run I shifted to playing all the roles as women. I no longer thought of the male characters as men. It became a matter of women with different personalities, some more masculine and some more feminine."

great person, someone with immense capabilities of wit and action, who is in a crisis and falling apart. When he says, "It hath made me mad!" to Ophelia in the nunnery scene, for that moment he's a boyfriend admitting something deeply true and terrible to his girlfriend, even though the moment before that line he was berating her brutally for her having betrayed him to Polonius and Claudius. Hamlet knows he's falling apart, and his inability to handle everything adds to the grief triggered by his father's death.

We could score out Hamlet's journey according to (1) when he's too much in his head, and (2) when he's in his Action Groove. He's too much in his head, for example, in "O that this too too solid flesh" or "To be or not to be." In these moments he feels stuck and unable to act. He is most in his Action Groove in the *Mousetrap* scene, where he manages to work the entire room moment to moment with dexterity and panache. We see him there at his most witty, most agile, most able to take action on the fly and achieve exactly what he intends to achieve. Then moments later he passes by Claudius praying (Act 3 Scene 3) and bam: he goes right up into his head, failing to take action. Hamlet's entire through-line can be scored according to Headiness and Action Groove. With this simple binary we can together track his psychological and emotional journey.

Ophelia

Her overarching journey is one of feeling she's everyone's pawn, that she never stands up for herself and does what people ask her to do, and is uncertain how to push back. She is very conscious of this, and it's making her feel she's going crazy. So when she eventually fakes her own madness and kills herself,[65] she's taking her life back by taking it. "You have all taken my life from me? I'll take it back. You have all made me feel insane? I'll perform that insanity right back at you and push it in your faces on my way out. You all denied me my voice? I'll hit you with a barrage of songs and monologues you haven't the wit to understand!" In this way we've rendered her very much like Hamlet. Their positions within this society make them different in decisive ways, however, which of course determine their actions and actions taken by others in relation to them.

---

[65] Mark Jackson: " See the section, ' Rehearsal—The Politics of Collaboration; below for additional details on Ophelia's faked madness."

66

Gertrude[67]

We'll play her much more politically savvy than is typically expected. She says little because she's smarter than saying too much. Her ability to listen and speak sparingly is a key to her ability to maintain power. The less she admits to, the less material she gives others to pin on her. The connection between her and Claudius is real, we must assume. That connection gradually unravels over the course of the stresses undergone in the play.

Claudius

Not a villain. He's a shrewd, ambitious politician who has done terrible things. His connection to Gertrude is real. That connection unravels over the course of the stresses undergone in the play as his ambition narrows his vision, while Gertrude's conscience opens up.

Polonius

Not an indulgent clown. He speaks far more than is necessary, for sure. But approaching him as a capable political maneuverer serves our purposes. We want the audience to take Polonius' contributions to the plot twists seriously. So, yes, he has a lot to say, but we'll make him a quick-thinking fast talker rather than a meandering orator.

All the characters...

...use language as their chief act. Speaking is their main means of taking action toward one another. It's their currency. They are very good listeners and excellent wits and speakers—with the exception of Rosencrantz and Guildenstern, of course. So we must embrace both the detail and the unrelenting rush of all they have to say. Our staging will support this, allowing the text to be the melody of the storytelling and the movement a baseline.

---

[67] Cathleen Riddley: " We had fabulous discussions as to whether or not Gertrude actually knew that Claudius killed Hamlet Sr., if she just didn't want to know so she could have plausible deniability, if she really enjoyed ' honeying and making love o'er the nasty sty.' Each of us had our little secret about Gertrude. And sometimes the Gertrude and Claudius would say what they were thinking in the ten seconds before the first entrance. Made for some tingly excitement."
68

Our general aim is to take all these characters seriously, to put their intentions and psychological journeys front and center, to not serve up the usual expectations that can make an audience not hear or see them deeply. Familiarity kills consciousness.

What We're Offering Our Audience

We need to get them on our bandwagon.[69] From the marketing, to the design and how we play our edit of the script, we need to communicate to them what we're all here to do: study this great play *Hamlet* in an experiential way. It's the principle that research is practice and practice is research, that "studying" does not mean only reading and thinking in an academic way. One can study a performance by experiencing it, whether once or repeatedly. *Hamlet* is a very familiar play. So many daily expressions come from it. Everyone can find a connection to it. This production will offer the opportunity to experience and consider the breadth of possibilities in the characters and the play. Ours is not a production that's about how clever the actors, director, or designers can be. It's about the play. We're doing the play. Watching the play. Listening to the play. Considering the play. Feeling the play. Appreciating the play, in our brain and in our gut. We need to articulate this to our audience with every aspect of our production, from the set to the acting to the program notes.

This is why I've been so insistent that ultimately what we're offering is not the roulette concept. The roulette concept is the wild rotating doorway by which we get into the play. But despite the massive challenge of the roulette concept, the play must still be the thing. It is so utterly familiar a play that sometimes it needs to be kicked up a new and steep mountain for us to feel its weight, its nimbleness, its possibilities.

---

[69] Kevin Clarke: " For me, this started in our preshow entrance, coming onstage as ourselves without artifice. It was a singular opportunity to unite with individuals in the house, people I knew and didn't know, and share the excitement electrifying the room from both sides of the downstage lip. Absolute magic. Soon after we opened I realized I could use this as part of my pre-performance process rather than just experiencing it as a moment of excitement."
70

We want our audience to share in our experience with this play, in their way: as participants with a job of equal importance to those of the artists.

The rest is all that.

Mark J

Rehearsal—The Politics of Collaboration

> I've been trying to imagine how on earth this can be rehearsed. I've been timid about attending, but spent this afternoon at Shotgun Studios and while I'm still not without some reservations I can see that they actually are going to do it! As far as I can tell they are doing the impossible. Today they did what I can only describe as a sort of round robin rehearsal of the nunnery scene and to be or not... Two of them would do the scene, there would be a break and some conversation with Mark, then the next two would begin. Amazing amazing amazing to see different actors doing the same scene right after each other and NOW I'm seeing the WHY of this. – *Carolyn Jones in a private email to a friend, February 2016*

What I appreciate about what Carolyn Jones wrote to her friend is that she acknowledges both the difficulty and the joy of the roulette task, and the inner conflict between apprehension and hope that arises from such a task. Arguably the one needs—and feeds—the other. And I believe it's no coincidence that Carolyn's comment ends with a reference to having begun to find meaning in the tension within these dichotomies.

Collaboration is hard. And it's worth it. As individuals who ultimately survive as social creatures, without collaboration we risk the gradual insanity that comes from isolation, lack of opposition, and lack of experience with sharing. As groups, communities, and societies, without collaboration we risk fascism—itself an insanity. Collaboration is hard for the same reasons democracy is hard. But we must persist in collaborating, and in creating the conditions for it, otherwise we will at least alienate ourselves from one another to some or another degree, and at most kill each other.

For artists and audiences alike, theatre is a practice place for collaboration

---

71

and democracy.[72] Rehearsal, more obviously than performance, is a laboratory for collaborative efforts in perpetual negotiation, visioning, renegotiation, and re-envisioning.[73]

Or at least rehearsal *can* be that! The average mainstream American rehearsal process, dictated by the pressures of capitalist economics, tends not to afford artists the time, space, or material resources necessary to exploit particularly extensive collaborative processes. One significant result has been too much thin and repetitive work, and a gradual conditioning of American artists and audiences to accept such work as normal—in other words to expect less and call it good. As the seasons pass, naturally it becomes less and less apparent why theatre is of value when it is so often so been-there-done-that-decades-ago, with season brochures straining colorfully to convince potential ticket buyers of a production's topical relevance, gorgeous sentimentality, or ALL-CAPS-FUN factor. It can make for very expensive nostalgia and, worse, the pretense of importance.

These are generalizations to which there are many exceptions. But how can one consider world theatre and deny the American theatre is years behind the forefronts of innovation? It's not because there aren't interesting American artists making great work. Theatre has simply not been central to our capitalist culture. Theatre's innate socialist implications, combined with its transiency and material expense, put it in fundamental conflict with capitalist expectations of value. So it makes sense that the moral, ethical, and—as an expression of morals and ethics—financial support does not exist to consistently provide new, unusual, aesthetically unfamiliar, critically engaged work the kinds of exposure that are either bought by explicitly commercial Broadway or Broadway-style product(ion)s or provided by a subsidized repertory tradition. By contrast, theatre communities within capitalist governments that yet retain significant aspects of socialism in their

---

[72] Mark Jackson: " As the current subject is rehearsal, here I'll focus on the artists. For the audience perspective, jump to the later chapter on that subject."

[73] El Beh: " This is a huge part of why I choose theatre making as my art-making specifically. Performance is my least favorite part of what we do, and in fact I was only really able to come to terms with this when I started doing longer runs of shows—especially with the gift of doing repertory for a year—and was able to reconfigure my view of the performance aspect as an extension of the laboratory."

74

governing and their social politics—such as Germany, France, Poland, and still to an extent the UK—are comparably more able to devote sufficient time to exploring collaborative processes and to experimenting with new ideas on a scale that might be experienced by significant numbers of people.[75]

In America it tends to be poverty that affords artists the time to work

---

[75] Mark Jackson: "In 2007 I had a conversation with Oliver Reese, then the Intendant of Deutsches Theater Berlin where Beth Wilmurt and I were performing at the time. Reese told me that in Berlin there is so much competition for audiences that theatres MUST experiment, in order to get audiences to keep coming back. It occurred to me that in America we have the opposite problem: to keep audiences coming back we must do the same handful of things, over and over again! When it comes to theatre (and perhaps other things) capitalism skews toward encouraging a mentality of narrowed, repeat buying, while socialism more readily encourages in theatre a mentality of broadened, new experiencing. This begs the question as to what ethical values are embedded in a given economic system. What does a society ultimately value: amassing capital or expanding awareness? Why do those two values tend to diverge from one another, and what does that divergence reveal?

"Of course, these binaries I'm positing are exception-ridden and risk romanticizing two highly complex systems. Socialism cannot claim perfection any more than capitalism can. Capitalism has its benefits just as socialism does. And in reality there is nothing romantic about either. And yet this acknowledgement does not negate the value of the inquiry. That value relates to Reese's challenge in Berlin. Just as practice is theory put into action, action often begins with an untried question. A question is an experiment: What will happen if...? Experiments take time, space, and other resources to explore effectively, allowing for the inevitable failures that open the way to insight. So we're back to the perennial question: what are our values, what system of theatre production will best support and manifest them, and how do we finance that system?

"Our current American system is a sand castle at high tide, begging for radical ideas and action. I don't have any to include in this particular footnote, or this book. But hopefully the radical approach of the *Hamlet* roulette helps as one spark toward further possibilities. And even Reese's predicament in Berlin provides a problem to strive for: How might we set up conditions that saddle us with a public mandate to experiment?"

at a more collaborative pace or to experiment toward innovation. Poorer artists heavily subsidize their own work by not paying themselves well. It is the rare exception—e.g. The Wooster Group, SITI Company, Elevator Repair Service—that has managed to secure the means to experiment in overtly collaborative ways over a significant period of years, and even these groups are partly dependent on Europe for a great deal of their opportunity and support and pay themselves less than any major American regional theatre. Artistic directors at the (economically) top American non-profit regional theatres are on public record paying themselves six-figure salaries that do not start with a one. This is obscene when one looks at what they pay their artists.[76]

I could continue off into a whole other chapter's subject here. The basic point is that national economic politics impact how a production is rehearsed, and yet we still have choice. Systems are made and can be unmade or remade. Very aware of this, The Shotgun Players, now considered a

---

[76] Mark Jackson: "Here are some relevant stats and commentary from a 2014 Howlround.com article by director Brian Bell: 'The Maxim Gorki Theater—the smallest of the six state-funded houses in Berlin—has an annual budget of €10.7 million ($14.2 million). This is comparable to the annual budget of the Steppenwolf Theatre in Chicago ($15,293,699 in 2012). With this budget, the Maxim Gorki Theater employs a resident acting company of sixteen actors, and produces ten main stage productions every year in addition to the shows in its repertory. Steppenwolf boasts an ensemble of forty-three actors, and produces five main stage shows per year with no repertory. Steppenwolf does a great job of promoting ensemble theatre as a value. But like most theatres, they do not produce enough work each year to offer their current ensemble full-time work.

'The common complaint from the American side is that the German theatres can only support a permanent repertory ensemble because of the public funding. But why can't American theatres with a similar budget do the same? As demonstrated above, the smallest theatre in Berlin has an annual budget comparable to Steppenwolf in Chicago, which is not even the best-funded theatre in the region or the country. So clearly, it's not just an issue of money. *It's an issue of how that money is being spent*' (Bell, 2014, my emphasis)."

77

medium-sized regional theatre, remains committed to embedding "longer" rehearsal processes into their evolving financial structure and the *Hamlet* roulette could not have been produced otherwise. I condition the word "longer" with quotes because a typical Shotgun rehearsal period—five weeks prior to tech—should be normal. But three-weeks is currently the American norm. *Hamlet* had six weeks prior to tech, then one week of tech, and three weeks of previews, totaling ten weeks prior to opening night. Add to that our two preparatory workshops and that's twelve weeks. This is exceptionally rare in the American regional theatre, and the sad fact is, although Shotgun increases its artist fees every year, the organization as of yet cannot pay artists a living weekly wage. The hope is that slow growth, rather than the more capitalist-oriented sudden spurt, will allow the company to continue steadily increasing its artist wages while retaining its collaborative ethic of providing proper time, space, and materials.[78]

Really, the *Hamlet* roulette needed at least two more weeks of rehearsal and even then things would still have been stressfully hurried. And yet in the time we had we were able to experiment with a range of collaborative processes, detailed in the previous section devoted to our rehearsal strategies workshop.

Before getting into examples of how those strategies played out, it's useful to contextualize them by charting the journey of collaboration from the early twentieth century to the teens of the twenty-first. The broad outline of this history helps illuminate our country's current political moment, with its heightened attention to diversity—a central concern of the *Hamlet* roulette that naturally impacted rehearsals.

In the early twentieth century when the Russian theatre director, Vsevolod Meyerhold, created his acting system, Biomechanics—featuring a series of highly physical exercises used to practice principles relating rhythm, balance, dynamics, tension, and release to acting—he drew partial inspiration from the American industrial engineer Frederick Winslow Taylor's theories of movement for factory workers (Gordon & Law, 1996: 34-36). Meyerhold riffed on these theories toward his ambitious aim of formulating a singular,

---

[78] Mark Jackson: " Also of relevant note is that Shotgun regularly provides the set from the first week of rehearsal. The rehearsal studios were architecturally designed to accommodate this possibility, and production schedules are based around it. Outside of Shotgun, with rare exceptions, I have only experienced this when working in Germany."

79

aesthetically inclusive acting system that would prepare actors for all possible styles of acting. Taylor's theories had aimed to accomplish a mechanized physical efficiency on the factory floor, which benefitted employers but was gradually recognized for its dehumanizing impact on workers. Naturally this hierarchical bias is easily located in Meyerhold's artistic work as well, complicating his intention to free the actor up for diverse possibilities.

Eventually, American theatre makers of the 1960s and 1970s rejected Taylorism's favoring of hierarchical benefit for more horizontal, humanizing modes of working. "Furthermore," notes choreographer and performer Martha Ruhsam in her essay titled "I Want to Work with You Because I Can Speak for Myself," "there were demands for more authentic experiences than those made by consumption and a resistance to alienation resulting from the standardization of goods and work processes as well as from the transformation of everything into a commodity" (Colin & Sachsenmaier, 2016: 82). Ironically, these impulses to free the individual, coinciding with revolutionary movements against mainstream social and political norms, resulted in many individual artists being granted cult-like guru status (e.g., Robert Wilson, Jerzi Grotowski, or Merce Cunningham), as well as communal collaborative groups nevertheless working to conform to a singular aesthetic or mode (e.g., The Living Theatre, Bread & Puppet Theatre, or the Suzuki Company of Toga).

Gradually realizing this persistent contradiction in and out of the theatre, by the time we reach the world-wide-webbed teens of the twenty-first century, when more information than one could possibly need or handle is more democratically accessible and the concept of experts and gatekeepers increasingly dismantled—whether by young people entering the workforce without formal education or the president of the country subverting the press via Twitter, or positive advances like the expanding societal awareness of cultural identity or new types of employee-friendly business models that encourage creativity—respecting difference has become of heightened interest throughout American society. Ruhsam observes:

> Today, collaborating artists are not unified by one socio-political vision or belief in a revolutionary overthrow of the prevailing political status quo and are not patronized by any authority. They are used to the daily negotiations of opinions, roles, modes of communication, and rules

of co-working that constitute a politics of collaboration. That's how they come into contact with the political dimension of their modes of working day after day in the here and now and have to *repeatedly agree anew on the rules of a specific collaborative project.* (Colin & Sachsenmaier, 2016: 83)

The italics are my own, emphasizing a theme that emerged in our *Hamlet* process, which kept changing as we learned what the roulette, our time-schedule, and one another's individual assumptions and expectations demanded of us. Negotiation of difference went beyond the expected cultural-political questions of characters being played by a cast of actors diverse in age, gender, and race, to differing ideas of collaborative practice. A given artist's personal notions of their individuality and agency sometimes came up against divergent understandings of our shared, singular task—meaning, we did not always agree on how to proceed. It was a question of democratic processes. How would we—this *particular* group—work together on this particular project?

Relevant to unpacking this, theatre scholar Laura Cull Ó Maoilearca, in her essay, "Since Each of Us Was Several: Collaboration in the Context of the Differential Self" (Colin & Sachsenmaier, 2016: 93-107), asks some useful questions about the task of negotiating collaborative difference. Helpfully, she makes the distinction between *individuality* and *singularity*, where the former references an individual person and the latter refers to a singular process involving individuals but not reducible to any one of them (98). When the distinction between individuals and their shared task goes un-clarified, conflicts of understanding can result in which we think we're accomplishing one intention together but really we're accomplishing different intentions. To begin with, the nature of a singular collaborative task, its own innate needs and demands, is defined in theatre by a complex of individual factors:

1. **The script** (Assuming there is one, as there was in this case). In addition to plot and characters, the script might dictate certain material necessities, such as specific props or scenic locations that need to be conveyed. When played, the script yields a general running time and this duration impacts choices of rhythm.
2. **The approach.** Often called "the concept," in American play production this is most typically determined by the director. I don't prefer the term "concept," even less "director's concept." I don't like the possessiveness of the latter. An approach, regardless of its

origin, must ultimately be shared by the artistic team, not seem to be owned by any individual. Also, "concept" on its own connotes theory, whereas "approach" connotes a process, a physical journey toward the eventual performance from some or another direction(s). It's the director's responsibility to help unite the artistic team in a shared, singular direction that yet considers each artist's individual approaches.

Further regarding theory, I'm a big believer in the practicality of it. My own measure of a theory's value is what it yields in practice. Rehearsal is theory, for example, aimed at the practice of performance.[82] One creates an approach to rehearsal with the aim to eventually arrive at an effective approach to the performance. Our *Hamlet* rehearsal strategies workshop, for example, was an explicit attempt to pose and test theories that might help us put the roulette mechanism into practice.

3. **Time.** In other words, the schedule. How much time do you have? How long is each session, how many sessions per week, over how many weeks? Is everyone available at the same time? How have the various tasks of production, including direct work at art-making, been organized within the time allotted?[83]

4. **Space.** What sort of space are you working in? Does it accommodate the dimensions of the space you'll eventually perform in? Do you have multiple spaces to work, allowing the group to split up and work on different things simultaneously? Space impacts time.

5. **Budget.** How much is it? How has it been allocated? Budget impacts time and space. Budget also expresses values. Do you choose to spend your money on people or on materials? Regarding materials, what technical equipment can you afford? What quality of material goods can you buy, and in what quantity? Budget impacts aesthetics. Aesthetics are containers for meaning(s). So, budget impacts content.

6. **Experience.** This is huge, and hugely difficult to quantify. Each artist brings their past with them into the present endeavor. They have

---

[82] Mark Jackson: " As Ruhsam observes, theory and practice are 'two fictional categories which are always already entangled' and can be put 'into a dialogue which reveals congruities, divergences and contradictions' (Colin & Sachsenmaier, 2016: 77)."

[83] Mark Jackson: " From playwright/activist Lisa Schlesinger: 'In the commercial world, time equals money but in a creative world time equals possibility' (Svich, 2015: 70)."

84

their knowledge, their biases, their developed tastes, their fresh eyes, their ear tuned by experience, their assumptions, their fears, hopes, ambitions, personal needs, personal codes of conduct, personal problems, personal gifts to offer in the form of talents and skills and points of view. They've done more or less of the kind of work the production demands. They've been involved in a fewer or larger number of projects of any kind, in various venues. They've studied this or that acting technique, directed or designed this or that sort of project.

7. **Zeitgeist.** Our current moment. Local, national, and international politics. The world we're living in and how we're choosing, or being compelled, to live in it. This is the greater, undeniable context around the above factors.

Reconciling these factors is the task of collaboration. That task is a question of the *how* of democracy, and it must be answered anew with each production.[85] Tensions between notions of individuality and of the shared nature of the collaborative task can arise from divergent expectations and their resultant (mis)understandings. Tensions increase if those misunderstandings continue to go unrecognized. Is one person ultimately deciding things, does each artist decide independently, or does consensus decide? How vertical, horizontal, or diagonal is this collaboration, this democracy?[86] These useful

---

[85] Mark Jackson: " For a larger discussion about democracy see the next chapter, 'Product(ion).'"

[86] Mark Jackson: " Given the employment insecurity and shifting power dynamics endemic to the American theatre— the hierarchical structures of which stand in contrast to the horizontal connotations of 'collaboration'—these are questions of perennial interest, whether a company is ensemble-based or the more typical multi-show-season-based. Relevant to these questions and to the *Hamlet* roulette, in a 1971 interview about the Théâtre du Soleil's collective creation process, Ariane Mnouchkine puts it succinctly: ' We don't gather together to decide to put a nail here or there, the person who decides is the person who knows where to put it... With our way of working, talent is easily shared, so there's no talent hierarchy, we're equal, but not identical... It would be wrong to describe this process as collective decision-making. It's a process of confronting evidence and solving the puzzle' (Williams, 1998: 26–7). Théâtre du Soleil's highly collective process and company structure does not make a perfect parallel to the *Hamlet* roulette. *Hamlet* was a production created within a basically hierarchically staffed theatre organization, but one with a notably uncommon emphasis in its company membership structure on opening up decision-making

questions can sometimes get stuck on a web of assumptions, spun gradually between each individual and the group they comprise, and go unnoticed until this web of differences becomes tangled. Then, perhaps out of well-intentioned politesse, not wishing to offend or rock boats, or merely wanting to stay on schedule, we might hold off confronting it, or simply avoid it, and this avoidance can begin to get embedded in the artistic results of the process since we perform whatever, and however, we rehearse. As Maoilearca asks:

> Do individual and collectively made works both run the risk—equally but differently—of allowing us to keep the unsettling force of difference at arm's length, of capturing its unknowable affects within our existing ways of thinking and acting? *How do we engage in collaborations in democratic ways that produce genuinely polyvocal results, rather than those in which one voice dominates or speaks on behalf of another...?* (Colin & Sachsenmaier, 2016: 95)

Again the italics are mine, highlighting a question that speaks to the *Hamlet* process as it evolved.[88]

---

processes to the room for discussion. This emphasis inevitably impacts individual productions in a given season, especially when they involve as many company members as *Hamlet* did. (Eight in total. And after the season was finished, three more of the *Hamlet* team were invited to become Shotgun company members.) So Mnouchkine's comment does resonate with the *Hamlet* roulette process, where actors had a direct voice in the edit of the text, in rehearsal split off into various rooms to work on the same scene at once, in performance took up one another's ideas and interpretations, and me all the while floating from room to room and person to person after standing before the assembled group to pass on the staging templates that were our most obvious shared base."
[87]

[88] El Beh: "This question, and my participation in it, were very much at the forefront of my mind and body during our process, and especially at the beginning of it. As one of only two people of color and one of only two queer identified people in our core acting ensemble, I found myself in a room where the bodies who had the most

For example, my increased use of staging templates, and my developing belief that the production's staging should be exact and largely shared from actor to actor, was intended on the one hand as an efficiency in response to our evident time constraints, and, on the other hand, a means of reducing the amount of variance the actors would need to respond to in performance, given the cast's reporting and my concurrent observation of their feeling increasingly overwhelmed by the scope of the task. Some actors found the precision of the staging restrictive. Attention among them to finding opportunities for individual flourishes heightened. Confusion as to what was to be shared and what could be individuated continued weeks into the run as we all made our individual and shared journeys toward understanding the project's variously objective and subjective demands. As Maoilearca observes:

> When I collaborate with others, I have to acknowledge
> and accept that what they can do with and to me will

previous experience with and knowledge of the text of *Hamlet* happened to be the white cis-gendered males. That in and of itself is not a surprising fact, but it was a great opportunity for me as someone who—both because and in spite of my minority history—has a tendency to listen more in large groups. I found myself both butting up against my own habits and feeling victim of a larger systemic oppression that I so desire to affect and change. How do I gently encourage those who have had the historical privilege and practice of holding the microphone to step back without silencing them, while simultaneously stepping up when they factually have more experience with the subject matter than I do? How do I just not get angry and shut down when I am enacting my part in the perpetuation of certain kinds of privilege, and how do I communicate most effectively to start skewing the trend? As practice is study and study is practice, this production's microcosm of a community provided a silver platter of opportunity to practice the type of communication I want to participate in and use to elevate our level of collaboration with 'genuinely polyvocal results.' Of course, as with everything else in our particular project, there was a large level of failure and surrender involved with this for me. Even with our extended rehearsal period we didn't have the time to flesh this aspect of our singular task out as much as I would have liked. But the opportunity and the challenges it presented my immediate body were indispensable."
89

be different from what I can do with and to them. What counts as a good way of working for me, may affect another body differently; what feels like an intolerably slow pace of working for me, may still feel too fast for my collaborator.[90] What is singular too, then, is the collaboration, the encounter, the relation which can be more or less successful, more or less productive or empowering for all those involved. (Colin & Sachsenmaier, 2016: 98)

In other words, our individual differences must be reconciled within the singular shared collaborative task. This is democracy.

To this challenge of reconciling individual desires and needs with a shared task, Ruhsam offers a useful perspective when she references the necessity of investigating…

…the space I call 'outside-of-self.' If artists dedicate themselves to a process of listening, negotiating, discussing and sharing, they oppose the obsolete idea of the artist as an inspired individual imagined as the original and lone author of an artwork. By committing themselves to the singular encounters that will evolve in the development of the work, artists are rejecting this conception of the artist impelled by romantic individualism. (Colin & Sachsenmaier, 2016: 78)

And here Ruhsam has stepped onto a common and problematic battleground in theatre between actors and directors. First, would we imagine the individual artist Ruhsam refers to in the quote above is among the actors or the director? An answer could depend on who one asks, but really it

---

[90] Kevin Clarke: " Here is where our common time deficit worked to our advantage. The unrelenting pace of our work kept us nimble in quick decision-making, which helped in our act of collaboration. We really had a shared collaborative pace. I sometimes wonder if our production would have still been as effective if we'd had years to really polish it. Perhaps then it would have just been 'another Hamlet' like those Mark mentions earlier in the chapter. Audiences often say they are interested in the backstage/rehearsal process. On our stage, more often than not, they were experiencing it firsthand."
[91]

could be either. And American culture, with its conflicted attitude toward the individual as at once an ideal and a suspect, complicates the question further. We admire unfettered individuality so long as it is tempered by modesty. We love our heroes and to then tear them down when they reveal their imperfection, which almost inevitably is our imperfection too. We want our leaders to follow us, until we get lost and then we expect them to have already taken the wheel. In base terms, Americans don't want to be told what to do, and yet don't want to be accused of egoism. It's an inner conflict of our national character as old as our Puritan roots, and it creates confusion and tension between actors and directors. Actors are often suspected of egoism simply because they wish to stand on stage. But that's their job. And it's really hard work to stand there well! Also, the nature of their job is to focus on their own particular role, not the whole,[92] and this lends itself to what either might be or might only appear to be narcissism. It's the director whose job is to look after the whole, to consider everyone else's jobs and to help unify their work. This lends itself to either what might be or might only appear to be a desire to control. And although directors are not literally onstage, their contribution to shaping the performance is, making that contribution difficult at times to identify. When that contribution takes on a recognizable trait or personality, directors may be said to have put their "stamp" on the work, which sounds at least a bit violent. The term *auteur*, typically used benignly by reviewers in reference to directors with a recognizable aesthetic, is habitually considered a condemnation by many artists, who sometimes use it as a synonym for *asshole* or even *abuser*.[93] Suspicion of the director's tyrannical motives is great. Suspicion of the actor's narcissism is likewise great. It's all very tedious, and, I would argue, stems from fear of unemployment and a sorry lack of any shared understanding of the sheer range of possibilities as to what collaboration can mean, and likewise the wide range of what the job of the actor and of the director can be.

How did these two dichotomies—individuality versus the shared singular task, and actors versus director—play out in our *Hamlet* rehearsals? Some

---

[92] Mark Jackson: " Of course, our roulette concept complicated this usual expectation that actors need only concern themselves with their part of the whole. Now they needed to consider every part in the script. And though they were still not responsible for design, direction, producing, or etcetera, playing all the roles demanded an expansive scope not usually asked of actors."
[93] Mark Jackson: " For an example see Hillman (2016)."
94

examples…

One example is a bit of staging for Gertrude in Act 4 Scene 1. We'd grafted this scene directly onto Act 3 Scene 4, in which Hamlet confronts Gertrude about her complicity in Claudius' murderous usurpation of the former king—her husband and Hamlet's father. In that scene we chose to have Gertrude also see the Ghost, so that her denial of it heightens her denial of her complicity in the crime. By the end of the scene she has sat down in a chair, emotionally gutted and in shock, staring out into the audience. She is still there when Hamlet exits, dragging the dead Polonius away, and Act 3 Scene 4 segues seamlessly into Act 4 Scene 1 with Claudius' entrance.

    Two staging details are of interest here. The first is what Gertrude does when she is alone between Hamlet's exit and Claudius' entrance. Some actors remained frozen in shock. Others took the private moment to release some tension and collapse into their hands, only to jerk back into tension a moment later when Claudius enters. The latter choice made a great marker on the through-line of Gertrude's journey from having buried her guilt to contending with it and rediscovering her conscience. Once this was recognized, most actors incorporated the gesture into their staging.

    The second staging detail relevant to this discussion is Gertrude facing out while Claudius is present and then also when Hamlet returns. When actors playing Gertrude stayed facing out throughout the scene, that single simple gesture expressed volumes about her shock and inner turmoil. So overwhelmed by Hamlet's confrontation and the appearance of her dead husband, looking at Claudius or Hamlet was too much stimulus to handle and she had to block them out in order to speak and to listen to them. Any even small glance to them would instantly lessen the stakes of the moment. It was debated whether the moment of Hamlet's re-entrance might be an exception. But when actors tried looking at Hamlet in that moment, it seemed to me the stakes did drop a bit. Whereas when they remained facing out but physically braced themselves for whatever might happen upon Hamlet entering, the stakes remained heightened and deliciously tense.[96]

95

[96] El Beh: " I think the latter was the most prevalent among us, at least for awhile, as this staging detail of Gertrude's was also an example of a handful of things we discovered during the run—or if my memory fails me and it was not during the actual run then it was certainly not until we were in front of audiences during previews and we had done multiple performances with various actors playing the

Debate about this constraint continued among some actors months into the run. Some kept in dialogue with me about it and others just went with their preference. In some cases there may not have been debate around the idea at all, but they'd simply missed the memo. So many notes were still swarming untethered in the air, lost to time and circumstance. It was hard for everyone, myself included, to keep track.

In any case, which choice was the best? Obviously I have my assessment. Did contrary choices ruin the scene? No. Did they lessen its clarity of stakes? I believe so. But I have no proof beyond my own senses and observations. In any case, it is a fine detail in the overall staging of the production that illustrates the level of detail to which everyone was willing to work. One can understand an actor feeling creatively bound by such a strict moment of staging. One can also understand an actor feeling emotionally freed up by it. The seven actors among the cast reported both feelings, and they each responded according to their leaning. This is democracy.

A more general example worth discussing is the overall strategy of the staging, which leaned on a minimalism based in tableaux and limiting the gestural vocabulary.[97] The staging grew stricter, more precisely set, as the process went on and as the staging's own storytelling language grew more evident and articulate—and, frankly, as it became apparent that the quality of acting was likely to remain uneven due to the randomized circumstance of the roulette, which disallowed consistency. The theory was that a clear and consistent staging would support the actors from one inevitable variable to the next. What if someone did not play Hamlet for months? The staging would still be there as a graphic hieroglyph of the given moment even though certain nuances might have faded in the interim.

So, for example, at one point I noticed that only Gertrude ever stood on a diagonal. Everyone else either stood in profile or facing directly upstage or downstage. This hadn't been intentional. But it made for a subtle yet crystal clear expression of her general political and personal stance—standing

---

role in different kinds of ways. It took time to discover what was evident about certain moments, and I loved the extended time the rep gave both the actors and Mark to come to those discoveries. The hard part was that the translation and communication of certain discoveries over time, of course, was not always foolproof."

[97] Mark Jackson: "The basic reasoning for this approach is also discussed earlier in this chapter in the section devoted to our rehearsal strategies workshop, and is further articulated later in this chapter in the section,' Notes, notes, and more notes...!'"

98

ready between others who are more loudly and definitely pronouncing their positions. In order to allow that staging detail to remain meaningful, it was important that Gertrude be the only character to stand on diagonals.[99/100/101] This single detail added yet another limitation to every actor's portrayal of every character, and such things only work if everyone participates. Everyone did. But I hope the point in relation to the individuality/singular-task and actor/director dichotomies is clear: the more shared limitations there are in the staging the less individuality there will be. For some actors such limitations were gold for mining emotion.[102] For others they were distractions, and as such a director's imposition. And so our particular democracy continued to find its way.

Ironically it was Ophelia, the character most controlled and determined by other characters, wherein the actors had their greatest overt opportunity for individuality. Our choice for Hamlet and Ophelia to perform *The Mousetrap*

[99] Mark Jackson: "Ophelia also had one or two instances of standing on the diagonal. Interesting that only the female characters did this."

[100] Kevin Clarke: "I don't believe it was in the original staging but rather emerged through Mark's notes, but Claudius, interestingly, takes a strong diagonal for a moment in Act 3 Scene 1. Claudius is in a nearly frantic state after the Nunnery scene and is looking to his wife for guidance on whether to take Polonius' advice to let Hamlet stay in Denmark. Some actors would turn only their heads to look to Gertrude for her input. Some didn't check in with her at all. But Mark, noting this important silent exchange, eventually directed us to turn full-body to Gertrude, which resulted in a diagonal. I always enjoyed this sly reversal of status and power, putting a 'feminine' stance on Claudius, throwing status toward Gertrude. It was a great example of 'staging equals storytelling', a tenet of our Minimalist approach."

[101] El Beh: "We actually had Claudius on another diagonal as well, in Act 4 Scene 5 as he approaches Laertes to tell him that Hamlet has killed Polonius. Like the diagonal for Claudius when he checks in with Gertrude about sending Hamlet to England after they witness his berating of Ophelia in the Nunnery scene, this expressed the same clear but completely oppositional intention of Gertrude's stance. Claudius was on a diagonal in moments of apprehension or doubt, exposing his vulnerability, rather than, like Gertrude, being at the ready with the agility to play all sides."

[102] El Beh: "[Raises hand!]"

as a duo granted Ophelia a virtuosic turn in the dual roles of The Player Queen and Lucianus. Her task was largely independent of Hamlet's, and so each actor could craft a unique approach without risking throwing a given night's Hamlet off. This moment was often greeted by applause.

Likewise, for her mad scene, though we eventually identified shared principles by which all the actors scored the psychological beats of the scene, they interpreted her songs and monologues in distinctive performance styles of their own choosing that brought out variable emotional and intentional emphases. This too became a virtuosic moment for Ophelia: her own outraged solo performance art *Mousetrap*, by which she accuses her abusers of their wrongs against her with a sophisticated creativity that eludes their narcissistic intellectual (in)capacities. By the time any of the seven actors reached Ophelia's final plaintive song, by whatever their individual approach, the audience was invariably pin-drop still.

And so our shared desire to grant Ophelia more agency than she is typically allowed by either the text or the average production manifested in our giving her seven distinct variations in the only two instances—in our edit, at least—where the plot provided outward openings from her traditionally restricted narrative confines. Ophelia and the cast's mutual desire for individual agency had found one another and embraced.

Ophelia's mad scene in particular provides a clear example of the uncertainty described above as to the balance of shared versus individuated elements in the production, and how this uncertainty dovetailed with perceptions of the actor-director relationship. During previews a couple of actors expressed a concern that the cast had become more focused on crafting their individual Ophelias than on Ophelia herself or her scene, and that this preoccupation was leading to choices that didn't make the strongest psychological or storytelling sense. The fact that actors brought this concern to me was a relief, I'll admit, as it meant I, the director, would not have to take sole responsibility for noting the phenomenon. I was by that point aware and sensitive to the frustrations my emphasis on shared staging was causing some of the cast, and to tensions arising from my notes.[103] So I was glad to know others were also concerned about how the relationship between individuality and our shared singularity was being negotiated. My personal inclination was toward the shared task, and I was frustrated when this was interpreted as a restriction of anyone's creative freedom—in other words, as undemocratic. The need for more shared staging than had been originally expected seemed evident, to use one of the mantras of our rehearsal strategies workshop. But what was evident to some was as evidently different to others, who would have preferred greater latitude for individual variance in the staging. The yearlong run was a yearlong negotiation of these varyingly evident differences. This is democracy.

---

[103] Mark Jackson: " More on notes can be found in the section, ' Notes, notes, and more notes ...!' later in this chapter."

One final, quite specific material example is the scripts used on stage in performance. Out of the rehearsal strategies workshop came a props idea that dovetailed with an existing scenic idea. Nina Ball's largely black set featured "HAMLET" written in large white capital letters. This bold gesture was meant to emphasize that the play was the thing. Having the actors carry black, hardbound copies of the script with their character track's names written on them in white capital letters might (1) reinforce the gesture made by the set, (2) support the minimalist approach, with the books doubling as other props—e.g. Ophelia's bundle of letters or the Gravedigger's shovel[104]—and (3) help get actors out of a jam when they inevitably went up on their lines in some significant way beyond the prompter's ability to help them. So the books were an artistic but also a practical idea.

Response among the cast, Shotgun staff, and company was quite varied. Only a minority initially recognized the range of artistic implications the books offered. Many assumed the books meant we were taking either a "staged reading" or "academic" approach, and it was difficult to convince them otherwise. Some viewed the books as a crutch. Some even suspected actors would use the books as an excuse to not fully memorize the text. Among the actors specifically, some embraced the books fully, while response from those who did not ranged from skeptical acceptance to committed protest. For the first few weeks of rehearsal, this variance stymied our collective ability to develop the use of the books. With some actors actively engaging their book and others as actively rejecting it, our creative momentum around them lurched awkwardly along for a time until finally, and not without some pushing, everyone had come to accept them.

Audience response to the books ranged from the practical—the books helped them remember which character an actor was playing—to the poetic—the characters were carrying their souls in their hands—to

---

[104] Kevin Clarke: "Or my favorite usage of the books: Rosencrantz and Guildenstern used them as THEIR scripts when tasked by the King and Queen to spy on Hamlet. Hamlet asks them why they've come and they don't know what to say and so check their scripts, delivering the most banal answer: 'To visit you, my Lord.' It was good for comic effect, but also it was a really nice meta-theatrical moment, as it was born out of a rehearsal where the actors actually couldn't remember the line and referred to the book."
105

an appreciation of their creative transformation into other objects. That audiences were volunteering consistently positive feedback about the books helped convince those in the building who still doubted their purpose.[106] Of course it had been my job as director to help everyone understand the intentions of the books and how to creatively explore them despite our differing perspectives on them, and I failed at that job for a long time.[107] That a director cannot succeed at their job alone is a relevant point. That an actor likewise cannot is as relevant. So, again, we have this relationship between individuality and a singular endeavor dovetailing with the relationship between actors and the director. And again, we see democracy finding its way through difference.

Beyond the individuality/singular-task and actor/director dichotomies, the other topic under the rubric of difference, and ultimately the more

---

[106] Cathleen Riddley: "It took a lot of discussion and reminders to accept that, in this context, calling for line in front of the audience was a GOOD thing and to be expected. But it was an endless cycle because it flew in the face of years of training and performance. The growth from the sometimes gut-wrenching need to call for line came in the form of acceptance that this would, from time to time, be needed, that we had the mechanism in place for a reason, and that the response from our audience seemed to range from forgiveness to elation. Also, since each of us at some point would take on the awesome responsibility of being on book when playing Laertes or the Ghost, it democratized the process. It wasn't 'I am on book for Cathleen,' it was 'we are on book for all of us.' It allowed me to stress less about the lines and to do the play. So failure on lines meant success in asking for a line, and I could move on."

[107] El Beh: "As I mentioned before, part of what I loved about the circumstance of the repertory was being able to witness directors allowing themselves to make discoveries over longer periods of time as we kept mining the material through the year. I think that at least part of the confusion and divergence around the use of the books was that it was hard to tell what was helpful for the story, the performer, and the audience until actually seeing it put into practice (imagine that!) and those three needs did not always coincide. The negotiation of what to prioritize in any given moment, based either individually among us or collectively, was also democracy."

108

politically meaningful one, is the currently heightened societal awareness of race and gender. Though age, a comparatively less hot-button issue, also had an impact.

Regarding age, interesting details occasionally came of certain casting combinations, such as a twenty-something female Hamlet berating a forty-something female Ophelia in the nunnery scene. Or the reverse scenario, whereby Hamlet is the older woman and Ophelia younger. Both offer subtle shades of meaning around ageism and competition between women. But the impact of age showed itself most clearly through the title character Hamlet during Act 5. The younger actors in the cast struggled with Hamlet's speech to Yorick's skull (Act 5 Scene 1), for example, as well as with the "fall of a sparrow" speech (Act 5 Scene 2). Both of these speeches and the material around them deal with questions relating mortality to letting go and forgiveness. It's in Act 5 Scene 2 that Hamlet finally answers his younger question, "To be or not to be?" with an answer that is the epitome of mature Zen enlightenment: "Let be." That is an epiphany people spend their lives struggling to embody. Mortality and its related concerns are not the sort of things one tends to dwell on too deeply in life until middle age, when the body starts its gradual decline and death becomes tangible. And so hearing David Sinaiko or Beth Wilmurt, for example, both actors of an age one never gets to see play the traditionally mid-thirties Hamlet, talk to their long dead childhood mentor of sorts, Yorick, and then arrive at the conclusion to let things be, takes on palpable waves of resonance that cannot be acted. The younger actors appeared curious and contemplative in these sections, whereas the older actors were grounded squarely in the profound and unromantic reality of them.

Easily the clearest example of gender and race impacting our choices comes from our work on Act 3 Scene 1. The scene begins with the distractingly famous "To be or not to be" soliloquy, in which Hamlet questions the value of life versus death. This leads directly into his confrontation with Ophelia, sent by Polonius and Claudius—themselves eavesdropping from behind a curtain—to goad Hamlet into revealing the true motives of his recent acts of seeming madness.

Nearly every word in this scene is famous. To get an audience to actually see and hear it we needed to take some care to make it particular. We separated the soliloquy's neon-sign of an opening line ("To be or not to be: that is the question") from the rest with a long, slow cross taken by Hamlet from downstage left to right, where he then stood to continue the text. His stance was very precisely staged: Hamlet's body remained in profile facing in the direction he'd been walking, off stage right, but he turned his head downstage to look out beyond the audience. Over the course of the soliloquy, his upstage hand very slowly reached up and out behind him, his fingers carefully feeling for something unknown.[110] Very simple, slightly odd, allowing the words to be the melody of Hamlet's quiet, searching ballad and the staging to be its grounding baseline. Meanwhile, Ophelia is onstage, tucked under an overhang upstage right and out of Hamlet's view. As Hamlet moves carefully through each image of his thoughts, Ophelia listens attentively and eventually crosses quietly and unseen to upstage center, where she finally interrupts him, announcing her presence with, "Good my lord. / How does your honor for this many a day?"

Having Ophelia listen in on "To be or not to be" is not an unprecedented staging in the history of *Hamlet* production. It supported our take on Ophelia as a kind of Hamlet herself: thoughtful, suicidal, too in her head at times to take action. So this solo moment for Hamlet became a duet, with Ophelia listening in on thoughts she too has had. But she is doing so under circumstances that compromise her ability to connect with her partner—she's there as a spy by order of the King and her father. And so with "Good my lord" she dutifully snaps herself into the action of her unwanted mission. At first Hamlet is relieved to see her and they embrace.[112] But as their dialogue progresses, Hamlet—by this point wary of anyone who crosses his path— soon begins to suspect Ophelia's odd behavior. When he then hears a noise from behind a curtain and realizes she is collaborating with his enemies, Hamlet erupts in a volcano of molten grief and outrage. The last person he

---

[110] Mark Jackson: "This staging was created out of our Schizoiding technique, detailed in the section, 'Rehearsal Strategies Workshop', above."

[111]

[112] Kevin Clarke: "Here, the Horatio/Ophelia doubling was notable for me. My therapist, in talking about dark spirals of one's thoughts, once said, 'Sometimes you just need a rescuing thought.' Hamlet is completely mentally stuck, desperate and suicidal at the end of both 'too too solid flesh' and 'to be.' In both instances, the rescuing thought comes in the face of the actor playing this double role, Horatio in the first instance and Ophelia in the second. I was always able to borrow and use the same relief I felt at seeing Horatio at the beginning of the play with this Ophelia entrance, which in turn beautifully set up Hamlet's arc of betrayal moments later in the nunnery sequence."

might still have trusted, and whom he loved, has now betrayed him too. Now he is alone.[113] He had already advised Ophelia to go to a nunnery and no longer be a breeder of sinners, and now he condemns her deception in a violent onslaught of accusations and insults, amidst which he quite suddenly and open-heartedly confesses, "It hath made me mad!" Losing his father and not knowing whom he can trust has driven him insane, and he's falling apart. With that he storms out, seemingly in pursuit of Claudius and Polonius who have fled from their hiding place.

Now alone herself, Ophelia's own explosive response to Hamlet's assault is telling. "O, what a noble mind is here o'erthrown!" she cries out. She does not lament his having berated her. She grieves the mental and emotional downfall of her partner whom she loves and respects. She identifies directly with his sense of betrayal, having been betrayed herself by her father when he asked her to betray Hamlet. And she too feels alone in this family of strangers who do not respect her voice. And so her grief here cascades from empathy and identification, not self-concern or self-pity. When she cries "O, woe is me," she is not asking us for sympathy but admitting her own emotional alliance with Hamlet's deep grief.[115]

---

[113] Mark Jackson: "Hamlet's mixed desire to be alone and yet have company he can trust is expressed throughout the play. 'Now I am alone' is something he says with some relief following his tedious, rather maddening encounter with his old drinking buddies turned spies, Rosencrantz and Guildenstern, in Act 2 Scene 2."
[114]

[115] Kevin Clarke: "A good place to talk about the gendering of emotion, for lack of a better phrase. This was a tough speech for me, and Mark and I discussed it several times. It seemed a place where the gender of the actor had an effect on the acceptable amount of emotional expression of the text. I would watch other actors in rehearsal and read their notes on a scene to capture greater insight for myself. And here was a spot where more outward or traditional displays of 'emotion' in the women received more positive reinforcement than the men. This makes sense when you look back at how we handled our own personal gender difference from our character. My older male Ophelia could not ape an affectation of a young girl lest she become a cartoon. So maybe there lies the disparity? I still never figured it out, but it was always interesting to me. I couldn't be outside myself to see how my own connection to the speech was actually manifesting itself."

The staging of this psychological escalation involved Hamlet walking slowly toward Ophelia, forcing her backwards toward the stage left edge of the platform, pushing her abruptly on the chest and arms and eventually screaming in her face. When the women played this scene together, as Hamlet they did not wish to engage their Ophelia with physical violence or to rail at her with too much verbal force. When a woman as Hamlet was up against a male Ophelia, this reluctance was also present though less so. The men as Hamlet had little hesitancy to push and rail. They were respectful of their acting partners,[116] but as men they felt freer to access violence.

Similarly with regard to race, one day in rehearsal when Kevin Clarke—male and white—was Hamlet and Cathleen Riddley—female and African American—was Ophelia, the question was raised by El Beh—female and Chinese American—whether for this racially charged casting arrangement we should consider a different staging that was less violent.[117]

So our own personal politics around gender and race prompted very useful discussions about the art we were making. What should be shown on stage? Do we condone behavior by depicting it? How to play a character's moment truthfully when it goes against one's own impulses or values? What are we saying about gender in playing this scene, wherein a male (as originally

The speech remained elusive and technical for me. Next time!"

[116] Mark Jackson:" At one rehearsal I even had to push David Sinaiko, an actor capable of great roaring, to release his ' It hath made me mad!' even more fully into Beth Wilmurt's teary face."

[117] Cathleen Riddley:" To El Beh's suggestion that we consider modifying Hamlet's attack on Ophelia when Ophelia is played by me, an older African American woman, I am so very glad that we didn't make that choice. White men assert power over Black women all the time. It's been happening forever. I don't think we should shy away from that on stage. And if our audience has feelings about that, great. Have those feelings. Have those discussions. In this moment, Hamlet is raging, and, in this moment, his Ophelia is Black. Though I never talked about this in rehearsal, and now wish I had, this occurrence of violence against Ophelia resonated as the violence against Black women during slavery. White men had all the power, could do what they wanted and not be held accountable, and the women had to take it or risk worse. But given that Ophelia has more agency in this version of Hamlet, she does take some of that power back in the Mousetrap and mad scenes. One other thing to be noted here: El Beh knocked me on my butt when she was Hamlet and I was Ophelia, so I think I had more to fear from my beautiful queer, tall, strong woman Hamlet than I ever did from Kevin!"

written) character berates and condemns a female character? What are we saying about race when we show a white man pushing an African American woman up against a wall? Are we obligated to be "saying" something? Is it okay to show without comment? What is our responsibility as artists to our audience? What is their responsibility to interpret and to contextualize?

I believed if we selectively adjusted the scene to tone down its violence— whether against women or people of color—we would be cheating our audience out of the conversation the scene had prompted us ourselves to engage in. The point of the roulette casting concept, and of having gathered a diverse group of actors, was to set possibilities in motion. I personally do not believe in the notion that audiences must be taken care of by artists, or protected from uncomfortable subject matter. Of course artists should advertise what their work is about, and audiences should find out what they're buying a ticket for. But one significant reason to go to the theatre is specifically to be triggered, to practice sitting in fictional unsafe spaces, so that in real life we might then better deal with them. We go to *Macbeth* to consider how we handle our ambitions, to *Richard III* to consider our collusion with unscrupulous but charismatic politicians, to Sarah Kane's *Blasted* to consider how we treat people with different power available to them than we have, to Penelope Skinner's *The Village Bike* to consider our prejudices about women's sexual appetites. So, one might say theatre is not a safe space, but a brave space.

In the end we kept the staging uniform from actor to actor. These situations did a great deal to advance my own understanding of that question I'd been asked so often by actors during the audition process: Why are you doing this? As the director Thomas Ostermeier has said, "My point in making theatre in the first place, is that I myself do not know who I am" (Boenisch & Ostermeier, 2016: 187). The first line of the uncut *Hamlet* is "Who's there?" The play opens with a question each character and each of us could rightly ask in the mirror. So another reason to make and to attend theatre is to figure out how to be better people despite our biases, failings, understandings, and lack of understanding. But how can we do this in the theatre if we remove what makes us uncomfortable, or what we don't agree with? On a personal scale, lack of opposition breeds ignorance, and on a larger scale, fascism. Too much opposition can be crushing. Healthy amounts of opposition can

118

oil and energize a democracy, as they can a creative process.

The Design

In this section designers Matt Stines, Christine Crooke, and Heather Basarab speak to the sound, costume, and lighting designs respectively. Not detailed here is the visual canvas, Nina Ball's set, or the shortlist of properties—hard bound scripts and Yorick's skull—created by Devon Labelle. Nina Ball's scenic designs often set a production in motion, and in this case her simple theatrical assemblage of two black platforms and two red curtains, with "HAMLET" printed in large white letters across the front of the upstage platform, announced the theatre-centric approach taken by the production and that the play would be the thing for the evening. Devon Labelle's handmade black clothbound scripts with the character's names in white letters reinforced the scenery's message. The three-color scheme of red, black, and white was echoed and expanded upon in Christine Crooke's flexible costumes. Matt Stines' sound design conjured the shades of emotion building up between the characters. Heather Basarab's lighting design helped us hear everything clearly, and despite the severe limitations put upon her by the repertory season she was able to squeeze some simple but effective nuance out of what she'd been given to work with. Altogether it was a very cohesive design, created by a group of people with a history of working together that allowed for the kind of shorthand that is difficult to explain but easy to rely on in practice. It's the kind of earned shared knowledge a collaborative group can trust to support them. It didn't mean we always agreed. It simply meant we could get on with it whether we agreed or not.

Sound—commentary by designer Matt Stines:

The very first thing I knew about this project was the casting concept. The second thing I knew was that the final sword fight between Hamlet and Laertes was going to be mimed, which seemed like a fine idea to sidestep the task of seven different actors learning how to fence, learning how to sell it, and all of them learning both sides of the choreography, all while learning every character track in this show. What's more, it offered the chance to really make these fights exciting beyond a concern for safety, since the actors didn't have the actual physical object to worry about.

But in the absence of the visual image of the swords in hand, the *sound* of the swords needed to be loyal to reality so as not to shortchange the excitement of the fight. In other words, it had to *look* as though the actors were wielding swords based not only on their mimed movements but on their sound. It became clear in the early stages of making these fights that it was even more on the sound design to sell the action than I'd thought. No matter how good the fight choreography might look with mimed swords, the visual alone would not harness the excitement of people chasing one another around with real swords. Interesting and theatrical as mime can be, Hollywood has greatly influenced our expectation for satisfaction and excitement in live performance. Why go to the theatre to watch a clearly fake fight with fake swords when you can watch relentless realistic violence on television in the comfort of your bed? And where sound design specifically is concerned, the standard surround sound systems in cinemas, video gaming, and home television viewing condition us to a heightened sense of sound location—the source of the sound in space. So in live theatre, the sound bar is now raised. To keep the audience engaged, a sound designer must ensure that the telephone ring is coming from upstage left, where that telephone is located. To be clear, I do not endorse this fidelity to realism in sound-storytelling across the board, but sometimes it's the right move. For example:

- Hamlet and Laertes hitting their swords as they cross from stage right to stage left, sometimes making contact, sometimes *barely* making contact, sometimes missing entirely—each contact with its particular cling or clang and each miss its particular swoosh.
- Laertes knocks Hamlet's sword out of his hand center stage, it hits and slides down a cinder-block wall and lands on the floor stage left.
- Hamlet manages to smash Laertes' foil out of his hand and it flies twenty feet out into the audience and lands in the aisle.

In each instance, location in space, the exact quality of the particular objects connecting, and with their particular force, were all important. Introducing sound to the sword fights provided the chance to have both the theatricality of artifice and the real excitement. The actors could choreograph essentially whatever they wanted because nobody needed to deal with a real foil or learn how to actually fence. So this particular acting company was given some acreage as far as creative freedom in choreographing these fights, and boy did that sadistic bunch of circus performers use every square foot of it. I had to chase them all over the farm with Mark whipping me to go faster. And the audience got the treat of hearing, and thereby feeling, the danger, because sound *is* movement.

Once I got past the initial anxiety of this moment's success being contingent on my contribution, it became a worthwhile four-way collaboration between the acting company, who created and performed it; Mark, the director, who oversaw the development; myself, who scored it; and the stage manager, Nikita Kadam, who ultimately executed each individual sound effect in real time based on each movement. (It's fair to say Nikita got just as much of a workout running this sequence as the actors playing Hamlet and Laertes did!) It was a serious undertaking, the most collaborative I've experienced, and the most particular and precise sequence of sound design of any in my career to date.

But it certainly wasn't the only challenge of this project. For my money, a score or a sound design is successful when it's specific not only to the script, but to every other aspect—to the genetic rendering—of the entire production. The casting in a performance doesn't typically change, let alone randomize itself each night. And the way music interacts with action and language naturally changes when different people are speaking and moving against it, even if the text and staging remain basically the same from actor to actor. Sound itself "appears" to change by virtue of the energies of the different bodies on stage. Each actor colors the sound in a slightly different shade. The goal for this *Hamlet* then was a sound design concept that could be at once chameleonic and yet specific for the actors. It had to exist outside of musical keys or modes. It had to be tonally neutral. It also needed to provide a sense of forward momentum for the drama. This production's rouletted casting generated a lot of interest. And in the technical variables of that, the sound design—where it went and why—needed to work for each actor in each role. They needed it like a chair to sit in rather than an extraneous costume piece to play with.

And let's just get real here: Shakespeare is fucking hard and fucking boring for a great many people, even if you appreciate his text. So the sound design, like the production, couldn't be stuffy or esoteric. We needed to invite the audience to get their heads in our game, to jump on and have fun and experience the excitement all the way through to the end. So the challenge: what device in music or sound art would act as a metronome, be neutral enough to allow any actor to drop into it, and also be exciting and different enough from the usual expectations so an audience would stay with us once the novel excitement of the casting passes…?

A drum set.

Great idea. Now all I had to do was remember how to play the drums, something I had taught to myself as a teenager but hadn't done seriously in ten years. With gratitude to friend and fellow soundman Theodore J.H. Hulsker for allowing me to steal bits of his drum set, and to Shotgun for providing me the physical space to practice, as well as dizzying technological advances in sound recording, I was able to get it all back in my body. I threw some mics down, hit record and played for two hours, brought various beats, samples, accents and bloopers to rehearsals, and repeated this process two or three times until each scene was supported with the proper tempo and voice.

There was the requisite amount of trial and error, but mostly, the drum set score worked. By the time tech rehearsals rolled around, the actors at least had a solid metronome in their bodies. I assume it must have been useful, considering they were still learning seven different tracks. I myself was pretty much done with my job by this point. Tech rehearsals for me are mostly about pragmatic discussions regarding timing with a lighting designer, or the scenic designer asking me to make the speakers disappear. Can this microphone pack fit somewhere in this person's costume? Can I gut this old radio and wedge a speaker in it? These sidebars with other departments are necessary, fun, and foster the village spirit. But I can't call it "collaboration," at least not artistically. At Shotgun we call it the art and practice of "collaborating on solutions."

Mark and I reflected on this project sometime after it opened, and he made the point that, while we spent forty hours a week together for nearly three months, we barely even talked. It was our tenth show together over eight years, and I think we were each worried about other things on this one than how we would collaborate. He knew I was going to give the show what it needed, and I knew he would tell me if I wasn't doing that. I barely got any notes on content. Collaboration happens in its own way. And this was the perfect example of the collaboration I'm personally most comfortable with.

I'm uncomfortable at the design meetings with the furrowed brows and the volley of obligatory compliments that fly with all the fervency of a cocaine bender. Because of my particular approach to my work, which mostly involves creating the composition and design in the rehearsal room alongside the actors and director, I often zone out or meditate at the designer roundtables. Interesting perspectives on the script begin to sprout at these meetings, sure, and obviously this is where all the designers can get on the same page about the vision. At some point, another designer is going to say something that wakes me out of my daydream and inspires my own work. And this particular design team had worked together, in whole and fractured arrangements, for some years now, usually with Mark J. They are indeed top shelf artists and humans, and they're a humbling bunch to work alongside of every time. But the rehearsal room is ultimately where collaboration happens for me. The rehearsal room allows for subtle, organic magic to happen over time, to marinate and cook slow and low. It's the best practice for my brain because it's less about theory (words) and more about real-time response (action), with the promise of intellectualization later on if one cares for that. Personally, I find word-storms get in the way of creating meaningful art and make me want to chain smoke. Too many cooks chatting in a kitchen doesn't always make the tastiest baked ziti. In Quentin Tarantino's *Pulp Fiction*, Mia asks Vince why we feel the need to "yak" about "bullshit" to feel comfortable. Vince replies that it's a good question. I agree. The silence is only as uncomfortable as you make it. And the rest happens to be silence, after all.

Costumes – commentary by designer Christine Crook:

Creating a successful production comes with blood, sweat, and tears, and the *Hamlet* roulette was no exception. Still, everyone needs a healthy dose of stress in their lives, right?! Challenging ourselves creates personal growth, and despite the arduous nature of creating this production, it's now remarkable to look back and see that somehow through all of this I managed to enjoy myself!

I pushed hard to be on the design team for this production of *Hamlet*. I had worked with Mark on many shows in the past and always felt deeply proud of the work. I appreciate that Mark devotes a lot of time to our pre-production process, and that we meet often, at a variety of coffee shops and cafes, to negotiate the details of the world we are building for the stage. Mark's approach often pushes the boundaries of realism and allows room for an edge of abstraction or stylization, and this is exactly the kind of work I want to be doing. That said, I am not always sure my own style suits him. I am a bit messy and wild and loud and unapologetically campy. Mark is very neat and meticulous. I think he has this kind of Eastern European minimalist aesthetic mixed with a dash of German Expressionism. With costumes he usually veers towards a clean contemporary look, and I don't usually get away with a lot of fantastical campy things with him.

So here we are designing this crazy production of *Hamlet* with this new radical concept of allowing each actor to play any role on a given night! Mark was interested in a focus on the text, and wanted to minimize the presentation of character details in the costumes to allow the words to be the most important thing onstage. He didn't want the audience to think too much about the costumes, and was clear that the costumes should never pull focus or create any kind of distraction. He of course explains this to me as I am presenting a wild, colorful array of extremely fantastical costume design ideas in my first preliminary collage of research images. Crestfallen, but not surprised, I pulled up my bootstraps and began to plan for a much simpler design world, writing this key word in my notebook… "STARKNESS."

With a cast of men and women who would be playing either gender opposite each other on any given night, Mark and I started with a proposal of removing any clear gender implications from their clothing. The costume design plan took shape with concepts based in androgyny, as well as visual cues to express hierarchy among characters. The base costume for each actor was inspired by an attraction Mark and I had to the contemporary white dress shirt. The idea was that a crisp white dress shirt would provide a simple bold canvas, and allow for layering of additional costume pieces that suggested an essence of military or royal status, as well as some necessities of gender and age.

The costume design also called for a very controlled color palette. I used a combination of red, white, blue, and green. This simple color language provided stability for the actors. In this world of instability, never having any idea which character they're going to have to play, the costumes were something for them to lean on. The actors explained to me that they used the visual language of the costumes (color, silhouette, etc.) to reorient themselves onstage. It was a constant in their inconstant world.

Creating this collection of costumes for a cast that could each play any character on any given night was certainly bewildering. There had to be a system! It was important to maintain the consistency of each look, no matter who wore it, so the actors could depend on that visual stability. Everybody had two pairs of pants and two shirts, and then there were different jackets and ties and vests and hats and glasses that composed the different characters. For example, if you're Hamlet, you wear green pants; if you're anybody else, you wear white. Despite this effort to simplify the ingredients, there were problems to contend with. How do you maintain a consistency with a design when each actor looks drastically different in the same clothes? One night a young woman is Ophelia and the next night a middle aged man! They are not ever going to look the same no matter how identical the clothing is. The biggest challenge in this respect was with Gertrude. The androgyny of her look felt powerful on the women, but the men just sort of looked like another version of Claudius.

Getting the right shoe on everyone was another one of my major stress points. The look needed to feel consistent on everyone, support their often very rigorous movement, and be durable enough to last throughout the lengthy repertory season. I think if we ask the actors they will recall the frazzled pain in my eyes as I lugged in mountains of shoeboxes on a daily basis to find that none of them felt quite "right."

Also, the idea of things feeling crisp and polished all the time, because of the characters being in a royal family, was difficult to maintain because of the amount of movement and sweating the actors were doing. Their crisp cotton dress shirts became damp and wrinkled very quickly onstage. Oh gosh, the quantity of sweat was a huge wardrobe issue! More than any other show I've ever worked on…ever. Those actors were working so hard, those costumes took a beating!

Remember how I said I had fun? Well, I really did! This group of actors, designers, and technicians was a blast to work with. I really enjoyed sharing this collaborative space where we all were working so hard to make this crazy production successful. Costume fittings are probably my favorite memory. I had to really negotiate with Mark and Nikita, our stage manager, to get time scheduled with our already over-worked actors. They came into the fitting room sweaty and slaphappy after hours of rehearsing and still they were so game to try anything! These were chaotic and hilarious events and we had so much fun together collaging different pieces of clothing to create character looks. The photos I took of the costume fittings are extremely entertaining as it's obvious how silly we were all being. Their time in the costume shop felt like a break from the rigorous rehearsals, and I enjoyed sharing that time with such an awesome group of people.

Once the show opened I was able to release it and let it run without me. I was always so proud of the attention *Hamlet* garnered and the success we shared with consistently sold out houses throughout the run. During the run I was able to begin reflecting on the process, and I realized how much I appreciated the challenge of editing myself and creating a bold yet controlled design world. It stimulates new design muscles to work outside of my messy, wild comfort zone. And, despite our mild divergence of style, my work with Mark always manages to maintain a flavor of Christine Crook in the end

125

product. So, over the years I have developed a great deal of trust and respect for the design process I have with Mark. I enter our work together with an understanding that he is going to push me and I am going to have to work hard, but it will be so worth it.

Lights—commentary by designer Heather Basarab:

Two of the things I love most about being a lighting designer are in complete opposition to each other. I love being part of an art form that means working together with other theatre artists and a live audience to create a communal experience. I love the democratic principles underlying and guiding the entire process.[126] However, I'm the first to admit I love the power that lighting gives me. I love providing both literal and figurative clarity that wouldn't happen without my work—the opportunity to heighten the choices of actors and my fellow designers, and to influence an audience's reception of those choices without their even realizing it.

Working on the *Hamlet* roulette project forced me to confront and recalibrate my default settings as a designer in a way I never have before. Through the *Hamlet* roulette process, I reevaluated the relationship of my medium to my collaborators—actors, director, and designers—reconsidering our common mandate to serve the work above all, but also considering how to allow for the support of each individual's struggle. I reevaluated my relationship to the audience, and the extent to which I am beholden to their experience of the piece. I had to let go of some of my control, trusting them to more actively take part in choosing how to engage and how to feel about each unfolding moment.

With this unconventional production of *Hamlet*, I was forced to decide between two antithetical yet equally justifiable approaches to lighting: either (1) provide way less structure and vision than I would ordinarily aim for, putting the focus of the production more on the process, and the power more in the hands of my collaborators and the audience; or (2) provide way more structure and vision, putting the focus of the production more on the play itself, and the power more in my own hands. I chose the first.

Lighting, like the investigation of character, develops through ongoing

---

[126] Heather Basarab: "Democracy could be defined as working together to steer the communal experience, both for those involved and those who are not. This is also a possible definition for theatre."
127

exploration of the text, deepening over time. In the *Hamlet* roulette, the actors continually reset, reimagining their characters as new combinations or new relationships unfolded. In a production in which the actors were wrestling with the text possibly more deeply—certainly more publicly—than usual, I experienced a strange dissociation. I felt obligated to pan out. Usually the lighting responds to the subtleties of the actors' choices: supporting the intention of the moment, pointing out little details, tracking their movements carefully. But lighting different actors for the same moment is like different people trying on the same clothes; the outfit looks different on everyone. Because of the variation in actor approach, I felt that I had to leave space, almost in a clinical way, and be the control factor, the constant in the experiment. I could have gone the other direction, defining the time, place, and mood more overtly, to give the actors an exoskeleton of support as they stretched into each evening's roles. But too much detail felt as if it would have caged them. (Although maybe, the nature of the story being what it is—so many trapped characters!—that would have been helpful.)

In working with other design elements, I felt more locked to the scenic, costume, and sound designs than ever, as they gave context to the lighting in the ways that the actors could not. I was responding to scenery and costumes for the composition of the looks, and to sound for the timing, since the actors were transitory. Usually the actors are the anchor, with lighting and sound keying off their timing. Here, Matt Stines laid down a rigid soundscape that established the pace and rhythm, and both the actors and I had to match it. I had to create an environment both flexible and stable, establishing a grounded space to contain the careening possibilities that might emerge off-balance each night.

I struggled with lighting the seamy underbelly of the task. How much do we want to see and acknowledge the actors waiting on the side of the stage, the sweat, the attempt, the struggle—the story within or without the story—the process itself? Does this do a disservice to the play? To the art of theatre? Does it keep us from connecting to the characters, even as we empathize with the actors? *Hamlet* addresses the importance we place on relationships. The *Hamlet* roulette explored this in a novel way, opening up not only the characters' relationships to one another, but baldly exposing the actors' relationships to their characters. Lighting is in the business of exposing, but also of exposition, and here I had to choose between the two. I felt that it was almost impossible to engage in storytelling with this production, as the framing device was almost always in evidence: we watched the actors take up the roulette mantle and teeter under its weight. The craft of theatre is often the diversion of attention, using sleight of hand to make it look easy, to keep the audience from even realizing the process so they can lose themselves in the story. But are the mechanics just as interesting? Do we want to remind the audience of what, typically, we would attempt at every moment to conceal?

In my usual relationship to the audience, I enjoy the insidious opportunity to influence their reception of a piece without their realizing why they are responding a certain way. Everything they see is literally colored by a filter that I create. In this project, I tried to remove that filter to a certain extent. This required self-control for me, but I felt it was important for the audience to be more active in making their own choices as the play unfolded, just as the actors had to reinvent their roles and relationships each night. My sister saw the show and remarked that she really appreciated seeing how hard it is to do this work, something that is usually deftly hidden from view.

Much of *Hamlet* plays out on an interior level, within the inner mind of the characters. And the roulette process was about personal exploration and challenge, the unique relationships between the individuals and the roles. My opting for a wider, more open, less personal design to allow each actor and each audience member the room to make the roles their own was an uncomfortable choice, a rebalancing of power. But this illuminated for me the amount of creative control I typically expect and crave as a designer and collaborator, and forced me to confront and buck conventions of my art that I haven't questioned before.

Previews / Opening / Roulette / Stress

> When I think back on the first preview what I remember clearly was that Megan Trout played Hamlet and we all sat on the edge of our seats. The audience held their collective breath, and then it just took off. Whatever missteps occurred were of so little consequence. I actually think the audience felt a conspiratorial sigh of relief realizing that, no matter what, the actors weren't going to be hung out to dry, that we were all having this grand adventure together. When the final curtain came

down we all rose, as one, and cheered and clapped and I
knew we were on to something really, really special.
—*Carolyn Jones, email to Mark Jackson, May 2017*

The first preview was a series of train wrecks, and among the most electric
nights of theatre I have experienced.[131] Megan Trout had the gift and the
burden of playing the title role for our first audience. It's likely she messed
something up in each scene, pulling curtains in wrong directions, misplacing
exits, dropping lines—my favorite being when she called for line, Kevin
Clarke fed her the line, "Ah HA!" and she promptly repeated "Ah HA!" with
exceptional commitment, eliciting a huge laugh from the audience who by
that point were fully on board for the ride. I have never contacted an actor
during intermission, but I texted Megan to let her know she was doing great
and to keep going. The entire cast was similarly in lightning-storm mode,
energy shooting wildly in many directions, alternately sparking fires and
sharp flashes of insight. Sitting in the back of the house, despite my own
nerves I could literally feel the audience staying with it—their silences, their
stillness, their bursts of laughter and collective gasp when Gertrude drank
from the poisoned cup. At the end when they leapt at once and en masse to
their feet it was not for a Broadway musical or a movie star playing the lead,
but for a raggedy production of *Hamlet* with very unconventional casting.[132]

Needless to say, this was encouraging. Yet we knew we had only just

---

130

[131] El Beh: " I distinctly remember the very specific bodily
sensation during the first preview of feeling like I was
wandering aimlessly around the stage all night with my
pants perfectly positioned just below my butt cheeks so
that my posterior was constantly blinding the audience for
the full evening. Amazing."

[132] Mark Jackson: "This from performance maker Katie Pearl:
'To say "the performance is the accident of my rehearsal"
requires that we believe that the process of imagining is
actually more important than the success of innovation.
This is not the same thing as letting go of rigor and
aesthetic standards. It is rather a re-focusing of values
towards the process of making rather than towards a
guarantee of product; it allows for an intentionality
to the process, recognizing that if care is put into the
making, the resulting product will "accidentally" reflect that
care' (Svich, 2015: 62)."

begun what would be a long and challenging year.[133]

One immediate challenge arose around how we were handling the roulette. Back during our last week of rehearsal and single week of tech, the cast drew roles out of Yorick's skull on each first of seven runs and this random casting arrangement would then determine a rotation that carried itself out over the next six runs, thus guaranteeing each actor one pass at each character track. During this period some actors chose to know in advance which characters they'd play at the next rehearsal, so they could prepare, and others elected to be surprised, to break the ice of the nightly randomized

---

[133] Cathleen Riddley:" There were times when I dreaded the audience drawing my name for Hamlet. The role was physically daunting to me, as the set was just, well, too big for me. The steps were high, I was unable to easily get on and off the raised platform, and I just can't move as fast as those darn kids and ex-gymnasts and dancers and such. Although just a circumstance of my age, height, and body type, feeling like 'oh my God, I don't know that I have it in me tonight' was a constant companion. The nights when I felt less successful—whether due to physical exhaustion or pain, struggles with lines, or because it had been a long time since I'd played Hamlet— were tough. I would often go home disappointed, and feel as if I had disappointed the audience and my company. I was, however, lifted up on one particular night when I got Hamlet, and I saw a group of young African American women in the audience who had been brought to the show by their professor sit straight up in their seats and cheer. No matter what occurred on that night, that was success. Audience members who often feel disenfranchised from the theatre were reached by virtue of the democracy of this process, and able to see someone who could easily be their mother but possibly even their grandmother throwing down some Hamlet. So, yes we are all Hamlet."
134

roulette experience.[135/136] We then had fourteen previews scheduled in order to allow our seven actors another two runs of each character track prior to opening. To guarantee this, we adapted the process we'd used in rehearsal: seven scrolls were made, each listing a different casting combination, and a member of the audience would draw a scroll from Yorick's skull. This guaranteed the actors their two shots at each character track while also preserving the roulette concept—until the last night, when only one option remained and the actors would know who they would be playing. A lot of discussion was had around whether to share this fact with the audience on that night or not. Megan made the point that if this put the integrity of the roulette in doubt, the integrity of the entire run might be compromised. And indeed there were some audience members openly expressing to us their doubts that we were really doing what we said we were doing. I was surprised by this skepticism. But it was evident. And so the uncomfortable decision was made to play off the last night as if it were unexpected.

That would have been the end of it had I not felt the cast could use

---

[135] Cathleen Riddley: "During our final period of rehearsal and tech, I was among the actors who chose to know what role I would be playing at the next rehearsal. Though some did not want to know, and I had much respect for that, as the oldest, least physically capable cast member (I have no shame about saying that as it's the truth), I wished to have just a bit more time to focus on one character at a time, albeit briefly. My stress level was sky high, as evidenced by my regular actor's nightmares, my waking and walking around the house at all hours, more frequent headaches and general anxiety. ('Why did you say yes to this project, Cathleen?') Just a little advance notice helped me focus my attention and do more thorough work. By the time when it seemed most were choosing not to know, I was initially deeply embarrassed to admit that I needed what might seem to be a crutch. In retrospect, if given the choice again, I would do the same thing. I was being honest with myself, and knew that, as I was already struggling weekly with impostor syndrome—the inability to internalize my accomplishments and a persistent fear of being exposed as a 'fraud'—knowing my character for the next rehearsal was a form of self-care."

[136] El Beh: "Regarding this, as I was so flatteringly quoted in *American Theatre* magazine online in April 2016 when talking about the reasoning behind this decision: 'I wanted only one fuckfest at a time' (Miller, 2016)."

137

another round of each character track, to solidify things a bit more before switching over from scrolls to the fully randomized tile roulette method.[138] With the tile roulette method, the audience draws not scrolls with a full cast list, but individual tiles with the actor's names. This meant it might be weeks, months, even *never*, before a given actor played a role again. But the acting was still very inconsistent, so I advocated the cast have at least one more guaranteed shot at each track.

It was not a comfortable discussion. There were conflicting ideas about why I was advocating for this. Some thought I had suggested it solely to accommodate the concerns of actors who were still feeling less prepared than they were comfortable with. For others, the fully randomized tile method was something they had for months been preparing to dive into fully and to now not do so as planned felt like a derailment. And then there was the significant concern, shared company-wide by degrees, about lying to one more night's audience, which we'd have to do again by extending the scroll-based roulette another seven nights. Some felt very strongly that this violated a contract we had with the audience. To my mind, doing another round of scrolls was in the long-term artistic interests of the production, and of greater importance than either the immediate desire to switch to tiles or the concern about lying one more time to one night's audience. But this made the majority of the actors angry, and they said so explicitly. Listening to their points, I did believe the need for everyone in the cast to feel ready had not been fully considered by those against the extension. I also felt frustrated by what I interpreted at the time to be a shift of emphasis whereby the roulette, not the play, had become the thing. Everyone was coming from a place of passion for the project. But the situation became contentious and feelings were hurt. The unusual stress of the production and of the impending repertory season—four more plays would gradually be added to the mix—was taking its toll and we each had our own relationship to handling the mounting pressure. For my part, I certainly said things I regret.

A day or two later our stage manager took a private poll of the cast, and most agreed to extend the scrolling period, despite their mixed feelings, if that's where the majority leaned. So we did just that. We all valued the

---

[138] Mark Jackson: " Even with one more round of scrolls the cast would still have had only five full runs of each role over the seven weeks of rehearsal and first four weeks of performances. Ideally, we'd have planned for at least seven rounds of scrolled roulette, guaranteeing all seven actors seven shots at the seven character tracks. Next time!"
139

contract we had made with the audience. And we all valued the quality of the work we were presenting to them. That these two values had come in conflict was a very interesting, and difficult, creative and ethical conundrum. One might not hope for such difficulties. But perhaps one cannot hope to never face them and also strive to accomplish great or unusual things. Is this democracy too?[140/141]

Notes, notes, and more notes...!

I had never in my directing career written so many notes for so many performances! But as we had discovered, when seven actors play all the

[140] David Sinaiko: "There were several very intense meetings. One always feels fatigue around tech, but the fatigue brought on by the logistical insanity of the roulette format exacerbated the stress that much more. But, no matter where each person came down on the issues with which we were struggling, I always felt complete confidence in the individuals in the group and in the group as a whole, in spite of the endless permutations and unknown situations to which we were consciously subjecting ourselves. We were just getting ready to start and we'd already come so far! We were embarking on a very complex journey—a marathon exercise in being ready. The readiness is all, right? Of course, it was very hard for us to know when we'd be ready to be ready."

[141] El Beh: "This pivotal conversation also illustrates the lovely overarching lesson of surrender that so serendipitously coincided with Hamlet's own letting be. A lesson that we got to practice time and time again throughout the year—sometimes, as in this conversation, in more concentrated doses than others. This unavoidable practice of surrender was a very large part of why I signed on to the rep to begin with and one of the most cherished of all the amazing practice opportunities afforded to me by both the roulette and the rep in general. To me, the surrender to not meeting expectations, the surrender to redefining expectations, the surrender to acknowledging the sticky and ever-evolving balance of being a true ensemble member, both contributing to and at the mercy of all members of a community, again weighing and balancing individual needs with the needs and desires of others and surrendering to the hope that any decision collectively made was made so because of a communal desire for the benefit of the whole, was all straight-up democracy."

roles everything takes seven times as long. I grew tired of taking notes, most of them repeats due to the roulette slowing down the cast's ability to practice and incorporate them. Some of the actors were likewise growing tired of receiving notes, while others ate them for breakfast. Confusions would arise as people took each other's notes, or lost track of a note given to the entire group for a particular role on a night they themselves did not play that role. It was very complicated.[142] And of course none of us had experienced anything remotely like this project before, so there was no point of reference for what was "normal" or what to do.

So, and in an effort toward keeping things democratic, after one performance I opened a discussion about how we should proceed with notes. The intent was that together we'd determine a single system, shared by everyone, for how to move forward in the coming weeks. At this point we were performing the show five times per week. Eventually it would turn to one time per week, when the second show of the repertory season opened. So, and with our now fully randomized roulette underway, how should notes be done, if at all?

One by one the actors unloaded their varied stockpiles of angst around receiving notes.[143] One actor said my voice was always in his head, and

[142] David Sinaiko: "There were hundreds of pages of notes, I'd wager. I still have them all! I had a different relationship with notes on this production than on anything I'd worked on previously, mainly because it got to be overwhelming. It was useful to remind myself that it was obviously overwhelming for Mark, too. So we were all feeling our way through it as best we could. It was complex: studying the notes for the track played the previous night knowing that it might be a while before playing that track again, AND studying the notes for the other tracks in preparation to potentially play them. Because of the volume and variety of notes we were receiving, I found the practical notes pertaining to what we'd actually done (e.g., 'It worked well to take the air out of X moment.') were easier to implement, or tuck away for the future, than notes about intention or interpretation (e.g., 'Gertrude should be sympathetic, but wary.') It's rarely the case that those types of notes are problematic, but, because of the peculiarities of this particular process, the practical notes were the clearest to manage and worked best for me."

[143] El Beh: "I think this was another case of everyone wanting what was best for the production but also being aware of their own personal limits and abilities, and understanding that those balances shift when long-term maintenance is involved. It was also another example of trying to create consensus within a vast spectrum of experiences and desires."

others nodded in sympathy. Another actor burst into sobs over wanting notes despite them making her feel like a failure.[144] It was a mass purgation of built-up anxieties and frustrations, all absolutely understandable but not leading to any plan. Once everyone had finished, the room lightened considerably and everyone began to chat and laugh and the meeting started to spontaneously break up. I stood up and said, "So what am I doing? There's no plan!" The couple of actors who'd heard me laughed, and one said, "Do what you want, Mark."

That wasn't what I wanted. But, democracy. The cast had elected not to vote.[146] So I did what each of them seemed to want according to their given purgation. Some I gave notes to regularly because they asked I do. Others I never gave another note because they did not want them. Others, who'd expressed mixed feelings, I only gave notes to when they asked for them. Of those, some I would first ask in turn what they were interested in hearing about and address only those things, while to others I volunteered whatever I had. As the weeks passed, if the nature of someone's response to notes seemed to change, I'd adjust accordingly, whether that meant offering more or less. I didn't like the inconsistency and ambiguity of these disparate systems, since it meant the rolling collaborative conversation was now lumpily distributed, with some actors not privy to discoveries and refinements being made

---

[144] Cathleen Riddley: "Yep, the one who burst into sobs was me. Throughout the process I had struggled with the fear of personal failure, which would by default also mean that I had failed the company. I was a Notes Junkie, afraid to get notes and afraid to NOT get notes. I spun around between wanting to take the notes in and do better, and fearing that I'd not be able to retain or implement them—especially not knowing which character I'd draw on any given night. When I got around to seeing that notes are just tools, I was better able to manage my relationship to them."
145

[146] David Sinaiko: "It's true, I think at that point, as a whole group, we just couldn't handle going through the process of making one more decision. At that moment, we just wanted to play the play and fully explore that phase of the experience."

between me and those with whom I was in regular dialogue.[147]

It's a good and useful thing for a director to step away for a time. But this was a highly unusual production that shifted tones and sociopolitical implications radically from night to night. I enjoyed being audience to it and didn't want to miss whatever great surprise might happen next! In any case, a trip to Europe provided an excuse for a good, necessary, productive few weeks away—I would guess for both me and the cast! Sometime after returning I attended the final performance of the summer. Now there were three productions in the repertory and the actors were very busy. I thought *Hamlet* had by then become quite diffused. Audiences were still packing the house and going mostly nuts, so my observation wasn't of much matter. And of course my perspective was informed by my unique relationship to the show. In any case it was a good time for it to go on hiatus for three months, so everyone could have a break, while the final two shows of the repertory rehearsed and opened.

Last thing on notes. Shortly after opening, to provide a quick reference for the cast's use as the season went on, I wrote two versions of an attempt to summarize our particular minimalism, to which each actor had their own relationship and understanding. I hoped something simple, used as a touchstone, might help unite their understandings over time. The first version outlined the principles in a fairly straightforward way, and the second played

---

[147] El Beh: "This felt to me to be a missed opportunity in our production, and was harder for me to surrender. Part of what excited me about the repertory was the possible longevity of our lab experience with this project, and with each other as an ensemble. Of course, there were lessons to be learned in how to deal with this eventual unevenness, but to me it also dissipated our ensemble on a certain level since this part of the journey of discovery was no longer shared and contributed to by the whole. It meant that the sky was no longer the limit and there was only so far we could grow in particular directions collectively. In the end, we're all human and there was only so much we each could take on with this beautiful monster—AND the rest of the shows we were doing for the rep—but I'll always wonder how much deeper we could have gone if we'd had the bandwidth to stick with that particular way of working that required more and more dialogue and discovery."
148

upon Polonius' advice to Laertes:

OUR MINIMALISM [v1][149]
as brevity is the soul of wit

Minimalism is high stakes.
It leaves you feeling naked on stage
because there is little to distract from the truth
and the truth is hard.

The language is your main means of taking action.
Be clear, simple, direct, and dynamic.

Keep the staging simple.
Hit your marks as marked:
time, space, energy, and intention.
Staging is storytelling.

Play the precise distance between you;
It conveys relationship, status, intention.

Your position is your psychology.
You're always in either profile, full out, or full back;
We can count on one hand how often anyone is in three-quarters.

The particular energy that drives your intention
oft' determines how it lands.

Lead with intention, let emotion follow
or we don't know what's happening.

Listen more. See more. Do less.
On stage as in life, nobody needs more stuff;

---

[149] El Beh: "Thankfully, we had multiple copies of this manifesto posted all over the theatre for the entire year. I loved it as a reminder not only for *Hamlet*, but found myself referencing it time and time again for the other shows I was involved with in the rep. Its lessons not only on minimalism but on good, responsive, listening-filled acting, are indispensable. And the brevity helps!"
150

And one can always stand to listen and to see more openly.
Familiarity and fear can tempt us to be clever and inventive.
Refine your performance rather than elaborating on it.

The play's the thing
The rest is silence

OUR MINIMALISM [v2]
as brevity is the soul of wit

Yet here, cast! On stage, on stage, for shame!
The audience sits in the pews of the Ashby
And you are stay'd for. Here, my blessing with thee.
And these few precepts in thy memory
See thou character:

Give thy lines your tongue,
And any unproportioned emotion the cork.

Be thou simple: so by no means simplistic.

Be aware of entrances to a scene, then being in,
Bear't that the staging may support your partner.

Neither clever nor inventive be;
For invention oft' loses both the scene and substance,
And cleverness dulls the depth of understanding.

This above all: to thine open ears and eyes be true,
And it must follow, as the night the day,
Thou canst not then be false to any moment.

Farewell: my blessing season this in thee!

The Run

In many European countries the repertory system is normal, and productions
may run for years. But in the American theatre, repertory is virtually unheard
of. Only the Oregon Shakespeare Festival, in Ashland, Oregon, maintains a
regular repertory production model and even then each production plays

in only one season, as with any regional theatre. Shotgun's twenty-fifth anniversary one-off repertory season was an exciting, taxing shock to the artists and staff involved, and alternately a thrill and a befuddlement to our audience. In this section, actors El Beh, Kevin Clarke, and Cathleen Riddley offer some thoughts about certain aspects of running the *Hamlet* roulette within the context of this unique season.

El Beh on playing the show 5x/week versus 1x/week:

The first time we would have to perform *Hamlet* after we had opened the season's second show, *The Village Bike*, therefore moving into the 1x/week rotation of *Hamlet*, was the thing of which I was the second most scared in the entire season—the first coming later when we would move into the full repertory of all five productions after having had over three months off from three of the shows.

We did not perform *Hamlet* during the intense two-week period of *Village Bike* tech rehearsals, previews, and opening. The first performance back felt incredibly discombobulating. I remember the difficulty of having to remember to not spontaneously bust into my *Village Bike* British accent during *Hamlet*, or, conversely, of calling "line!" during *Village Bike* performances where this wasn't an option. Also, being in a slightly familiar yet all too different world—still at the Ashby Stage but the set designs were completely different—was a surprisingly confounding physical experience. And we now had not only the seven tracks of *Hamlet* but our characters in an entirely different play to hold and manage. Though all of this was somewhat obvious and anticipated, I could never really have known how crazy it would feel until we went through it. The camaraderie of the ensemble and the opportunity to stay the course together was also palpable.

The *Hamlet* roulette was not like traditional productions, in which a little time away from the play could add some freshness or spontaneity when perhaps things start to get stale. We never had the chance for that kind of staleness with our roulette, even at 5x/week. So the 1x/week schedule further pressurized the already seemingly impossible task. Part of the real beauty of theatre performance to me is getting to experience its ephemerality through its repetition. Through the lessons of fleeting moments, a longer journey and a longer sustaining lesson evolve. My relationship to the longer journey had to evolve once we were at 1x/week and the repetitions were fewer and farther between. We simultaneously became gradually more fallible—drifting further away from certain core concepts—and yet more comfortable and confident each week that we pulled it off, *and* more frightened every week that went by that we hadn't touched a given role. The larger lesson was certainly about surrender, but I'm sure there was a lot of learning in the retention of all that material over time. That's part of the beauty of active practice. Sometimes you're just in it and doing it and the ripples of its effects go further than you have the scope to recognize in the moment.

Kevin Clarke on playing the show 5x/week versus 1x/week:

What stands out foremost about playing the show 1x/week was that I had performed in *The Village Bike* the night before and been at rehearsal all day for *Grand Concourse*, then had an hour off to wolf down some food before diving into our *Hamlet* warm-up games and fight call. And then sometimes I played Hamlet that evening. I couldn't just switch off that day's rehearsal—many times the big discoveries of a rehearsal come after you leave the studio and have a moment to reflect, make notes, read notes, review. So to switch gears abruptly would shortchange the rehearsal process I was in for *Grand Concourse*. And yet I had to get ready for *Hamlet*. So my normal show prep—the things an actor does during the day or shortly before a performance to get ready—got left by the wayside by necessity. There were days when I really didn't know exactly who or where I was. Then again, the whole repertory scenario is an actor's dream. Things got considerably easier when we entered full repertory in the winter, and I was no longer trying to learn a new show during the daytime.

El Beh on the hiatus and playing the show during full rep:

The three-month hiatus from the first three shows, and then playing *Hamlet* alongside all five shows, was, as I said, the thing I was the most scared of for the entire year. There was so much to hold, so many drastic changes in short periods of time. Part of why I was afraid of doing a repertory season—which is also why I participated in it—was that holding so much might result in a lack of depth in performance. While I think that fear at least partly came true, I'm sure that with the gift of the season's length there also came a depth of which I'm still not even aware. More than that, it offered the audience the chance for multiple viewings over time, which, like the roulette concept of our *Hamlet*, allowed for them a deeper study of each play in the season. Things throughout the repertory got messy for sure. But the feedback we received from most audience members who had season subscriptions was that a similar type of generosity that accompanied *Hamlet* bled into the rest of the season. The sheer magnitude of the task was a recipe built for failure, so when we were able to deliver even more than expected, we were met with kindness and gratitude. And so this communal working together on both sides of the stage was also the practice of coming together toward a larger common goal of generosity and effort.

Kevin Clarke on the hiatus and playing the show during full rep:

The three-month hiatus was a welcome break. During that time I did spot checks in the background of my brain for the material from each of the three shows I performed in—all of which were on hiatus while the final two shows of the season were getting underway. But putting things back on their feet was tricky. There was confusion about the schedule, actor availability, and plans for brush-up rehearsals.[154/155] Generally these rehearsals were a mess of hodgepodged and self-guided work with whomever could be there. This was not the best way to get a show like the *Hamlet* roulette back on its feet! That said, some of my best brush-up rehearsals were working one-on-one with another actor, as it allowed time for just two of us to confer and confirm some of the specifics, especially details that had gotten lost by the end of the initial repertory, whereas with more people in the room there was less time to confer.

During the full-repertory run I definitely noted a collective softening of our commitment to our Minimalism. As we all became more familiar with some aspects of the show, we became, as actors often do, "freer." Most notably, gesturing started to creep in in a more naturalistic manner, whereas earlier we had stripped away much of this in support of the language and the communication between characters. I both caught myself doing this and observed it in others. During the initial 5x/week run of *Hamlet*, Mark, having worked with me for years, brought to my attention my habit of building physical bits of varying intricacy, which didn't really belong in our streamlined staging. In other shows, these bits had been—when appropriate, discussed, and refined—welcome. But they didn't have a place here. Having been personally and privately noted about it early on, I was able to refer back

---

[154] Kevin Clarke: "This was the case with multiple shows in the repertory season, not just *Hamlet*."
[155] El Beh: "Ideally we would have had seven pick-up rehearsals of *Hamlet* at the end of the hiatus in order to give us all a chance to run each track before jumping in front of an audience again. Schedules and resources and life eventually determined that we got three, with not a single rehearsal having everyone present. More surrender. More making it happen with what was available."
156

to this note as a touchstone and reminder to play within the constraints of our system. Of course I slipped, and I was grateful for the reminder. I was a believer in the Minimalist principles we were exploring, and in honesty was a bit saddened to feel us loosen our collective grip on the rigor of constraint during our full repertory performances.

Final thoughts from Cathleen Riddley:

As we were approaching the last two months of the run, I sustained a physical injury that made it unwise to continue in the roulette and run the risk of drawing one of the more physically demanding roles. I was wearing down under the full rep. I was extremely sad about this, and once again the specter of failure reared its head. In considering whether I should withdraw entirely and have our understudy, Caleb Cabrera, do the remaining performances, Mark told me that, whatever I decided, I was, and forever would be, a part of a once-in-a-lifetime experience and that I would cross the finish line with everyone else. After talking this through, the decision was made that I go on "modified duty" for my own wellbeing and play one character track—Ghost/Gravedigger—for the remainder of the run. This would be explained to the audience each night, everyone else would continue with the roulette, and the integrity of the roulette would remain intact.

I'm glad I chose not to withdraw, and to be on that stage with my beloved cast through our final bow. In all of my failures, the success was that we experienced it, we shared it, I was a part of it, and we did it. And I learned that self-care is an aspect of the creative process that should be honored. A true gift was that, when I most feared that I was letting the cast down, I received an outpouring of support like I never would have dreamed. I was reminded that I was a vital part of this family. We were in this together. We got there—wherever there was—together. And as always, the journey is what it's all about.

Final thoughts from Kevin Clarke:

On closing night, we were each "awarded" the prop book of the character we had played most frequently throughout the run. I received Polonius. We were also given the wooden tile bearing our name, used nightly to draw our role out of Yorick's skull. I was immediately struck by the weariness of these objects, how they were each a bit smeary and smudged in their own unique ways. The book bore the signs of nights of constant handling, throwing, dropping. Although I had seen my tile I never really interacted with it. The tile's edges were rounded and sanded smooth by design. Now in my hand, it immediately reminded me of beach glass and for a moment I thought it had been worn smooth from use in the selection process. The thought prompted me to reflect on its use. It occurred to me that at each performance a different individual in the audience had reached in and pulled out my name. And each night I'd play whatever part they had "chosen" for me. All these people had helped to shape a huge part of a year of my life. This unusual act of random connection with so many audience members steered the completely unique course of my performance journey. I found myself moved by this simple object bearing my name. Receiving this on closing night had an unanticipated and powerful impact on me, and I do consider it more sacred relic than keepsake.

"Drunk *Hamlet* Roulette"

Three months after closing night, the cast reassembled at the request of Shotgun board member Tami White, who at the company's annual fundraiser had bid on an auction item by which the winning bidder chooses a play and Shotgun organizes a reading, either at the theatre or the person's home. Tami asked that we do *Hamlet* at her house, drunk!

So with no formal rehearsal or preparation—just the deeply etched memories of a year's work—we gathered, ran the sword fights sober, tossed a few drinks back and went at it. The audience sat on various benches and chairs in Tami's backyard and, when the action moved inside, her living room. The actors adapted the original staging on the fly, incorporating the upstairs windows as well as the particular entrance and exit opportunities afforded by the layout. I'd arranged a nine-bottle whiskey flight, with whiskies chosen for specific characters or speeches, to keep everyone greased. By intermission the cast and many in the audience were properly tanked, and for safety I asked the cast not to drink in the second half. They didn't, but the spirits were freely flowing in their bloodstreams by then. Out of this came some genuinely hilarious moments, genuinely bad moments, and genuinely *good* moments! I was amazed by how much of the text everyone could remember. Their improvised riff on our original staging was delightful. And they managed to render a few bits with all the finesse one would hope from any performance. Kevin and Cathleen's Claudius and Gertrude unleashed their full passion, at one point making out on Tami's living room couch, which Megan's embarrassed Polonius awkwardly interrupted to share Ophelia's news of Hamlet's madness. David's Ghost was exceptionally focused and strong, and he found new moments to haunt Hamlet through various windows and glass doors. Nick's Ophelia was genuinely moved, and moving, when he tenderly approached Hamlet after overhearing "To be or not to be," which the night's Hamlet, El Beh, had just rendered with all the care and attention of the best nights of the run. For the climactic mimed sword fight, I approximated Matt Stine's sound design by banging and scraping a metal pot and spatula together, with members of the audience spontaneously vocalizing some sound effects of their own.

No doubt the whiskey made it all seem better than I remember it—the cold night air warmer, the mosquitoes less pesky, the outrageous acting more believable. Beth had told me beforehand that she was genuinely worried she might suffer some form of PTSD by returning to the show. Yet somehow this too-soon revisiting turned out to be the only way I can imagine coming back to the show—unrehearsed and inebriated, not only inviting failure but fully embracing it in a bear hug and dancing it off its feet around an entirely unfamiliar dance floor. "Drunk *Hamlet* Roulette" did nothing to further Shakespeare in production, nor our production's implications of diversity and democracy. But it made for an uncommonly literary drinking party, and a weirdly fitting coda to an experience that greatly warranted a night of cutting loose. By taking our *Hamlet* roulette out for a round of drinks, perhaps at the very least we shook off any remaining tensions from what had been a very stressful year.

Final Casting Tally:

	BETH	CATHLEEN	DAVID	EL	KEVIN	MEGAN	NICK
3/31	Claud	Polo	Ghost	Gert	Laer	**Hamlet**	Oph
4/1	Ghost	Laer	Oph	Polo	Claud	Gert	**Hamlet**
4/2	Laer	Gert	Claud	**Hamlet**	Polo	Oph	Ghost
4/3	Gert	Oph	Polo	Ghost	**Hamlet**	Claud	Laer
4/6	**Hamlet**	Ghost	Gert	Claud	Oph	Laer	Polo
4/7	Polo	**Hamlet**	Laer	Oph	Gert	Ghost	Claud
4/8	Oph	Claud	**Hamlet**	Laer	Ghost	Polo	Gert
4/9	Gert	Laer	Oph	**Hamlet**	Ghost	Polo	Claud
4/10	**Hamlet**	Oph	Claud	Laer	Polo	Gert	Ghost
4/13	Laer	Claud	Ghost	Oph	Gert	**Hamlet**	Polo
4/14	Oph	Ghost	Polo	Claud	**Hamlet**	Laer	Gert
4/15	Claud	Polo	Gert	Ghost	Laer	Oph	**Hamlet**
4/16	Ghost	Gert	**Hamlet**	Polo	Oph	Claud	Laer
4/17	Polo	**Hamlet**	Laer	Gert	Claud	Ghost	Oph
4/20	Laer	Polo	**Hamlet**	Claud	Ghost	Gert	Oph
4/21	Ghost	Laer	Claud	Gert	**Hamlet**	Oph	Polo
4/22	Polo	Oph	Ghost	**Hamlet**	Laer	Claud	Gert
4/23	Oph	Gert	Laer	Ghost	Polo	**Hamlet**	Claud
4/24	**Hamlet**	Ghost	Gert	Oph	Claud	Polo	Laer
4/27	Gert	Claud	Polo	Laer	Oph	Ghost	**Hamlet**
4/28	Claud	**Hamlet**	Oph	Polo	Gert	Laer	Ghost
4/29	Gert	**Hamlet**	Claud	Polo	Laer	Oph	Ghost
4/30	Claud	Gert	Polo	**Hamlet**	Oph	Ghost	Laer
5/1	Gert	Ghost	Claud	**Hamlet**	Polo	Oph	Laer
5/4	Polo	Laer	**Hamlet**	Ghost	Gert	Claud	Oph
5/5	Gert	Ghost	Oph	Claud	Polo	Laer	**Hamlet**
5/6	Gert	Oph	Polo	Ghost	Laer	**Hamlet**	Claud
5/7	Laer	Gert	Polo	Ghost	Oph	Claud	**Hamlet**
5/8	Gert	Claud	Polo	Ghost	Oph	**Hamlet**	Laer
5/11	Claud	Ghost	Polo	Laer	Oph	**Hamlet**	Gert

	BETH	CATHLEEN	DAVID	EL	KEVIN	MEGAN	NICK
5/12	Oph	Ghost	Laer	**Hamlet**	Claud	Polo	Gert
5/13	Ghost	**Hamlet**	Claud	Gert	Oph	Polo	Laer
5/14	Claud	Polo	**Hamlet**	Oph	Gert	Laer	Ghost
5/15	Claud	**Hamlet**	Laer	Gert	Ghost	Polo	Oph
6/10	**Hamlet**	Gert	Oph	Polo	Claud	Ghost	Laer
6/17	Laer	Gert	Ghost	Polo	Claud	Oph	**Hamlet**
6/24	Gert	Polo	Oph	Claud	**Hamlet**	Ghost	Laer
6/30	Oph	Gert	Laer	Ghost	Polo	**Hamlet**	Claud
7/1	**Hamlet**	Claud	Oph	Ghost	Gert	Laer	Polo
7/21	Polo	Claud	Oph	**Hamlet**	Ghost	Laer	Gert
7/28	Ghost	**Hamlet**	Polo	Oph	Laer	Claud	Gert
8/4	x	Claud	**Hamlet**	Gert	Polo	Ghost	Oph
8/11	x	Claud	Oph	**Hamlet**	Gert	Ghost	Polo
8/12	x	Polo	Oph	Ghost	**Hamlet**	Gert	Claud
8/18	Laer	Oph	Polo	**Hamlet**	Claud	Ghost	Gert
11/25	Polo	Claud	Gert	**Hamlet**	Oph	Laer	Ghost
11/30	**Hamlet**	Oph	Ghost	Laer	Polo	Gert	Claud
12/4	Laer	**Hamlet**	Gert	Ghost	Polo	Oph	Claud
12/7	**Hamlet**	Ghost	x	Claud	Polo	Oph	Gert
12/11	Claud	Ghost	Laer	Gert	**Hamlet**	Polo	Oph
12/14	Oph	Ghost	Gert	Claud	**Hamlet**	x	Polo
12/18	Laer	Ghost	Claud	Oph	Polo	**Hamlet**	Gert
12/20	Claud	x	Ghost	Oph	Polo	**Hamlet**	Gert
12/31	**Hamlet**	Ghost	Oph	Laer	Gert	Claud	Polo
1/3	Oph	x	Gert	Polo	**Hamlet**	Claud	Ghost
1/4	Claud	x	Ghost	Polo	**Hamlet**	Oph	Gert
1/13	Claud	x	Polo	**Hamlet**	Gert	Oph	Ghost
1/14	Gert	x	Ghost	Oph	Polo	Claud	**Hamlet**
1/18	Polo	Ghost	Gert	Claud	Laer	Oph	**Hamlet**
1/22	**Hamlet**	Ghost	Laer	Polo	Claud	Oph	Gert

An "x" means that actor was out for the night and understudy Caleb Cabrera went on as Laertes.

Backstage logistics:

Our stage manager, Nikita Kadam, created this spreadsheet and posted a large printout of it in various locations backstage to help the actors stay on track. This is a black and white rendition of the original color version.

REHEARSAL CHUNKS		1.2A - Press Conference	1.2B - H&H Reunited			1.3 - Laertes Send Off		
Page #		1	4	4	8	8	9	10
Act.Scene.Sub		1.2.1	1.2.2	1.2.3	1.2.4	1.3.1	1.3.2	1.3.3
Sub Duration		4:57	1:47	3:09	:19	1:26	1:24	2:32
Hamlet			Hamlet			5:22		
Rosencrantz	Claudius	Claudius		23:17			23:17	
Guildenstern	Gertrude	Gertrude		23:17			23:17	
Ophelia	Horatio	Ophelia	Put on Coat x->HL	Horatio	Take off Coat and put on USL chair		Ophelia	
Laertes		Laertes		5:15		Laertes		DSR
Osric / Priest	Polonius	Polonius		6:41			Polonius	
Gravedigger	Ghost	Ghost	DSL Chair **ON BOOK**; Leave when Laertes exits and go to HR Vom					

	1.4 - Hamlet Meets Ghost					2.1 - Tricking Polonius		2.2A - Ophelia Letters
	12	12	13	16	18	19	19	20
	1.4.1	1.4.2	1.4.3	1.4.4	1.4.5	2.1.1	2.1.2	2.2.1
	:54	1:31	3:57	2:37	1:27	:16	1:58	4:00
			Hamlet					Claudius
				23:17				
				23:17				Gertrude
						Ophelia		
		Horatio; sit on SR stair when Ham makes you "leave".						
					DSR Chair; Sitting in France ON BOOK after Ghost leaves.			Polonius
			USL Chair					
						DSL Chair		
x-> HL Vom	Ghost on Railing	Ghost x-> Stage		2:37	Ghost			

2.2B - Except my Life	2.2C - Denmark's a Prison			3.1 - To be or not to be & Nunnery Scene			
23	25	26	29	30	31	34	34
2.2.2	2.2.3	2.2.4	2.2.5	3.1.1	3.1.2	3.1.3	3.1.4
2:17	:08	5:13	4:17	:21	6:26	:45	1:05
Hamlet				:21	Hamlet	1:50	
2:17 x-> HR	Rosencrantz		MSR Chair	Claudius			
2:17 x-> HR	Guildenstern		MSL Chair	Gertrude			
	USR Chair			Ophelia; Exit USR and be ready at USC for cue to enter for play within the play.			
DSR Chair; Sitting in France **ON BOOK.** Exit after Gertrude to USR.							
Polonius	USL Chair				Polonius		
DSL Chair				DSL: Have your book ready to be grabbed by Hamlet after Polonius is killed.			

3.2A - Play within the Play				3.2B - Play on this Flute		
35	35	36	41	42	45	46
3.2.1	3.2.2	3.2.3	3.2.4	3.2.5	3.2.6	3.2.7
1:34	:23	6:49	:20	3:29	:38	:39
			Hamlet			
1:34 x-> HR Vom	Claudius		:20 x-> HL	Rosencrantz		:39 x-> USR
1:34 x-> HR Vom	:20 x-> HL		:20 x-> HL	Guildenstern		5:23 x-> USL
Ophelia; Exit USR and be ready at USC for cue to enter for play within the play.				USL: Standing		USL Chair: Exit after Laertes to USL.
DSR Chair; Sitting in France **ON BOOK.** Exit after Gertrude to USR.						
1:58 x-> HR Vom	Polonius		3:49	Polonius		:39
DSL: Have your book ready to be grabbed by Hamlet after Polonius is killed.						

3.3 - Claud Prays/ Hamlet gets Revenge			3.4 - Queen's Closet				4.1 - Claudius Mad/To England!		
46	46	47	48	48	51	52	54	55	56
3.3.1	3.3.2	3.3.3	3.4.1	3.4.2	3.4.3	3.4.4	4.1.1	4.1.2	4.1.3
:29	1:57	2:18	:19	4:11	1:20	2:07	1:55	2:06	:39

2:26

Claudius

Hamlet — 1:55 — Ham

Claudius

Gertrude — :39

5:23 x-> USL

MSR Chair: Have your book ready for Hamlet to grab.

USL Chair: When you exit - exit after Laertes to USL.

DSR Chair; Sitting in France **ON BOOK.** Exit after Gertrude to USR.

Polonius — 4:15

Polonius — Ghost

4:40   DSL Chair: Exit after Ophelia to USL

DSL: Have your book ready to be grabbed by Hamlet after Polonius is killed.

4.5A - Ophelia Gone Mad								4.5B - Claudius Manipulates Laertes/Ophelia Drowns			
57	57	57	57	59	59	60	61	64	64	65	65
	4.5.1	4.5.2	4.5.3	4.5.4	4.5.5	4.5.6	4.5.7	4.5.8	4.5.9	4.5.10	4.5.11
	1:31	:46	2:03	:28	1:06	2:49	4:33	:20	:05	1:37	:19

Character / timing blocks:

- 2:17
- Gertrude
- Claudius — 15:33
- Gertrude
- Ophelia; Open curtain to first spikes — 1:31
- 4:48
- 1:34
- 4:33
- Ophelia
- 4:53
- Laertes
- Ophelia — 1:56
- 8:05
- 11:19 x-> HR Vom
- DSL Chair with YORICK'S SKULL **ON BOOK**

INTERMISSION

5.1A - Yorick	5.1B - Funeral		5.2A - Wager is Made			5.2B - Duels and Death	
65	70	72	73	74	76	77	80
5.1.1	5.1.2	5.1.3	5.2.1	5.2.2	5.2.3	5.2.4	5.2.5
7:46	5:32	:10	1:34	2:50	1:31	5:28	3:21
	Hamlet	:10		Hamlet			
	Claudius			6:05		Claudius	
7:46 X-> HR							
	Gertrude			6:05		Gertrude	
7:46 X-> HR							
	Horatio	:10			Horatio		
8:05 x-> HR Vom	Laertes			6:05	1:31	Laertes	
HR ON BOOK	Priest ON BOOK		1:44	Osric		Osric	USR Chair
Gravedigger					DSL Chair ON BOOK		

Questions:

What makes a good question? And what does "good" mean in this context?

How does what we call *process* impact what we call *product* in live theatre? Though we distinguish them, how do they relate over time—if they do?

Regarding vertical, versus horizontal, versus diagonal collaborative processes, first: what are they? Second: what are their obvious and less obvious differences? And finally, what are their use(s)?

Product(ion)
Mark Jackson[1]

The "product" is not on stage.

By nature of the roulette task that was the engine of this project, in performance, as it had been in rehearsal, the 2016 Shotgun Players product(ion) of *Hamlet* was in key respects approached more like a devised performance than a play. With that in mind, rather than using this chapter to chronicle the production's staging and acting choices from one scene to the next, examples of which appear elsewhere throughout this book, I'll explore certain particularly striking sociopolitical products of that staging and those choices.

Many people have articulated, in many ways, this maxim that the "product" is not onstage. It emerged as phrased here in my own consciousness from working in devising and performance-making circles where expectations of "process" and of "product" intermingle far more messily than in traditional mainstream theatre practices and venues—by which I mean practices and venues related to the production of plays.[2] It's reasonable to suggest that the average American theatre participant, whether behind the scenes or seated

[1] All footnotes in this chapter are by Mark Jackson unless otherwise noted.

[2] The terms "devising" and "performance-making" continue to be defined, refined, and redefined by practitioners and academics alike. For simplicity I'll suggest here that the most basic feature distinguishing this broad range of work is that it does not begin with a play written by a playwright, or then get created in accordance with the linear production models typical of mainstream play production. Highly diverse work by a wide variety of international artists—600 Highwaymen, Action Hero, Bryony Kimmings, Elevator Repair Service, Forced Entertainment, Gob Squad, Pina Bausch, Robert Lepage, SITI Company, Sleeping Trees, Teatr Zar, and The Wooster Group, to name a mere few—have all been considered under the "devised" and "performance-making" rubrics. For more extensive discussions of devised theatre and performance, see Bailes (2011), Colin & Sachsenmaier (2016), Daniels (2014 & 2015), Harvey & Lavender (2010), and Lehmann (2006).

in the auditorium, expects a performance to be the finished product of a private rehearsal process, that this finished product is what audiences buy tickets to experience, and that the experience is contained entirely within the given stage space and performance running time.

Devisers and makers of performance, who exploit process, failure, and broken expectations of form in order to get at something true of the human experience, have long questioned the idea of product as separate from process. Dancers, for example, do not act as if they are sweating. They produce real sweat because they are engaged in the process of an actually exhausting task. Like watching sports athletes, when we watch dancers we are witness to and aware of their actual effort, their actual breathing, their actual physical struggle to balance despite gravity and to persist against fatigue. Emotions and ideas arise from a physical engagement with concrete tasks (the choreography), allowing the audience to interpret and to imagine the meaning(s) of those tasks. Very generally speaking, traditional theatre, by which I mean plays, tends to eschew this aspect of performance in favor of the fictional world of the play. Actors in plays pretend to do what they are doing, particularly in the physical and emotional realms, and meaning tends to be defined predominantly by the artists.

These are gross generalizations with significant omissions and limitations, made not to weigh a value judgment but only to illustrate the broad difference of expectations when it comes to distinguishing what I've referred to here as plays versus devised performances. With the latter, the "product" is often considered more explicitly to be off stage, in the audience and their responses. The audience is typically expected and relied upon to be a decisive participant in the making of a performance's meaning. In this way the audience co-authors, or co-creates the event, defining it open-endedly between them and without any singular authorial finality.

After the eleven-week hurtle of formally rehearsing, previewing, and finally opening the Shotgun Players *Hamlet*, alongside the surprises and learning-curveballs of running it, the varied nature of its impact on audiences soon emerged. Initially I was disappointed that the roulette held such a prominent sway over the experience. I had hoped audiences would forget about it within ten minutes and simply enjoy a great production of *Hamlet*. But by following closely the ongoing direct and indirect feedback from audiences,[4] my understanding of the production's implications gradually

---
3

[4] I attended far more performances of this *Hamlet* than I normally do of productions I direct, and this allowed me to sit amongst many audiences and eavesdrop as well

began to circle around the questions of this book: failure, expectation, possibility, and democracy. I became fascinated by how audiences were engaging with, responding to, and reflecting on these issues through the performance, and that so many came back to see the show two, four, six times even.[5] I also felt compelled to consider the necessary impossibility of arriving at final fixed conclusions—necessarily impossible in order to allow for the production's key offer: perpetually diverse experiences and perspectives. Questions arising from those experiences and perspectives form the basis of this chapter:

- How might such an expected theatre text—a familiar "classic"—performed in an unexpected way compel us toward a more actively critical consideration of our experience?
- If we assume an audience to be some sampling of the larger citizenry, whose varied conceptions of democracy, diversity, failure, and success at once reveal and impact their values, ethics, and daily social and political choices, what does the *Hamlet* roulette—particularly in the blurred line between its perceived failures and successes—imply to its audience?
- What implications does the *Hamlet* roulette make with regard to conceptions of artistic and experiential quality, and do these at all relate to practical notions of democracy and diversity?
- How does this production of *Hamlet*—a famously revered dramatic text with all the expectations, preconceptions, and traditions that come with it—attempt, succeed, and fail to compel its audience toward an actively engaged, consciously democratic interaction with their experience of the play, and, by implication, each other?

If you're the sort who doesn't wish to hear about what's going to happen next but rather dive right in, skip down now to the section below titled "Can we make 'un-expect' a verb?" But for those who like maps, I'll first outline

as engage them directly in conversation. Also, The Shotgun Players solicit written feedback from audiences online and typically each performance is followed by at least a handful of privately submitted responses. Over time these written responses start to reveal trends.

[5] Sally Picciotto saw the show thirty-one times, and Carolyn Jones thirty-six. We dubbed them the "super fans."

[6]

what's to come:

To address the questions above I'll begin by placing the production within the context of the "post-dramatic" theatre genre,[7] articulated by theorist Hans-Thies Lehmann (Lehmann, 2006), to explore the key role the rouletted performance situation itself played in how the Shotgun *Hamlet* was received by audiences. Whether and how post-dramatic elements freed up the audience to respond to Shakespeare's most famous play in more diverse and unexpected ways will then be explored by way of philosopher Jacque Rancière's democratic notion of the "emancipated spectator" (Rancière, 2009), which assumes the audience to be active participants alongside the artists in making meaning of the performance event.

In the next section I'll examine the impact of failure—itself one of post-dramatic theatre's key creative elements—on the audience experience of the *Hamlet* roulette, relating the production to insights about failure by theatre-maker Sara Jane Bailes (Bailes, 2011). How failure contributes to democratizing the audience experience, how it perhaps even serves as a means toward determining alternate democratic understandings, and how the notion of failure as "productive" confronts the impact capitalist expectations have on the audience experience, will then be considered through two lenses. The first lens is German theatre director Thomas Ostermeier's efforts to subvert what he calls "capitalist realism" with his conception of a "new realism" freed from capitalist-oriented dramatic structures (Boenisch & Ostermeier, 2016: 3). The second lens is the philosopher-duo Gilles Deleuze and Félix Guattari's provocative critique of capitalist democracies, in which they goad us to reconsider our accepted systems of democratic order (Deleuze & Guattari, 1983 & 1987). I'll relate their provocations to the *Hamlet* roulette by returning to Rancière and his own critique of democracy, specifically

---

[7] Very simply put, "post-dramatic theatre" refers to a wide range of theatre and performance that doesn't make a dramatic text—i.e. a play—the center of its focus, but tends to emphasize image and sound and often uses language in ways other than to further a narrative plot through dialogue between characters." Post-dramatic" is distinguished from that other broad and more widely referenced category," postmodern," by its particular emphasis on a questioning and heightened consciousness of the relationship between theatre and traditional ideas of drama and of dramatic narrative structures (Lehmann, 2006: 1-2, 23-25).

8

as it relates to chance, authority, and notions of freedom (Rancière, 2006).

In the third and final section of this chapter, I'll describe five other theatre productions that have attempted, without use of the roulette casting concept, to achieve similar impacts on their audience's sense of democratic perception, participation, and engagement. By noting the commonalities of all six productions, I hope to point outward beyond this book toward still other possible means of engaging audiences as active free agents in the making and maintenance of diverse perspectives.

By this route I'll arrive at an elusive conclusion, itself a rolling question and not a fixed answer: What might we take from experiences inside the theatre that could be applied toward our lives outside the theatre? It is arguably for our lives, after all, that we go to the theatre—to better them, to expand them by, among other things, practicing failure in a room of strangers whom we must confront in shared space and time. This concluding, if not conclusive, question as to what might come of it all outside the theatre starts with the umbrella-question that hovers over this entire book: How did the Shotgun *Hamlet* roulette—indeed, did it at all—help these gathered strangers, whether artist or audience, question their expectations and practice failure, possibility, and democracy?

Can we make "un-expect" a verb?

William Shakespeare's *Hamlet* is arguably the most expected theatre text there is. By this I mean it is the most known. People who have neither seen nor read *Hamlet* might nevertheless quote it, even without knowing. Those who do know the play have likely accumulated some amount of expectations about it—that it's boring, a masterpiece, a political drama, a family drama, existential, funny, serious, intimidating, overrated, or endlessly... etcetera, etcetera. Such familiarity can create its own inaccessibility, limiting one's conception of the play's possibilities and thereby stifling an expansive creative engagement with it. Shakespeare being widely pedestaled, a common assumption about his plays is that only specialized experts of one sort or another, whether academic or artistic, can explain or define them, let alone understand them in performance. But how might *Hamlet*—this exceptionally expected theatre text, this perhaps too-familiar "classic"—performed in an

9

unexpected way, compel us toward a more actively, consciously democratic and critical consideration of our experience? Paradoxically, to provide theatre audiences with such an opportunity, might a play as familiar as *Hamlet* actually be necessary? By approaching a famous drama in a "post-dramatic" way, to use Hans-Thies Lehmann's term, might audiences be freed of their expectations and of the assumed hierarchy of expertise, and activated to consider more openly, more democratically, and less rigidly their possible range of experiences alongside those of others?

In her introduction to Lehmann's *Postdramatic Theatre*, translator Karen Jürs-Munby describes the concept as not simply "a chronological 'after' drama, a 'forgetting' of the dramatic 'past', but rather as a rupture and a beyond that continue to entertain relationships with drama" (Lehmann, 2006: 2). In line with this paradoxical pairing of rupture and continuum, the *Hamlet* roulette was as simultaneously burdened, buttressed, and dependent on our deep cultural familiarity with *Hamlet* as any more traditional production. But rather than rupturing expectation by deconstructing Shakespeare's drama, the *Hamlet* roulette deconstructed its traditional casting by nightly randomizing the cast of four women, three men, and among them their varying races, ages, and gender orientations. In addition to randomizing the demographic resonances of the characters, this deconstructed casting also made the real-life drama—of the actors leaping into roles they'd only just found out they'd be playing—as important to the artist and audience experience as the text of Shakespeare's drama itself.

This relates directly to post-dramatic theatre's use of the performance situation itself as the material *of* performance. Jürs-Munby's observation that post-dramatic theatre "often focuses on exploring the usually unacknowledged anxieties, pressures, pleasures, paradoxes and perversities that surround the performance situation" speaks to the impact of the roulette casting on the effects and affects of this production of *Hamlet* (Lehmann, 2006: 4).

The question has been asked of me, and by me, whether the Shotgun Players *Hamlet* would have worked without the inherent dramatic pressure of the roulette aspect. As far as the edit of the text, the design, and the basic staging approach go, I believe these choices might together indeed also support a viable "normal" production of *Hamlet*. However, the overall quality of acting in the *Hamlet* roulette would likely not have been acceptable in a traditional production. That is no slight on the cast's achievement. But actors calling for line well into the run of a production, and the irregular

---

10

limitations the roulette task placed on their ability to delve deeply into each character's through-line of intentions, meant their acting was uneven and sometimes lacked psychological depth. This issue was intentionally mitigated by the simplicity of both the staging and text delivery, which together sought to allow Shakespeare's language to speak as much for itself as possible and thus relieve the actors of the burden of consistent emotional engagement.

But the fact remains this production *did* feature the roulette approach. And feedback from audiences and critics made it evident that the roulette was a major aspect of the experience(s) of and response(s) to the production, with acting flaws time and again having been explicitly acknowledged, forgiven, and even celebrated.[12] The spectacle of the actors themselves, scaling the steep slope of their task in full view, alternately succeeding and failing, injected the production with a significant and particular energy. This non-fictive human spectacle offered an element of reality often actively denied by traditional productions that aim to maintain the illusion of a closed and perfected dramatic world on stage. The post-dramatic nature of the *Hamlet* roulette casting concept helped further open up possibilities for assessing and responding to what was particular about its offer, and may prove useful toward applying the lessons learned within the context of this very particular production to future productions that do not feature the roulette concept but perhaps seek to achieve a similar range of possibilities by other means.[13]

Likewise, this post-dramatic approach to *Hamlet* opened up possibilities for freeing audiences from their usual expectations of what *Hamlet* is or should be, namely its assumed innate authority over their perceptions, and their own passivity as spectators to it—or to any other play for that matter. In *The Emancipated Spectator* (2009), Jacques Rancière questions certain common notions about the artist-audience relationship, wherein the passivity and ignorance of audiences are presumed alongside the artist's charge to activate and educate them. Citing the theories of Bertolt Brecht[14]

11

[12] Reviews of the Shotgun Players *Hamlet* by critics from the major Bay Area publications as well as bloggers are included in the Bibliography.

[13] This potential is addressed more specifically below in the section titled "Alternative games in the casino-theatre of democracy."

[14] Bertolt Brecht (1898-1956) was a German playwright and director whose theories about de-familiarizing the familiar in order to compel audiences to respond more critically continue to be a significant influence in world theatre.

and Antonin Artaud[15] as the two dominating paths taken by contemporary theatre makers toward engaging audiences—with Brechtian theory tending toward intellectual engagement and Artaudian theory toward kinesthetic-emotional engagement—Rancière proposes a third route toward "a theatre without spectators," by which he does not mean "a theatre played out in front of empty seats" (2009: 3), but one where the spectator is presumed active. Here Rancière is arguing for a theatre where, to view is to act; to see is to participate and to potentially choose; where the spectator is assumed—by audience and artist alike—to be inherently active. Despite their not acting on stage, audiences act from their position off stage by constructing the performance through their perceptions and responses—translating signs, drawing conclusions, anticipating possible outcomes and meanings, making connections between the various things seen on stage as well as between those things and their own life experiences (2009: 13). Approached in this way, the spectator in the theatre might be freed from the now generations-old assumption of their passivity and ignorance, and a more truly democratic theatre-going experience might be achieved.

Also useful to consider here is Rancière's positive conception of the ignorant schoolmaster, the titular subject of his previous book (1991), which he refers to indirectly in *The Emancipated Spectator* when there he equates the "stultifying pedagogue" to the artist who presumes the authority to define (2009: 12). By contrast, the "ignorant artist," we might say, would not teach as expert of the performance but rather facilitate an event wherein the spectator might be compelled to participate in developing their own expertise—of the experience, of its methodology, its subject and implications. This relationship puts artist and audience on a more equal creative plane.

Such an attempt to compel greater creative equality was a central concern to the *Hamlet* roulette project. The strategic juxtaposition of the most familiar classic play on Earth with a nightly de-familiarizing of its casting was a juxtaposition of the expected and the unexpected. The actors on the stage platform and the audience on the opposite platforms, their individual seats,[17]

---

[15] Antonin Artaud (1896-1946) was a French actor whose vision of the "theatre of cruelty," with its passionate embrace of the irrational, spiritual, and visceral possibilities of theatre, was a major influence on twentieth century theatre.

[16]

[17] Steven Berkoff once referred to a chair as a stage, implying that an actor does not merely sit passively in a chair onstage but can rather fill it as if it were the stage itself. I am recalling this from memory, and have not been able to locate the specific reference amongst the several books of Berkoff's I've read.

were all put in a position to rely on something more than a familiarity with the text in order to make meaning of the event. The humanity of the actors, their fallibility and their effort, was recognized and highlighted. Indeed, audiences reported that actions traditionally considered embarrassing failures in theatre (e.g., an actor fumbling a line or misplacing an entrance) in this context were appreciated when the actor openly pressed on in the wake of their failure, itself committed in the spotlight for all to consider.

And so, just as the definition of failure was brought into creative question by the *Hamlet* roulette, the privilege of interpretative control was put on the table and, alongside it, assumptions of the cause/effect binary (Rancière, 2009: 14). The causes scripted by Shakespeare did not produce their traditional and expected effects, but rather compelled a variety of possible effects according to the individual interpretations of the various spectators. By highlighting age, race, and gender in the casting; and by making these highly politicized demographic factors a nightly matter of chance rather than of appointment or voted election; and, further, by making an awareness of the intentionally accidental relationships between chance, demographics, and this most traditional of play-texts a central subject for the spectator's consideration, in these ways the *Hamlet* roulette sought to practice something of Rancière's third option, wherein not consensus but individuality and difference unite the community of artists and spectators who have gathered to together create a singular event, allowing each person to appreciate the distance that exists between them and each other (2009: 17). "That is what the word 'emancipation' means," states Rancière, "the blurring of the boundary between those who act and those who look; between individuals and members of a collective body" (19). In other words, the *Hamlet* roulette offers the potential to practice democracy. Whether or how any one of us exploits that potential is then another question.

Democracy: the failure of success or the success of failure?

As an artistic tool, failure—whether as concept, experience, or outcome—can serve many functions, from subject matter to creative motivator to a means by which theory yields practice. "There's pedagogy in failure," observes Sara Jane Bailes in her seminal book on the subject, *Performance Theatre and the Poetics of Failure*. "We learn by mistake, by accident, and by getting things wrong" (2011: xix). Failure provides an opportunity—one that is, crucially, counter-intuitive to generally accepted assumptions of progress and of success—for artists and audiences to question the full range of implications

18

and outcomes in any given attempt, including the very language we use to assess these implications and outcomes. Questions about what works; what defines "working"; who defines what works and what is not working; what the value of an attempt's intended goal is; whether it is the right goal; what constitutes "right" in the given instance; how assessments of "right" and "working" might be tied to intention, to notions of value, to social ethics... These are the kind of productively provocative questions that a confrontation with failure offers those engaged with art.

Bailes also acknowledges failure's political force. "According to the hierarchy of success there is but one way to succeed, whilst there are countless ways to fail" (xx). Failure, Bailes suggests, flies in the face of capitalist expectations of individual achievement and of competition resulting in winners and losers who are often divided along lines of cultural identity (16). Rather than prescribing any one notion of success, failure poses "success" as a messy question to be explored. By exposing what is wrong in an endeavor, failure begs the question of what the "right" course(s) of action might be. A consideration of failure invites a democratic process by which multiple perspectives and possibilities might influence the eventual outcome(s). Similarly, failure raises the question of responsibility for what goes wrong and right in addition to who determines "wrong" versus "right." This is an opportunity for democratic engagement.

The *Hamlet* roulette invited the question of its success and its failure and, in doing so, hoped to prompt a parallel question of the successes and failures in our everyday lives, including debates around the impact that age, gender, and racial diversities have on how one person or group of people responds to and interprets another; notions of value attached to tradition versus innovation; and related notions of value around open versus closed definitions, and how these definitions influence our social-political choices, actions, and opportunities. These are questions of the processes and effects of our hierarchical capitalist democracy. Recalling Rancière's recognition of the active spectator freely connecting the spectacle onstage to the spectacle of offstage reality (2009: 13), we might even ask, how realistic—or even real—are capitalist democracy's promises of opportunity, gain, and authority?

We can address this question about capitalist reality by heading back through the stage door into the theatre. In a relevant echo of Rancière's call for a third option to Brecht and Artaud when it comes to the approach and

19

outlook taken by artists toward audiences (2009: 3-5), the German theatre director Thomas Ostermeier articulates his notion of a "new realism" in contemporary theatre as an antidote to a now dominating "capitalist realism." He writes:

> [The new] realism is more than the simple imitation of the world as it seems. It is a view of the world with an attitude that demands change, born of pain and wounds which are the trigger for writing because they demand revenge for the blindness and the stupidity of the world. The attitude of [this new] realism attempts to portray the world as it is, not as it looks. It attempts to comprehend realities and to reconfigure them, to give them a form. This attitude attempts to use the recognizable in order to provoke surprise and astonishment. It shows processes, by which I mean actions that have consequences.
> (Boenisch & Ostermeier, 2016: 16-17)

This explanation by Ostermeier of his new realism begins with a reference to an existing, older capitalist realism—briefly defined here as "the simple imitation of the world as it seems"—that itself promotes inaction and a satisfaction with surfaces. "Capitalism has," he believes, "no problem with the fact that human beings perceive themselves as objects with neither identity nor capacity to act, and to see this idea of humanity represented on stage" (Boenisch & Ostermeier, 2016: 22).[21]

In hopes of compelling audiences toward critical consideration and active change, Ostermeier strives for a new realism that uses theatrical means to depict not the surface of our reality but rather the reality of what drives us internally. Toward that end, based on my own direct experiences seeing

---

20

[21] Writer Mark Fisher, in his book *Capitalist Realism: Is There No Alternative?*, defines capitalist realism more broadly, beyond theatre, as "the widespread sense that not only is capitalism the only viable political and economic system, but also somehow that it is impossible even to imagine a coherent alternative to it" (2009: 2). This definition coincides with Ostermeier's, as well as with the impulse of his "new realism" to challenge the assumed inevitability of the capitalist worldview and to promote critical imagination.

his productions of Shakespeare, Ibsen, and contemporary authors like Sarah Kane and Marius von Mayenburg, each of Ostermeier's productions share an acting style that appears basically natural and therefore "realistic" while at the same time verging into theatrically expressive moments highlighting the structure of feeling inside the characters. Furthermore, this simultaneously critical and emotive acting is never conducted within a stage design that depicts reality in its literal minutia but rather expressively selects concrete, recognizable material details in order to highlight sociopolitical concerns— whether it's the bourgeois modernist couches and large glass windows typical of Ostermeier's Ibsen productions, or the singular architectural metaphors of his Shakespeares, such as the stage-wide dirt field that gradually turns to mud in his 2008 *Hamlet*.[22]

The Brechtian roots of Ostermeier's conception of a new realism can be seen in his reference to realism as an attitude rather than an aesthetic, with the inference that the aesthetic form it takes arises specifically from the political attitude toward provocation and change; but also in Ostermeier's comment that new realism shows processes by which actions have consequences, a comment that is arguably a paraphrase of Brecht. Nevertheless, Ostermeier's emphasis on an intellectual consciousness does not forgo Artaud's emphasis on the role of emotion. Intellectual and emotional awareness are dual strategies for Ostermeier in his new realism's attempt to activate audiences.[24]

In retrospect, one could say the *Hamlet* roulette was, albeit unintentionally, an example of Ostermeier's new realism. Despite Shakespeare's poetic language and formal iambic pentameter, the acting in the production was not "classical" but rather straightforward and unadorned by overtly poetic intonation. The staging featured expressive moments that departed from literal reality in order to convey a character's internal reality.[25] The stage

---

[22] Ostermeier's 2008 *Hamlet* is discussed in more detail below in the section titled "Alternative games in the casino-theatre of democracy."

[23]

[24] It is debatable how "new" Ostermeier's conception of realism is, not only given Brecht but particularly Meyerhold before him. If not literally or entirely new, Ostermeier's realism is perhaps at least a new emphasis in response to contemporary concerns that have developed since Meyerhold and Brecht.

[25] For example, when Hamlet accidentally happens upon Claudius praying alone in Act 3 Scene 3, after Hamlet notes that he could kill Claudius right then, we staged the killing. Hamlet stabbed Claudius repeatedly and gorily, with bone crunching, blood splattering sound effects and

design, comprised solely of dual level black platforms with "HAMLET" announced on them in white, and dual red curtains, emphasized the consciousness of performing amongst Shakespeare's characters, as well as their—and the play's—use of theatre as both mechanism and metaphor.[26] There was a near constant underscoring of percussive music, reflecting the pulse of the main action. Of course the production's most prominent feature, the roulette casting, immediately recognized the possibility that almost anyone in the audience, regardless of age, race, or gender, might connect with the intentions, actions, and circumstances of the play, and by extension that anyone might—by virtue of the immensely challenging task of playing Hamlet on short notice—succeed or fail at these intentions, actions, and circumstances.

Alongside Ostermeier's critique of capitalist realism it is useful to consider Gilles Deleuze and Félix Guattari's two-part provocation on the schizophrenia of capitalism, *Anti-Oedipus* (1983) and *A Thousand Plateaus* (1987). Together these books ask us to contemplate the further implications of systems we accept as normal, orderly, and, as such, good and productive. What is "productive" about our orderly capitalist systems, for example? What exactly do they produce? Answers would necessarily vary, and in their variations reveal the multiplicity of experience that capitalism produces despite what one might generally assume to be its chief goal: to move capital upward toward a single point. But capitalism creates other movements as well—or motions, which we might rightly call commotions—among them pollution, poverty, inequality, shame, prejudice, and violence.

In *Anti-Oedipus*, Deleuze & Guattari compel us to question our assumptions of such systems by metaphorically removing their organs and rendering them a "body without organs," a system-less system by which possibilities are not fixed within a determined structure but are allowed to flow freely and perhaps endlessly (1983: 9-16). Similarly, in *A Thousand Plateaus*, Deleuze & Guattari propose the rhizome, a thick subterranean root with myriad shoots that sprout endlessly into new plants, as a primarily horizontal and ever-outwardly-reaching alternative process to that of the tree, from which all roots and branches depart, reach a single endpoint, and can be traced back to the central, vertical, readily visible trunk (1987: 8, 21). With their two metaphorical dis-organizations, the body without organs and

---

a sharp lighting change. Then just as suddenly the lights returned to normal and Claudius was again quietly praying, with Hamlet behind him wondering whether to take action. For a moment we'd gone inside Hamlet's head and witnessed his fantasy murder.

[26] Famously, it is through theatre that Hamlet seeks to "catch the conscience of the king" (Act 2 Scene 2).

27

the rhizome, Deleuze & Guattari prod us to reconsider the expectations, preconceptions, values, and ethics that are produced in us by the vertical, linear, capitalist systems in which we daily engage. "Groups and individuals contain microfascisms just waiting to crystalize," they assert. "Good and bad are only the products of an active and temporary selection, which must be renewed" (1987: 9-10). Consciously playing the mischievous trickster, they structure their books in loops, varied repetitions, meanderings, and unfinished lines of thought in order to demonstrate in their writing the concepts they propose.[28] It makes for difficult reading, while also making the authors' point. By structuring their own writing with a schizophrenic logic, they complicate their explanation of their ideas—explanation being an expected purpose of an academic book—with their demonstration of them—demonstration being one expected task of a practical work of art. In these ways, Deleuze & Guattari's books are examples of art practicing what it preaches. Form and content share authority, and, by intentionally upsetting expectations of in this case how an academic book "should" read, they invite the reader to more actively engage, participate, even struggle, to make meaning.

This approach relates to the *Hamlet* roulette, which originated as a fantasy that a troupe of actors might learn all the roles in the most famous play on Earth and on the night of the performance draw the role they are to play out of Yorick's skull. Taken seriously, the implications of this roulette game transcend gimmickry to embody questions of how a familiar play, itself a structured system, can be re/de/un-structured to disrupt that system and the systems of expectation by which artists and audiences experience, assess, and respond to it. Deleuze & Guattari's conceptions of rhizomatic, organ-less, disorderly processes of perception emphasize attempt over accomplishment, journey over destination, and failure over success—namely, the breadth of possibility found in a system that fails to cohere as expected.[30] Similarly,

---

[28] " We are writing this book as a rhizome. It is composed of plateaus. We have given it a circular form, but only for laughs" (Deleuze & Guattari, 1987: 22).
[29]

[30] " We live today in the age of partial objects, bricks that have been shattered to bits, and leftovers. We no longer believe in the myth of the existence of fragments that, like pieces of an antique statue, are merely waiting for the last one to be turned up, so that they may all be glued back together to create a unity that is precisely the same as the original unity. We no longer believe in a primordial totality that once existed, or in a final totality that awaits us at some future date. We no longer believe

the *Hamlet* roulette un-systematized the experiences and responses of the artists and audiences involved, opening up democratic possibilities in theatre making and theatre reception, and implying like possibilities in life outside the theatre where the hierarchy of capitalist democracy arguably reigns and, among other things, defines success in our culture. As Ostermeier writes, the conditions of contemporary neoliberal capitalism call for our "telling the stories of individuals who fail in society, in the world, in their lives —today, in the here and now" (Boenisch & Ostermeier, 2016: 15). The *Hamlet* roulette told such stories through Shakespeare's characters—most notably the title character who fails for most of the play to exact the revenge he seeks, eventually succeeds in coming to a philosophical peace with his inaction, but then, in the end, finally fails to resist his father's demand that he uphold the patriarchal order by responding to violence with violence, resulting in a slew of deaths, among them Hamlet's own.[32] Alongside this scripted story of Shakespeare's, the *Hamlet* roulette simultaneously told a spontaneous story of failure through the efforts of the actors, making the audience hyper-aware of both at every moment.[33]

---

in the dull gray outlines of a dreary, colorless dialectic of evolution, aimed at forming a harmonious whole out of heterogeneous bits by rounding off their rough edges. We believe only in totalities that are peripheral. And if we discover such a totality alongside various separate parts, it is a whole of these particular parts but does not totalize them; it is a unity of all of these particular parts but does not unify them, rather, it is added to them as a new part fabricated separately (Deleuze & Guattari, 1983: 42, my emphasis).
31

[32] For an interesting discussion of *Hamlet* and other Shakespearean tragedies as early critical protests of the violence-based patriarchal order, see Gilligan (2003: 213-16).
[33] Christine Murray, audience member: " I was completely exhilarated by how many layers of awareness I experienced during the mimed swordfight of *Hamlet*. There were the stakes of the narrative of *Hamlet* the drama, and on one level I was fully invested in those characters and what was going to happen to each of them. As the swordfight unfolded, I was also impressed by the cleverness of how that scene was staged, and how fresh and powerful and profound it was to witness that climactic duel without the phony realism of the actors having prop swords in

To further consider the potential of this dual-level storytelling for making some democratizing impact on its audience, it's useful to look again to Rancière, specifically his articulations of democracy. In *The Hatred of Democracy* (2006), Rancière brings into question the nature of democracy—its inherent and problematic contradictions, the historical western conceptions of it, and the role chance plays or might play in its execution. A central point of Rancière's regarding democracy's contradictions is that it must be governed at all, given that in its full and free form democracy is not singularly coherent but rather pluralistically individualistic. Rancière describes democracy's chaotic nature as "the disorder of passions eager for satisfaction" (2006: 6), further noting in a provocative assertion that "a good democratic government is one capable of controlling the evil quite simply called democratic life" (2006: 7). To be effective as a system for societal organization, then, democratic chaos must be contained by some ordered form of governance, typically formulated around notions of authoritative legitimacy—e.g., wealth over poverty, experience over inexperience, formal education over its lack, age over youth, or notions of birthright. Each of these principles of legitimization suggests a hierarchy, whereas pure democracy is much more rhizomatic, more horizontal. Of all this, central to the *Hamlet* roulette is Rancière's discussion of chance, his question of authoritative legitimacy, as well as his comment that "freedom also means the freedom to do wrong" (2006: 6).

With regard to chance, Rancière posits whether, for example, drawing lots might actually be the more democratic procedure for collective decision-making, if also the most upsetting to those who favor one among the many existing hierarchies of power (2006: 40-41). Though not an unproblematic suggestion itself, democracy by lot is an intriguing notion. Voting, for example, pits sides against one another, resulting in winners and losers of the given debate who might then harbor animosities leading to active

hand. I was also deeply aware of the stakes for the actors themselves, and the technical skill it took to execute that choreography with perfect precision, to remain in synch with the bits of audio of the swords clashing together. And then I was doubly (triply? quadruply?) aware that each actor had to know BOTH SIDES of that swordfight, and had to respond with the same intensity and authenticity and accuracy to the energy of a different, random scene partner each night. On top of all that, I was buzzing with awareness that as an audience member I was aware of all of those things at once. It was one of the most thrilling moments I've had as a viewer in the theatre" (Murray 2017).

34

conflict despite "the people having spoken." Whereas when drawing lots, chance is responsible for the outcome and therefore nobody can blame any other body for it. Might the results of a decision made by drawn lots be more widely and peaceably accepted? In the context of the *Hamlet* roulette, this did appear to be the case. Neither any authority figure nor a general election had decreed who shall play Hamlet—the prized role of roles—on any given night. Chance decided the actor drawn from Yorick's skull in the moment of drawing, with the audience present to oversee the procedure in collective witness. Whomever chance dubbed Hamlet for the night was inevitably the recipient of great affection and good will from cast and audience alike, the daunting Sisyphean task being innately understood.

The decisiveness of chance connects to the question of authority. No casting director, Shakespearean scholar, or other traditional authority figure in the theatre profession had determined a given night's casting in the *Hamlet* roulette. And so in one sense, as actor/director Steven Berkoff asserts, the actors could not be miscast (1989: vii). Indeed audiences tended toward accepting them as they were, even relishing in their particularities. Of course, prior to the production there was a traditional casting process whereby I, as director, assumed the authority to select seven actors I deemed fit for the task. This mix of controlled and uncontrolled processes of determination further connects to Rancière's assertion of the contradiction inherent to democracy, that it is a chaos of individualities in need of some singular corralling in order to be effective as a process of social organization.

Finally, there is the point about the freedom to do wrong granted to us by democracy. Rancière offers the example of the rioting in Baghdad after the American military brought democracy to Iraq by force (2006: 6). Describing this instance of democracy as a "crisis," Rancière states that democracy "signifies the irresistible growth of demands that put pressure on governments, lead to a decline in authority, and cause individuals and groups to become refractory to the discipline and sacrifices required for the common good" (2006: 7). Obviously, a cast of actors playing out *Hamlet* by lots is not at all equivalent to a society in unrest following a severe military intervention, and I do not wish to debase the seriousness of the latter by relating it to the former. But the principle, at least, seems productively transferable. In the *Hamlet* roulette, crisis was averted by the collective recognition of the task at hand as an unquestionably difficult one. Whether by empathy or sympathy, the audience tended to unify and cheer the actors on. Errors and failings were accepted and the will to succeed was celebrated. Chaos and

35

wrongdoing added to the positive excitement. In the realm of the *Hamlet* roulette—a simple and relatively safe realm as compared to governments and wider societies—a democracy of chance, led authoritatively by chance, and celebratory of failure, played itself out like a "circus of daring," as critic John Wilkins called it (2016), offering artists and audiences an opportunity to practice a democracy based in acceptance and an embrace of difference rather than in conflicted, democracy-defying struggles to establish singular authority.

Alternative games in the casino-theatre of democracy

I've been discussing how this rouletted production of *Hamlet* attempted and might have succeeded/failed to compel its audience toward an actively engaged, more consciously democratic and rhizomatic interaction with their experience. But as a model for production the roulette approach is potentially a limitation. Applied to other plays in subsequent productions there is the obvious risk of it becoming a too-familiar novelty gutted of its impact.[36] There are also the limitations it places on an actor's ability to succeed artistically beyond some (un)certain point. A consideration of additional productions that have in other ways consciously combined the expected and unexpected, thus compelling more democratic engagement and diverse responses among their audience, might help to identify commonalities and germinate further approaches for future productions and performances. Productions I will reference include the 2001 Deutsches Theater Berlin *Emilia Galotti*, the 2008 Schaubühne Am Lehniner Platz *Hamlet*, the 2012 Third World Bunfight *Exhibit B*, the 2013 Theatre Group Seongbukdong Beedoolkee *Medea on Media*, and Jamal Harewood's 2014 *The Privileged*. This sampling is by no means exhaustive and one might also consider other even more radically different performances. But the current sampling might begin to identify those qualities, principles, and approaches that tend to compel the democratic openness the *Hamlet* roulette proved to do in its way.

---

[36] Coincidentally, during the process of my writing the first draft of this chapter, an article was published in *The Village Voice* about a production of Branden Jacobs-Jenkins's play, *Everybody*, an adaptation of *Everyman*, in which the ensemble of actors drew roles by lottery each night. That production ran from January 31 through March 12, 2017, at The Signature Theatre in New York (Felton-Dansky, 2017). I was unable to see it.

37

Emilia Galotti

Gotthold Ephraim Lessing's 1772 melodrama, *Emilia Galotti*, remains a staple of the German repertoire. Michael Thalheimer directed an extraordinarily radical new production at Deutsches Theater Berlin in 2001, which toured the world during its eight subsequent sold-out years in the DTB repertory. Thalheimer trained as an actor before turning to directing. In his rehearsals, the actors are sometimes included in the dramaturgical and editing process of the text, and consistently involved in devising the staging. *Emilia Galotti* is among the most refined examples of Thalheimer's approach to classics, which typically features an extensive cutting of the original text, a scenic design offering an evocative and provocative space in which the action unfolds rather than depicting any literal place(s), highly emotional acting contained within the pressure cooker of a limited gestural vocabulary, and explicit attention to the contemporary political rationale for producing the given play. That his distinctive productions are arrived at collaboratively between him, the actors, and the designers comes as a shock to those critics of his work who assume such precision in theatre must only come from an "auteur"—usually male—director bending everyone else to his vision.[38] Critics continue to resist the notion that this is not the case with Thalheimer, despite his collaborative process being well documented.[39] This resistance perhaps speaks to an inner-conflict in democratic cultures: between concepts of individuality versus community, dictation versus consensus, and other manifestations of the individual versus the group as they relate to agency, choice, freedom, and opportunity.

In its original form, en route to the lush rose of its classic melodramatic status, *Emilia Galotti*'s plot makes a thorny stem for contemporary feminism to hold. The title character is literally traded and carted about like precious freight between the men in her life. Her father has promised her hand in marriage to a prominent young count until the prince, a much more politically advantageous marriage prospect, is smitten at first sight of her. The prince, himself already scheduled to marry a countess, has Emilia kidnapped en route to her wedding and his henchmen voluntarily murder her fiancé. Moral conundrums between personal and political passions ensue in rapid succession until, in the end, Emilia advocates to her father that he take her life to save *his* honor, which he does.

The Deutsches Theater production turns this final scenario on its head.

---

[38] For an example of such shock, see Feingold (2005).
[39] For two examples of this documentation see Boenisch (2008) and Kalb (2009).
40

An exceedingly streamlined edit of the dialogue allows Emilia to directly confront her father with her outrage over how he and all the men have treated her like an object who stands for nothing and is good for nothing (Lessing, 1991: 134). Emilia does not beg, but rather defiantly dares her father to kill her. The father exits, leaving his gun (a contemporary substitute for the original dagger) on the ground. Emilia picks the gun up between her fingertips and meanders slowly upstage, surveying the left and right walls made up of floor-to-ceiling doors, now all open. Literally every door in life is open to her. Which shall she choose? A crowd of bourgeois ballroom dancers enters, and Emilia, center stage, disappears amongst them as they waltz past. For German audiences, who are exceedingly familiar with the play, this open ending punctuates the production with the finality of Nora's door slam famously "heard around the world" at the climax of Ibsen's *A Doll's House*. Only here it is a gunshot that fires loudly—crucially, without the trigger of the actual gun ever being pulled! Emilia overpowers the patriarchal violence directed against her through a highly articulate, openly outraged and succinct verbal confrontation, sending her literal patriarch shamefaced into the wings, before she herself then slips off into possibility center stage.[41]

Parallels to the Shotgun Players *Hamlet* are evident, though the Deutsches Theater team relied on nothing like the roulette concept in order to achieve the awakened consciousness in their audience. They played upon their audience's familiarity with a classic play to heighten attention to contemporary concerns. The original text was drastically cut; noticing its plot as originally scripted takes place in the span of one dawn to dusk, Thalheimer and the actors edited the text to the bone of the action and delivered it at a fiercely rapid speed in order to embody the destructively rash impulsiveness of the male characters. The set of polished plywood evoked a palace with its height and a bourgeois fashion show runway with its narrow depth. The characters, dressed in contemporary Italianate chic, made long entrances from a black open doorway upstage center, underscored by an

---

[41] I can't help but think here of our Ophelia, and the sanely calculated solo performance we made of her traditionally "mad" scene. (Act 4 Scene 5) Though we did not alter things so much as to have Ophelia live—the plot could simply not continue—we made her suicide intentional. When Gertrude relays Ophelia's death to Laertes, we staged a cinematic crosscut to Ophelia abruptly shooting herself in the head. This meant Gertrude's famous "There is a willow grows aslant the brook" speech to Laertes, in which she recounts Ophelia's accidental drowning, is a lie spun to protect Laertes from the gruesome truth that Ophelia blew her brains out on purpose. (We'd initially staged this with her drowning herself with a garden hose. Horrifying as it was for some people, the image persisted in getting too many laughs and so we eventually changed her suicide method to a handgun.)

infectious, foreboding, romantic waltz by composer Michael Galasso, which played in variation virtually nonstop for the full 75-minute duration of the production. In the shocking silences between rapid-fire volleys of percussive dialogue, spare and specific gestures conveyed explosive emotional subtexts. All of this demanded an extraordinarily keen verbal, physical, intellectual, and emotional precision from the actors, and audiences were aware of their effort alongside that of their characters (Boenisch, 2008: 40). Through these simple means a familiar play was rendered unfamiliar, its innate romanticism exploited to trigger intellectual consideration. The production compelled audiences to reconsider the famous melodrama and to revise the expected original message of female sacrifice to an unexpected declaration of female revolt against unchecked male desire. Like the dual awareness of the characters and actors, classic melodrama and present reality also coexisted in the experience of the production. One felt at once swept up in the play's headlong dramatic rush and yet mindful of the political implications of that rush.

Hamlet

Thomas Ostermeier directed *Hamlet* at Schaubühne Am Lehniner Platz in 2008. Since then the production has played continuously in Berlin and at festivals around the world, demonstrating itself to be of interest to a diverse global audience.

The set design is minimalist: a stage-wide square of dark dirt, a single curtain of gold beads spanning stage left to right, and likewise a platform supporting a long table and chairs that can slide up and down stage over the dirt. The lead actor, Lars Eidinger, is a major stage and screen star in Germany and so when audiences there attend the production they follow both Hamlet and Eidinger-as-Hamlet.[43] As staged, Eidinger strays from the scripted text at will and interacts with his audience. At the performance I attended, for example, when a couple in the front row walked out during Eidinger's rendition of the "O what a rogue and peasant slave am I" soliloquy, he broke from the text to offer up their expensive seats to anyone farther back who

---

42

[43] When this *Hamlet* is performed abroad, the Schaubühne itself, more so than Eidinger, can rightly be called a "star" of the international festival stage and is received as such. So we might say that when international festival audiences attend the production they follow both *Hamlet* and Schaubühne-as-*Hamlet*.

wanted a better view but had not been able to afford it. The incident proved a spontaneous dramatic gift. First, it fit rather perfectly into the substance of Shakespeare's soliloquy, which takes Hamlet from a consideration of actions by actors on stage versus actions by people in life to a realization that by putting on a play and inviting Claudius to sit front and center he might "catch the conscience of the king" (Act 2 Scene 2). Secondly, Eidinger himself drew attention to capitalist economic class politics by pointing out that two people who, like the royal characters Claudius and Gertrude, could afford a better view could therefore also afford to abandon that costly view when it was not to their liking. Eidinger then invited two people with less economic resources to stay and enjoy the opportunity. This intersection of Hamlet, Eidinger, and the audience remains among the most memorable moments of the production for me—and it only happened on that night! However, Eidinger's fluidity between the text and the given audience sets up the continuous possibility for this kind of spontaneous real life "drama" alongside the scripted drama. At its essence this is not unlike the *Hamlet* roulette's reliance on its audience's awareness of the actors as actors, who together spontaneously—by virtue of the roulette mechanism—play in that night's particular casting combination for possibly the only time ever.

Interestingly, Ostermeier's *Hamlet* also quite consciously draws on post-dramatic understandings found in Shakespeare's play. Ostermeier writes:

> If we look at some of the ingredients of Shakespeare's writing, a lot of things are involved that qualify as post-dramatic theatre according to Lehmann. Not least, we are presented with a mélange of different genres and different media, and already in Shakespeare, we find the use of different registers of speech: highly elaborate, very poetic verse, and a completely different language that addresses the groundlings in the pit. Shakespeare was greatly fascinated with popular culture, which is another aspect of post-dramatic theatre. He mixed popular culture with high cultures; comical scenes follow tragic scenes. When he introduces allusions to the political context of his time into the gravedigger scene, *Hamlet* becomes stand-up comedy for a moment... Furthermore, scholars provide us with insight on how he put his plays together by sampling different, well-known sources... And not stopping there, he even presents us with a hero of a revenge tragedy who refuses to take revenge – the

---

44

major twist Shakespeare gives to the tradition of revenge
tragedy in his play. This is postmodern eclecticism *avant
la letter*. (Boenisch & Ostermeier, 2016: 189-90)

Ostermeier's comment about Shakespeare twisting revenge tragedy
tradition would seem to echo Thalheimer's approach to *Emilia Galotti*,
whereby the traditional misogyny of melodrama was turned against itself.
In general, Ostermeier goes to great lengths to make his *Hamlet* relevant to
its immediate audience, incorporating among the production's strategies a
freedom for his actors to respond as themselves and in their own language
to the actions and comments of those assembled on a given night. Through
all these means, like the *Hamlet* roulette project, Ostermeier's *Hamlet* also
attempts, succeeds, and fails to accommodate a more democratic range of
immediate and diverse responses.

Medea on Media

I saw the South Korean Theatre Group Seongbukdong Beedoolkee's 2013
Medea on Media on tour at the 2014 Sibiu International Theatre Festival in
Romania. The sold-out performance took place at midnight in a cramped
basement theatre where my feet hung in the air from my knees, jammed
uncomfortably up against the hard chairs in front of me. The late hour and
my utter physical discomfort no longer mattered once the production was
underway. The production's energy, invention, humor, seriousness, and
its cast's precarious and utterly effective balance of skilled and unrefined
performing resulted in an uncommonly stirring experience, compelling in me
a feeling of wanting to run away and join the Theatre Group Seongbukdong
Beedoolkee circus.

Medea on Media channels the story of the immigrant Medea's obsessive,
finally murderous love for Jason through a variety of media genres. Medea
is depicted as a kind of Quentin Tarantino badass making her way through
a simultaneously stark and gaudy, sober and hysterical world populated by
ultra-violent, sharply ironic, pop-culture-saturated cut out characters that,
as performed by this cast, nevertheless have souls. The title of the piece
sounds like Medea jacked up on a drug, and indeed our contemporary pop
media world pulses through the veins of the piece at a crack addict's heart
rate. An early scene is done in a fully committed replication of traditional
Korean theatre. The confrontation between Medea, Jason, and his new

---

45

bride is then done like a *Jerry Springer* episode, with full-throttle slugging and hair pulling. Medea's decision to commit murder is enacted like an action videogame, with the performers perfectly executing choppy, digital videogame-hero-styled movements. The final showdown between Jason and Medea is a Tarantino gunfight in a maze of mimed hallways. The closing epilogue is a kind of *Korea's Got Talent* in which Medea, the winner, sings an old fashioned song. All of this is performed on an open white square of stage surrounded by black floor and walls, under banks of cold florescent lights, with all necessary props and costumes lined up in full view stage left and right.

The various pop culture performance modes are approached with enough iconic verisimilitude for us to recognize the reference, and yet director Hyuntak Kim tweaks the genres such that they transcend mere parody to create an organic, serious, truthful, and genuinely surprising theatre world. Between scenes, all acting is dropped and in silence the cast efficiently prep for the next scene, at which point an electrical switch seems to get thrown inside them and they leap into the next high-energy performance mode. The Tarantino gunfight was staged in an intricate way by which the performers mixed up conventions—of when they look at the audience to "look" at each other versus when they *actually* look at each other; when they lean back-to-back to convey being on either side of a wall and when they leave space for a mimed wall; how they share one space to be in different places; or how the chorus follows the action as if they were in a gunfight as well, each sputtering their traditional choral commentary individually as they die of Medea and Jason's stray bullets. All of this gives the outrageous action a real sense of suspense. Throughout everything, no matter how outlandish, there is always a sense of the performers playing it straight. They never quote what they do. They do it. Even operatic death convulsions with melodramatic last words are handled with complete seriousness of intent. And the largely black-and-white color scheme creates a flat, sober atmosphere in contrast to the hyper energetic comedic playing and the bold splashes of color in the prop and costume designs.

Here again we have a single, simple open space used to convey multiple places. The audience is made aware of the actors alongside their characters, appreciating both simultaneously. A familiar story is told in an unfamiliar way: the dramaturgy of the original having been radically reconceived to reconstruct the classic Greek episodic structure out of multiple pop culture media genres. And actors use very precise physical gestures and staging to convey their characters. Each of these elements provides gaps for the audience to participate with their imaginations. The problematic gender politics the original *Medea* traffics in are here—and fittingly—at once ridiculous and utterly serious. The production's overt commentary on how our various genres of contemporary media create gender role stereotypes and propagate those that have existed for millennia successfully puts pop culture's own often shallow irony toward a deeper use. In this production Medea's bloody triumph—killing her children, her ex-husband, and his new bride—somehow feels like exactly what *should* happen. That's sick—like the media. And the audience loved it. *That's* sick—like the media.

Exhibit B

Third World Bunfight, a politically engaged theatre company based in the Republic of South Africa, premiered *Exhibit B* in 2012 and subsequently toured Europe. I attended a performance in Wrocław, Poland, during the 2013 Dialog Festival. Presented there in the dark brick halls of a semi-dilapidated former brewery, *Exhibit B* departs from the above three productions in that it is more live art installation than theatre performance, employing local non-performers who rehearse twice for three hours each session to prepare for this simple but by no means simplistic piece. Nevertheless it makes a relevant and interesting example here.

 The audience is taken twenty-five at a time into a cramped, dimly lit cement room and each given a number. We are told not to speak with one another, not to take photographs of the exhibit and not to use our phones. Our numbers are then called in a seemingly random order, which feels ominously systematic as one by one we are let through a second door that shuts behind us with a foreboding clang. Once inside the exhibit, it is for us to wander at our own pace through a collection of installations featuring African performers posed in tableaux as in a museum display. Some displays are recreations of actual displays given in the African "human zoos" that toured Europe in the nineteenth and early twentieth centuries. Other displays depict contemporary local African immigrants or people who died of suffocation during deportation. Statistics are often listed about the person: where they came from, where they now reside, height, weight, etcetera. In one display recreating an actual historic exhibit of lopped-off heads, a handful of live singers kneel inside boxes so that their heads appear as on a platter and pedestal. They sing a beautiful African hymn for the dead. Black and white photos of the actual historic exhibit are displayed on a wall behind them. Broken rows of old red velvet theatre seats are arranged before them so that one may sit and listen to the music. In the brick setting of the

47

old brewery, it felt like being in an abandoned church or crypt.

A key gesture of the piece is that the performers all look their spectators directly in the eye. Sometimes I found it embarrassing to meet their gaze. Sometimes I felt ashamed. With other performers it was more comfortable to meet eyes, but never comfortable enough for me to linger long. Some of them seemed to look at me angrily, accusatorily, some with pity, one with a kind of regretful kindness, while still others seemed entirely blank or uncomfortable themselves. These are all my interpretations, of course, influenced by my own biases and life experiences. For me, this element of eye contact and eye evasion defined the piece. It was a literal confrontation, and not with trained actors who know how to pretend. These were non-actors who did not need to pretend to be anything other than who they were, even when costumed as someone else from another time. At the performance I attended in Poland, every spectator was white while every performer, of course, was black. This, too, was a strong element of the piece and contributed to its impact. There was a palpable feeling of the historic African human zoos the piece acknowledges and protests still being on display in our contemporary world. And in fact they are: in pop culture and in daily life.

Connections to the *Hamlet* roulette are indirect yet discernible. To compel its audience toward intellectual and emotional engagement *Exhibit B* uses the spectator's awareness of the performers as people, an extraordinarily precise and limited physical vocabulary based in tableaux, a familiarity with classic and contemporary—in this case real-life white European depictions of African—narratives, and a venue that provides space rather than depicting place. A heightened awareness of race in particular, and gender as well, is at the forefront of the experience, and is achieved by interpretable action and demonstration rather than explicit commentary. Unlike the *Hamlet* roulette or the other plays discussed in this inquiry, spectators are granted agency over time and space by an immersive venue dotted with many small "stages." This means the spectator must interact with the venue physically, which offers democratic choice as to where to be, when, and for how long. As a result the piece overall can last two minutes or two hours depending on how long an individual elects to linger. This elected duration itself then speaks interpretably to one's position in relation to the racial subject of the work.

The Privileged

Veering in yet another distinctive direction than *Exhibit B* from the classic-text basis of the other performances discussed here, Jamal Harewood's uncommonly powerful work of performance art, *The Privileged*, explodes the concepts of failure, expectation, possibility, and democracy by way of means relatable to all these productions despite clear and extreme formal divergences. As such it makes a very interesting example of the extremes to which performance might take these principles.

I saw *The Privileged* during the 2017 N.E.W. Festival, produced by students of the Theatre-Performance Making MFA program at California Institute of Integral Studies (CIIS), a joint project of CIIS and the UK-based University of Chichester Theatre Department. Harewood is a 2014 graduate of the Performance MA at Chichester, where *The Privileged* was first developed, and has been touring the piece internationally since then. He was invited by the Theatre-Performance Making MFA students to present two performances of *The Privileged* in their festival, which featured their own work alongside that of other San Francisco Bay Area and international artists over four days at CounterPULSE, one of San Francisco's significant venues for alternative dance and performance. This means the audience for *The Privileged* likely walked in with distinctly eclectic expectations as compared to audiences entering The Shotgun Players, Deutsches Theater, Schaubühne, or even the Sibiu International Theater Festival; The N.E.W. Festival audience was a healthy mix of students and friends of students with members of the Bay Area theatre-making and -going community, all coming specifically to see new, often unfinished, mostly student-made, but also professional performances. *The Privileged* is now long since a "finished" professional piece—though I must quote "finished," given the extent to which Harewood compels his audience to create, let alone to finish, certainly to define, the performance.

The audience enters the theatre and finds no ushers or crew. Rather than sitting in the auditorium, forty chairs await them onstage arranged in a square under white florescent and LED work lights rather than traditional theatre lighting. Within the square of forty chairs lies a person in a cartoony polar bear suit, surrounded by scattered broken bits of Kentucky Fried Chicken filling the air with their familiar scent. Placed randomly on ten of the forty chairs are manila envelopes, each numbered one to ten. The audience sits. The polar bear appears to be asleep. After a long silence with some smilingly uncomfortable shifting and murmuring, someone with the envelope marked "1" is finally moved to open it. It contains an explanation from the absent zoo keeper, who tells us the polar bear, named Cuddles, is a teenaged male animal who has been in captivity so long he's lost his natural instincts and will need our attention. We're told that Cuddles is generally friendly but if he ever does become violent we are encouraged to leave the enclosure. We're then asked to nominate a member of our group to wake Cuddles up. Once awake, Cuddles walks curiously along the single row of audience that surrounds him, allowing them to pet him and occasionally settling in with one person. Wariness in the audience gives way to a cooing enjoyment of the domesticated beast.

Other instructions in other envelopes follow, including a playful game of "Red Light Green Light," with an audience member nominated to be the prey and the group who voted, along with Cuddles, serving as predators. A turning point then comes when we're asked to nominate three additional members of the group: one to remove Cuddle's feet, the second his skin, and the third his head. Cuddles' animal instincts kick in as the first person attempts to pull off his feet. Harewood indeed becomes quite forceful with us in his physical agitation. And with violence now shimmering in the air between Cuddles' defensiveness and our mandated threat to his physical body, the debates begin. Should we do what the instructions say? Should we vote about it? Does the person charged with the task charge ahead or refuse?

The next dramatic turning point comes when someone finally gets Cuddles' head off and the human face of the artist is revealed. Both nights I saw the piece, the head came off second and the skin third. The revelation of Harewood's actual face came as a shock each time. Then the removal of his skin, revealing his naked body, clenched the room in a veritable fist of tension. Debates mounted. Most people seemed to continue to invest in Harewood as Cuddles. Only a few were willing to acknowledge aloud that he was the artist and the rules and tasks assigned to us were his creation, not an absent zoo keeper's mandate. We're eventually instructed to firmly command Cuddles to eat, but to just as firmly stop him from over-eating. The debates and moral conflicts escalate.

If and when audience members leave, they have the option to enter a second space that has been set up very like the first, only without the fried chicken and its fatty stench. There, audiences find one envelope, some pencils and blank paper. In the envelope are suggestions for how a conversation about the piece might be conducted. Those suggestions were barely followed at either of the N.E.W. Festival performances, so heightened was the racial and moral tension in the room. On the first night, toward the end of part one in space one, an African American man said, "Everyone who is not Black needs to leave." On the second night at the same juncture, an Asian woman said, "Only people of color can stay." Harewood told me afterwards that he's

50

never heard that kind of comment outside America. Our country's particular racial history makes it a very interesting destination for *The Privileged*.

In my own experience and observations of the piece, it was ultimately impossible to take a single firm position on the situation or the various audience responses. Everyone seemed culpable. Everyone seemed pretentious. Everyone failed to be "right" or "good," regardless of race or gender. I myself was no exception. With *The Privileged* Harewood has created a perfect trap. Placed under the spotlight of his theatrical work of performance art, any statement or silence becomes suspect. White women slowly and tenderly touching Harewood/Cuddles' beautiful, naked, glistening black skin, hoping to stop him from over-eating his KFC, come off as descendants of plantation owner's wives taking care of their husband's property and hoping to have sex with it. Black people seeking to defend Cuddles/Harewood come off as absurd in their possessive protection of the actor wearing his cartoony polar bear suit. Righteous do-gooders, cynical naysayers, and silent passives alike all come off as equally fallible. All our racially oriented blind spots, biases, fissures, and oversights glare center stage under the deadening clear florescent and LED work lights. I was struck by how many people seemed to want to own and to define Cuddles/Harewood, as well as the extent to which people performed their agendas for the assembled audience. One soon realizes the title of the piece refers to us, the audience, that we are the central character, recreating the worst of democratic society without too much actual pressure to do so, demonstrating the great difficulty we have contending with our racially driven social systems and expectations.

In relation to the present inquiry, how does Harewood accomplish all this? He immediately subverts our expectation that we will be entertained in any usual way. The show does not start until we do something, does not end until we leave, and in between the possibilities are entirely up to us. We determine the running time, the "plot," the dialogue, and the precise content. He plays with our dual awareness of him as both the performer and the character he performs, granting us the choice to acknowledge either, and revealing our strong desire to side with fiction—including the fiction of our own voluntary performances of our moral or sociopolitical agendas. He limits his own physical vocabulary at first to those that mimic a polar bear, and then a scared innocent "savage." He arranges the empty space very specifically, calling it an "enclosure," conjuring a zoo while he nevertheless emphasizes the fact that we're in a theatre unadorned by any special theatrical signifiers—e.g., the "scenic design" is comprised of a single row of forty chairs

51

arranged in a square around scattered bits of KFC. Harewood plays upon our human love of tamed beasts, our fondness for viewing them as children who want to play with us—their superiors and masters. He effortlessly juxtaposes this with our familiar, and uncomfortably parallel, racial concerns. Our varied familiarities with American racial narratives unfurl from our mouths like scrolls announcing our personal histories with the subject. Attention to the odd performance-situation's sociopolitical resonance at once explodes and implodes, creating a beastly moral conundrum itself impossible to tame. As such there is something hopeless about the piece: Is Harewood suggesting a post-prejudicial world is impossible? And yet the piece allows space for hope: Can we recognize our insurmountable complexity and accept it not with apathy but with renewed momentum toward moral evolution? Or is Harewood himself asking no questions at all? Does he merely provide us a highly charged circumstance in which we are free to buy, sell, accept, reject, leap into or walk away from our fictions, our realities, our truths?

In summation, elements all five productions share with the *Hamlet* roulette include:

- A heightened awareness of the performer alongside their character(s).
- A highly specific, often spare, physical vocabulary in the staging.
- A scenic design comprised of a single space, which, between the performer's actions in relation to it and the audience's imaginations, is transformed into the production's various places.
- A radical dramaturgical approach to familiar material.[53]
- A conscious playing upon audience familiarity with the given subject.
- A heightened attention to the sociopolitical relevance of the material.

52

[53] Jamal Harewood's *The Privileged* is perhaps an exception here. Though it has a dramaturgy improvised by the audience in response to the rule structure Harewood provides, it does not draw on familiar material in the sense of a play, or, as *Exhibit B* does, of a past form of entertainment that itself seeks to capture distinct micro-narratives.

Considering these commonalities together, connections to those ideas put forth by Lehmann, Rancière, Bailes, Ostermeier, and Deleuze & Guattari, which in the preceding sections of this chapter I have related to the *Hamlet* roulette, begin to emerge:

Each production places high technical demands on its performers, courting their failure to conform to traditional expectations of quality and of theatrical form. Similarly, their precisely limited physical vocabularies, which fail to meet common expectations of a complete realism, allow room for psychological interpretation and other meaning-making on the spectator's part. Meanwhile, the failure of the open scenic spaces to fully depict literal places forces spectators to create in their own imaginations the locations indicated by the performers' words and actions. These elements together encourage the learning opportunity attributed to failure by Bailes (2011: xix). What precisely one learns is up for debate. But altogether these six productions would seem to indicate that at least something one might learn is that expectations broken in some unexpected way have a heightened potential to render us more receptive to the unexpected possibilities of experience that emerge from the rupture. Crucially, it is the human failure on the performers' parts, and the resulting dual awareness of the performers as performers alongside their fictional characters, that compels the audience to recognize and consider their own human potential to fail at meeting expectations, and, by implication, to succeed at discovering new possibilities within themselves and others.

Lehmann locates this crucial dual awareness of the performer and the performed among the key means used by post-dramatic theatre to compel an audience's fuller awareness of their experience (2006: 4), further noting how performance "has the power to question and destabilize the spectator's construction of identity and the 'other'—more so than mimetic drama, which remains caught in representation and thus often reproduces prevailing ideologies" (2006: 5). From this observation of Lehmann's it is only a short step into the rhizomatic, de-organized chaos of endless democratic possibility promoted by Deleuze & Guattari (1983 & 1987). Their repeated emphasis on forgoing the centralized conclusions typical of capitalist thinking encourages a further and broader consideration of our democratic processes over an immediate or even final acceptance of them. In other words, they ask that we live always in the middle of the question (democracy/diversity) and not at the end-point of the answer (capitalism/singularity).[55] Combined with

54

[55] " Let us summarize the principle characteristics of a rhizome: ... It has neither beginning nor end, but always a middle (*milieu*) from which it grows and which it overspills" (Deleuze & Guattari, 1987: 21).

Ostermeier's intent to question the impact of capitalist societal structures on audience perception and reception, and his exploration of means to forge a practical approach to theatrical "realism" that embodies not the singular surfaces emphasized by capitalism but the more pluralistic internal reality of the human experience (Boenisch & Ostermeier, 2016: 16-17), a circle of critical thought is mapped back through Deleuze & Guattari to Lehmann's reference to a consideration of the "other" cited above. Had Lehmann written his book more recently than 1999, or had it been translated into English more recently than 2006, one might guess a more explicit reference to current sociopolitical concerns about diversity and empathy may likely have been made. Even without that explicit terminology, Lehmann's comment clearly implies a need to consider diversity with empathy, and the power performance has to help us do so by de-familiarizing familiar material, subjects, and modes, and, in doing so, effectively politicize our attention, by which I mean heighten our critical attention to the (formerly) familiar—be it a play, a person, an ideology.[56]

And here I return to the very title of this book: *Playing* Hamlet *Roulette: Failure, Expectation, Possibility & Democracy*. It is my hope that a consideration of these six productions and other like examples, as well as of the implications of their commonalities in light of the ideas of Bailes, Deleuze & Guattari, Lehmann, Ostermeier, and Rancière explored above, might together aide in the conception and consideration of various other means by which theatre and performance can use failure to break expectations in an effort to open up more democratic considerations of diverse possibilities.

---

[56] " In place of the discredited enlightenment model in which the audience gains moral and sentimental education from a night out at the civic or national theatre, we might be able to develop a model of performance as an ethical encounter, in which we come face to face with the other, in a recognition of our mutual vulnerability which encourages relationships based on openness, dialogue and a respect for difference. This represents a shift in terminology in which the theatre of moral instruction gives way to performance as ethical practice" (Ridout, 2009: 54).
57

Epilogue: "Don't draw conclusions."

That is something I once advised a group of students in a Devised Theatre course I teach at the American Conservatory Theater. My advice came about in response to a habit this group had of leaping immediately to hard and fast conclusions about their experiences, be it a five-minute video clip of a live performance they'd just watched or a short performance created in class by one of their peers. Their seemingly youthful expediency with regard to solidifying opinions based on limited experience, rather than taking the time to develop points of view based on a network of gathered experiences and references, strikes me as a habit not at all limited to the young. Quick conclusions are easier to conceive and perhaps more comfortable to hold—certainly they are easier to "sell"—than more prolonged processes of consideration and reflection that do not seek either an immediate product or a final result. And there we have a philosophy that might be as useful to our considerations of real life as it is to our considerations of theatre—the latter being rehearsal for the former.

Even among theatre makers the rush to produce conclusions might arguably be a product of habitual capitalist structures, which encourage a rushing of capital upward toward some single point. A more democratic—and therefore alternately and irregularly more frustrating and more enlightening—approach might indeed be to linger in a rhizome of questions: How far is an audience willing to go with their forgiveness of failure? What constitutes productive, creative failure and what is simply failure? The *Hamlet* roulette, for example, may have succeeded at being good theatre while failing to be good art. This brings into question the difference between an experience (theatre) and expectations of its quality (art). What are the values and intentions of theatre versus those of art, i.e., of experience versus expectation? What do these questions about failure and expectation in relation to the theatre-going experience and to notions of artistic standards mean in relation to wider notions of possibility, democracy, and diversity? Crucially, what from our experiences in the theatre might we apply in our real lives outside the theatre? And when it comes to either theatre or art versus life outside of either, can we really say which is theory and which is practice? Must we even?

Hamlet famously asks the question, "To be or not to be?" and then spends the rest of the play debating it.[59] Eventually Hamlet concludes neither to be nor not to be, but to "Let be." Perhaps this insight helps us here. Perhaps

---

58

[59] Or perhaps avoiding it!

it is indeed useful to sit with a set of un-expecting questions beyond the final bow, and, for some debatable amount of time thereafter, to let conclusions be. Is this a failure, or one possible means toward a more diverse democracy?

Questions

Is there a performance you have seen—whether a play, dance, performance art, or other form—that made you aware of your relationship(s) to the audience around you? How and in what way?

If a performance surprises you by not meeting your expectations, why might this be a good thing and why might it not?

Assuming failure is worth considering, is there a performance you have seen that did not compel you to think or to feel anything in particular? How did it achieve this lack? Was the failure the artists', yours, both?

The Audience
Sally Picciotto

With annotations by Carolyn Jones, Chard Nelson,
and K.M. Soehnlein.

Preshow speech
Mark Jackson

> Performances are not one-way delivery systems shoveling
> content and meaning from artists to audiences. In a strict
> sense, performances themselves present no ready-made
> meanings at all... [Rather,] performances may energize
> people to make hundreds, even thousands, of blends and
> meanings. (McConachie 2013: 73)

> The common tendency to refer to an audience as 'it'
> and, by extension, to think of 'it' as a single entity risks
> obscuring the multiple contingencies of subjective
> response, context, and environment which condition an
> individual's interpretation of a particular performance... It
> is important to remember that each audience is made up of
> individuals who bring their own cultural reference points,
> political beliefs, sexual preferences, personal histories,
> and immediate preoccupations to their interpretation of a
> production. (Freshwater 2009: 5-6)

> There is something particular about theatrical
> spectatorship that offers ways of talking about ethics—
> and, specifically, thinking socially and politically about
> ethics—that no other cultural practice seems to offer... The

---

1

> theatre is a place where we know that there is a difference
> between how people seem and how they are, but it is also
> a place where we pretend not to know the difference...
> All the same, people do come to theatre looking for
> truth. (Ridout 2009: 14-15)

Sally Picciotto is a mathematician. She saw the *Hamlet* roulette sixteen times between April and August 2016, and then fifteen more times from November 2016 through January 2017, totaling thirty-one out of the sixty performances. She did not come that often because she knew I would one day ask her to contribute to this book, nor because she was a critic reviewing the production.[3] In her essay below she explains why she kept coming back, and what came of it.

I asked Sally to contribute to this book for the obvious reason that her frequent attendance is highly unusual and makes her evolving perspective unique.[4] As if to demonstrate Nicholas Ridout's comment above, Sally's observations point to ethical questions about assumptions we make—in that blurry space within the triangle of actor, role, and audience—around gender, age, and race. Sally's account also certainly corroborates McConachie's suggestion that meanings might be made more by audiences than performances. Further regarding that, and in line with Helen Freshwater's comment, I've asked other audience members who came multiple times to augment Sally's perspective with their own, in order to reflect something of the diversity of experience had by people not involved in the creation of the show until the point of their arrival as audience to it—at which time, as Rancière would suggest, they joined the ranks of collaborators making meaning of the event (2009). A consideration of the *Hamlet* roulette without these perspectives would be woefully incomplete.

2

[3] Mark Jackson: "The Shotgun Players encouraged critics to see the production three times, in order to have the intended experience. Only one critic, John Wilkins of KQED, saw it three times. One other critic, Claudia Bauer of the San Francisco Chronicle, saw it twice. The rest, as far as we know, saw it once."

[4] Mark Jackson: "Carolyn Jones, a real-estate agent and Shotgun Players board member, saw the production a similar number of times: thirty-six."

Sally's Notes

First Impressions

Mark says, "We are all Hamlet," but I had never seen someone like me playing him. When I first heard of the project, I felt excited about the possibility of seeing a woman play Hamlet—particularly when I learned that the cast included four women and only three men, even though only two of the characters in the play are female.[5]

A couple of months before the first previews, subscribers were invited to a table read-through of the script. When I first saw the actors at that reading, I realized that some of them were older than others, which got me interested in the idea that actors would also be playing against type in age. I also remember being surprised when Kevin[6] said that Gertrude was the character he was most excited to play.

I attended the show for the first time with some friends who were visiting from out of town during previews. We were all exhilarated to see a woman (El) play Hamlet, and we found her very compelling.[8] At the

---

[5] Chard Nelson: "In some sense I guess I was excited about the opposite prospect from Sally's: I had only ever seen Hamlet portrayed by people basically like me. I too was intrigued by what different insights might come from a whole different kind of Hamlet."

[6] K.M. Soehnlein: "That would be Kevin Clarke, my husband, the main reason I attended this show nine times (a large number for me, though dwarfed by the experience of the author and other annotators of this essay). When I asked Kevin why he was so excited to play Gertrude, since she really doesn't have a lot of lines, he replied, 'Because she's always listening.' Seeing the show so many times allowed me to pay closer attention to how much acting goes on in response to other actors—and how in this production, an actor's quality of listening would change drastically based on whom one was listening to, which was different every night."

[7]

[8] K.M. Soehnlein: "The first Hamlet I saw was David, the oldest male cast member. I remember thinking that an older man playing the part of a younger man was not the most radical casting twist—Olivier was forty when he played the college-aged Hamlet—but I quickly saw that

time, I wondered whether I was more sympathetic to Hamlet because he was played by a woman. I also noted that Ophelia's death being grotesque comedy (suicide by garden-hose drowning) probably angered me less than it otherwise would have because she was played by a man (David)—making it feel less like disrespect toward a female character, of which there are so few in Shakespeare.[9]

I understood from the program notes and from what was said at the reading that Mark wanted to get away from the play being all about the actor playing the title role, and make it about the whole play again. That first time, I noticed that the production didn't merely broaden the focus to the whole play but actually emphasized the text's commentary on theatre more generally, on acting and performance. The fact that actors occasionally needed to ask to be prompted for a line didn't bother me at all; it felt consistent with what the production was about, because this staging drew attention to the fact that it was a play.[11] It was performed for us, but the characters also performed

---

the hard-earned wisdom that comes with age leant a less brash and more seasoned quality to the character. Rather than the impulsive behavior of youth—what the younger actors, in general, brought to the role—this 'mature' Hamlet conveyed a sense of midlife bitterness. His hostility toward the errors of his 'elders' contained a long lifetime of resentment. I saw this to some degree as well with the other older actors, Beth, Cathleen, and Kevin, all of whom imbued the young Hamlet with a degree of world weariness, though in individually distinct ways."

[9] K.M. Soehnlein: "The first Ophelia I saw was El, and the hose-drowning read as comedy, but misplaced. I didn't see it as disrespect toward a female character, particularly; it just seemed like a prank, not suicide. Part of it was the garden-variety green of the hose, an incongruous color amid a production design heavy on red, black, and white. I was relieved when the change was made to depict her suicide with a gun. No one was laughing anymore. The gun raised other questions, though, like was Gertrude's lovingly rendered 'willows speech' a big lie, since we'd just seen the brutality of Ophelia taking her own life?"

10

[11] Chard Nelson: "My first viewing was the final dress rehearsal, right before previews, with Beth as Hamlet. She was definitely not comfortable yet, calling for lines a lot, and I must admit that I had some serious doubts that

for one another. Hamlet, of course, performs madness, but this production made it more explicit: he and Ophelia acted out the play-within-the-play for Claudius, Gertrude, and Polonius. So not only could any actor play Hamlet, but Hamlet was also an actor.

All of these themes (casting against type, gender politics, and meta-commentary) came up repeatedly in my observations about subsequent viewings, with new insights and ideas developing and deepening over time.[13]

Second time[14]

After seeing a performance one week later, I noted how very funny this production was for a tragedy. Even though I responded differently depending on who played which part, I noticed how much stayed the same—not just the staging but many of the more striking gestures—despite the different

---

night, both about whether the whole roulette casting would work at all, and whether calls for 'Line!' would be too distracting. This was the first (but as it turned out, last) time I felt this show might fail."
[12]

[13] Chard Nelson: "I hadn't realized how meta-theatrical the production was going to be. I got new insights about theatre, acting, direction, and drama virtually every night. It all felt like a master course in the possibilities of theatre."
[14] K.M. Soehnlein: "The second time I saw the show, Kevin played Hamlet. Hooray! I'd feared I'd never see him in this role, a distinct possibility given the roulette casting, but here it was, and on our anniversary, no less. In fact, after Kevin's name was drawn for Hamlet from the skull and I loudly cheered from Row D, Mark informed the audience that it was our anniversary, which seemed to have the effect of infusing my personal viewing experience into what those around me were experiencing from their seats, too. This was an aspect of the production that I came to cherish: we all seemed to be in this together, the audience aware not only of the process the actors were going through, but of each other, partaking in this high-stakes game. As such it felt more like going to the circus, gasping together at a high-wire act, than simply seeing a 'play.'"

cast configuration.[15] However, this time I picked up on a couple of essential details of the Shotgun Players' interpretation that I had missed the first time, and that perhaps most people would not notice on their first viewing:

1. Ophelia was in cahoots with Hamlet from the start. On second viewing, I actually parsed what was happening in the transition into Act 2 Scene 1. Ophelia and Hamlet met behind the transparent curtain and mimed a conversation in which he indicated madness, she grabbed her own wrist, and they embraced. That is, we saw her and Hamlet coming up with the story she would tell her father. Then she burst out from behind the curtain, shrieking "O, my lord, my lord, I have been so affrighted!"

2. Ophelia, too, was only *performing* madness in Act 4 Scene 5. Why else would she dishevel herself on stage in front of the audience and check to make sure that her appearance was suitable for seeming to be mad, rather than just coming out onstage already mad? This was a rather radical choice that emphasized the textual similarities in their situations and gave her more agency.[17]

---

[15] Chard Nelson: " I had imagined the ever-changing cast would produce a wild and chaotic atmosphere. But I quickly realized that would be impossible, that most of the staging and pacing had to be very carefully coordinated or nothing would work. The discipline of all seven actors having to form their own versions of all seven roles within the constraints of the shared structure was mind-boggling."

[16]

[17] K.M. Soehnlein: " Regarding Ophelia. I saw nearly every member of the cast play this part, and the question of 'performing madness' was one that felt unresolved to me. Was it up to the actor to decide how much of Ophelia's madness was real versus put on? This moment where she disheveled herself for the audience was sometimes played for comedy—Ha ha, see how I'm acting crazy? Now you're in on it, too—and sometimes treated more gravely—Please understand, I'm doing this as a way to cope with the terrible, powerless situation I'm in. And sometimes the actor seemed to strike a more 'meta' note: Where is

A second viewing also added further to my understanding of this project's central theme of performance: I noticed how the frequent breaking of the fourth wall reinforced the play's references to acting. For example, Polonius instructed us when to applaud during Claudius' opening speech; Hamlet exhorted us to watch how Claudius responded to *The Mousetrap* and then to cheer and jeer with him when Claudius stopped the play; Ophelia asked us whether she looked sufficiently crazy at the end of intermission and requested our help in calling Gertrude out onto the stage. Hamlet also broke the fourth wall during his performance of *The Mousetrap* in order to interact with his onstage audience. The characters repeatedly drew attention to the presence of an audience, reminding us that the characters themselves, not just the actors, were all performing.

By this time, Ophelia's suicide-by-hose had been replaced by a gun-to-the-head suicide; however, since I saw a different actor playing Ophelia I assumed the change meant that each actor had a different suicide method. Because I saw Kevin as Ophelia four times in a row, I continued in that erroneous assumption until my sixth viewing! Also, his face became the default image in my head for Ophelia. This gives a pretty clear sense of how successful the against-type casting could be: my subconscious accepted that this man is what Ophelia looks like.

After the second time I saw the show, I was already feeling a little obsessed with it. At that point I intended to see it at least a couple more times. Little did I know![19] I ended up seeing it several more times over the initial run, partly because I wanted to see a woman play Ophelia. Improbably, I did not get to. I would not, in fact, see a woman play Ophelia until the repertory run and the eighth time I saw it. The probability of seeing only men play Ophelia seven times in a row is well under 1%. I began to understand how people get addicted to gambling: "I have to try again, because maybe *this* time..."

---

the dividing line between my performance of Ophelia and Ophelia's performance of madness? Think about it! That meta-uncertainty struck me as the richest way to enter into her plight."
[18]

[19] Chard Nelson: " I knew before the show was even staged that I would have to see it a lot. I didn't know what 'a lot' would entail. I eventually lost count, but my final total was about eighteen."

The next few times during the initial run

As I grew more familiar with the production, I started to notice more elements that I hadn't consciously registered at first: Ophelia listening intently to Hamlet's suicide ideation, which was perhaps what later gave her the idea of killing herself; the fact that each actor sang a different song as the gravedigger.[20/21] I also started to have preferred roles for each actor, as I saw them play more parts.

During my sixth viewing, I started noticing the responses from other people in the audience, particularly gasps of shock and horror at the mention and/or depiction of Ophelia's death and murmurs of dismay when Gertrude drank the poison.[23] Knowing that others were so completely engaged made me enjoy it even more, and it also gave me more of a sense of what the production felt like for an audience member who was not already familiar with the play. This was the first time I went to see it by myself. As a result, I ended up talking to some strangers in the audience. Discussing the show with other audience members turned out to be an unexpected bonus of

---

[20] Chard Nelson: " I loved the moments where the actors expressed a little of themselves, but in a way that wouldn't throw off the necessary structure of the staging. Having each actor choose a grave-digging song was a lovely touch."

[21] K.M. Soehnlein: " One night, the actor sang lines from 'Purple Rain.' Prince had just died. In the dark, I choked up. Good night, sweet Prince."

[22]

[23] K.M. Soehnlein: " Every time I watched this scene (where Gertrude drinks the poison) I heard gasps of horrified shock, a reminder that for some in the audience, this was a first-ever encounter with *Hamlet.* This struck me as akin to having your first encounter with a human face be a cubist portrait by Picasso. Would a traditionally cast, unedited, hands-off *Hamlet* ever be enough, after experiencing it in all its deconstructed glory at the Ashby Stage?"

returning to see it so many times.[24]

Repertory Performances through the summer[26]

The seventh time, I felt excited and happy as soon as I entered the theatre and saw the familiar minimalist set after a few weeks' break. This was when I realized that I was hooked and didn't want to miss any more performances if I could possibly help it.

I kept track of the casting configurations I saw on multiple spreadsheets. Yeah, I know, I'm a nerd. In fact, my training is in mathematics, so the randomization aspect of the project fascinated me. I spent several days calculating how many actors, on average, would play the same role they played the previous time. When I finally got the answer, I was stunned: it was exactly one. In fact, it turns out that this can be shown mathematically—no matter how many actors there are! So even if there were ten actors playing ten roles, or a hundred actors playing a hundred roles, the average number of actors playing the same role as the last time is always one.

A related question is: what is the probability that nobody repeats the

---

[24] Chard Nelson: "This was one of the areas where audience members in general felt empowered as participants in the show. It started with having them pick the casting from the skull, and from there on they seemed to feel invested in the show and wanted to express opinions and ask questions. There was definitely some kind of bonding that went with the roulette ritual that played out in the lobby. I can't recall any play that had audience members so engaged and wanting to talk to each other about plot points, about acting, about the whole process. Particularly when put in the context of the repertory season, where all the actors not only had to master all of *Hamlet* but also simultaneously handle one or more parts in other plays, audience members were awed and often, frankly, disbelieving. It's a bit like seeing Penn and Teller, where even after they tell you how they tricked you, you still can't believe it happened."
25

[26] Mark Jackson: "When *Hamlet* was joined by Penelope Skinner's play, *The Village Bike*, in June of 2016, it played once per week while *The Village Bike* played four times per week. The third play in the repertory, Heidi Schreck's *Grand Concourse*, was then added to the mix in July of 2016, and *Hamlet* continued once per week."

role they played last time? It turns out to be almost exactly equal to the probability that exactly one person repeats the role they played last time: just under 37%. The probability of four actors playing the same roles in two consecutive performances is only about 1.4%, but I saw it happen twice. Unlikely events do occur![27/28]

The probability of an entire configuration being repeated at some later date is actually much higher than one might expect. If we start counting on opening night, after the fourteen preview performances, then the probability of at least one full configuration being repeated at some point in the first forty-eight performances is 20%. By the eighty-fifth performance that probability is over 50%, even though there are 5040 different possible configurations.[29] It was still surprising, however, that one unlucky soul who showed up to see the play for the second time on June 30th happened to end up with the same configuration they had already seen on April 23rd; that probability was only one in 5040 (less than 0.02%).

In early summer I made myself a "bingo card" on which to mark which actors I had seen in which roles. Each role had a row, and each actor had a column. I also posted my responses to each performance on a blog. I reflected that it's rare to see a show where the illusion is broken before the play even starts, rather than afterwards during the curtain call. The actors are not in

---

[27] Chard Nelson: " I had the good fortune to see all seven actors in the role of Hamlet in the first seven times I saw the show. The probability of that is 0.6%."

[28] K.M. Soehnlein: " I'm grimly reminded that the likelihood of Donald Trump winning the White House was marked by Reuters on the morning of the election to be around 10%. I'm also reminded of how the political context of seeing Hamlet after November 2016 transformed the play itself, perhaps most emotionally in Act 3 Scene 4, where Hamlet confronts Gertrude with the portrait of the former king ('what a grace was seated on this brow') and the new king ('like a mildewed ear, blasting his wholesome brother'). I suspect I was not alone in that Berkeley audience, in the last days of the Obama administration, in finding potent resonance in the line 'What judgment would step from this to this?'"

[29] Sally Picciotto: "This is mathematically similar to something called the Birthday Paradox: in a group of twenty-five people, the chance that at least two people share a birthday is over 50%."

30

	EL	KEVIN	NICK	CATHLEEN	DAVID	MEGAN	BETH
POLONIUS	X	X	X		X	X	
GHOST/GD	X /	X			X	X	X
LAERTES	X		X	X	X	X	X
GERTRUDE	X	X		X			X
OPHELIA		X	X		X /	X	X
CLAUDIUS		X	X	X /	X	X	X
HAMLET	X		X	X	X	X	X ✓

character when they first come on stage for the roulette drawing.[31] Each one leaves as soon as they know their role, taking their labeled, bound script with them, to put on their costume and prepare mentally. Once the casting has happened, the director makes a few announcements, and then some music starts, which acts as the countdown.[32] Right as the song is ending, the actors file out on stage in character—except the Ghost/Gravedigger, who sits off-stage-left but visible to the audience—and just after the song's last note sounds, the house lights go out at the same moment that the stage lights come on, and the play starts. It's sort of like... BAM! Let the illusion begin.

It was all a reminder that theatre is a collaboration, a contract between the audience and the performers: we agree to accept the illusion they are presenting for us, and we recognize our active role in this because the illusion is thin: We saw the casting happen, the actors are carrying labeled

---

[31] K.M. Soehnlein: "This process was never not exciting to watch unfold. It infused this most familiar classic play with fresh suspense, every time."

[32] Chard Nelson: "Particularly at some early performances, I heard audience members talking who hadn't been aware of the random casting aspect of the show. Reactions ranged from disbelief that the casting was real, to being upset or disappointed about the way it came out. Later on, especially as more people were coming for repeated viewings, the talk was more about what/who was the same or different from previous viewings, and what that might mean."

33

scripts, they occasionally ask to be prompted for a line… so who cares if some characters' ages and genders do not match those of the actors playing them? It is up to us to believe in it anyway, and we do, maybe because the characters themselves ask us to participate right from the very first scene.

But they clearly aren't just performing for us. Each character is also putting on an act for the other characters. Thus, there are several layers of illusion and self-reference here, all of which is openly acknowledged, and all of which is still based in the text—containing, as it does, a play-within-a-play that influences the plot of the play.

Eighth through eleventh times: More about typecasting

The eighth performance I saw happened to be a very traditional configuration:

Polonius/Priest/Osric:	El
Ghost/Gravedigger:	David
Laertes:	Beth
Gertrude/Guildenstern:	Cathleen
Ophelia/Horatio:	Megan
Claudius/Rosencrantz:	Kevin
Hamlet:	Nick

Only El and Beth were playing against type, and it made me think a lot about typecasting. This was the first time I saw a woman playing Ophelia, an experience I had eagerly anticipated because of how society does not generally allow young women to express rage, no matter how justified. I really wanted to see how this production's interpretation of Ophelia would affect me when a woman played her.[34]

Of course, it's hard to know how much of my noticing or understanding something on the nth viewing is because of seeing it repeatedly, and how much is due to a particular casting configuration,[36] but this performance

---

[34] Carolyn Jones: "One of my favorite bits of casting was the Ophelia/Horatio combination. It is the only time we see the same actor play both a man and a woman in two important roles. It also required instant costume changes alongside instant gender change. It never disappointed."
[35]

[36] Chard Nelson: "This is an excellent point. At some point I had great uncertainty about whether it was the permutations and combinations coming into play or just my growing familiarity with the text and the staging that made me notice new things every night. And this wasn't

got me thinking…

Beth had pointed out in a discussion that in the "nunnery" scene, Ophelia is upset by Hamlet's verbal abuse and threat of physical violence, but further traumatized by the fact that there are three witnesses who neither intervene to protect her nor express afterwards any concern or compassion regarding the effect the confrontation may have had on her. Perhaps due to Megan's acting—though it could have also been the chemistry between the actors or just my own repeated viewings—I finally understood Ophelia's motivations in the next scene: She cooperates with Hamlet on his *Mousetrap* play—performed by the two of them in this production—because she, too, is angry at Claudius, Gertrude, and her father. She, too, wants revenge on them. She may even blame them for Hamlet's abusive behavior toward her and for their breakup, because he knew they were being watched and she could see that it looked to him like she had betrayed him. In a way she *had* betrayed him, but as a young woman, her behavior and choices are far more constrained than his, a fact that Polonius even points out earlier in the play:

> … For Lord Hamlet,
> Believe so much in him, that he is young
> And with a larger tether may he walk
> Than may be given you… (*Act 1 Scene 3*)

At the end of intermission, after applying her "mad" makeup and messing up her hair in front of us, Megan's Ophelia looked like a rebellious, goth teenager, which underscores how intentional her unravelling is. In fact, I noticed even more parallels than I previously had between her scene of performed madness and Hamlet's in the "nunnery" scene. Not only does she echo a lot of the same gestures and movements that she saw him do, but she—quite literally—physically re-enacts his role in that scene, intimidating Claudius the way Hamlet intimidated her, using his body language but

---

just an audience phenomenon. Especially toward the end of the final repertory run, I could see that the actors had been incorporating little bits of each other's portrayals. Just a look or gesture or a bit of emphasis or pacing that I'd recognize as someone else's. As they all got more comfortable with the whole process, they were clearly trying new bits either of their own devising or borrowed from each other."

37

different words.[38] She expresses rage in a way normally embodied by men—in fact, in a way previously embodied by Hamlet—and she does so with the conscious intent to discomfit the King she holds to blame, even if Claudius completely misses how much of her "madness" is anger directed at him. Her defiant determination and action are an effort to reclaim control of her life. She wants to walk "with a larger tether," even if only to her death. And because a woman was playing Ophelia this time, lacking the implicit power we associate with men, it felt more significant, more exciting, and ultimately more heartrending to see her do so.[39]

However, the deeper resonance I felt with this Ophelia is not a sign of inferior acting on the part of the men in that role. How I respond to the performance says as much about me and about our surrounding culture as it does about the actors. It may have been difficult for these men to embody the powerlessness experienced by a young woman being used as a pawn, but maybe it's just that it is hard for me to look at a white man and see disenfranchisement.

As another example of how subjective this all is, I noticed how powerful Claudius was when played by Kevin—in the sense that he appeared to exude power almost effortlessly, especially in the first chunk of the show. But later, as Claudius' fear and guilt grow stronger and as his relationship with Gertrude deteriorates, Kevin exhibited more and more of that repugnant male dominance that comes from insecurity. I noticed how gendered those qualities are far more when Kevin played the role than when anyone else

---

[38] Chard Nelson: "This was a recognition I came to rather late in the run. I came to feel this was one of the most brilliant aspects of the staging."

[39] K.M. Soehnlein: "This production's choices around Ophelia's character are brought out something I'd never considered in previous encounters with *Hamlet* on stage and on screen: that her awareness of her powerlessness motivates her actions. She is a young woman trapped inside a fortress (if 'Denmark is a prison' for the royal heir *Hamlet*, imagine what it is for her), and what few options she has are chained to the greater power of the men in her life: father, brother, lover. As such, I came to see her suicide, and the pose of madness she adopts (in this iteration) leading up to it, as an act of resistance, a taking hold of fate when there is no other powerful option available. However, even though I settled into that interpretation, I don't know if the production fully did."
40

did, and I wondered whether he is good at embodying power because of being a middle-aged white man. But then I also wondered—how much of it is Kevin's *acting*, and how much of it is that we are culturally conditioned to *expect* power—and those who abuse it—to look like that?[41/42]

This was the second performance in a row in which Kevin played Claudius and Cathleen played Gertrude, and the way their dynamic shifted as the play progressed was almost imperceptibly gradual. In other configurations, I'd noticed the major turning points, but this time I noticed its development in each interaction they had. At first he seems to seek her guidance in their dealings with her son. But as her compassion for both Hamlet and Ophelia increases, and as he begins to fear Hamlet more, their relationship becomes more and more strained. He begins ordering her around more and referring to Hamlet in a hostile tone as "your son" when he talks to her, and the seeds of doubt Hamlet planted in her head about Claudius begin to grow. She starts to distrust his intentions toward Hamlet, and finally, in an act of insubordination to her husband, unknowingly drinks the poison he intended for her son. It was a masterful performance by both of them.[43]

Given the randomized casting, the actors only rarely had the luxury of playing a given role opposite the same other actor. This means that the dynamics and chemistry between the characters had not always been fully explored in a given configuration. I thought that the subtleties of the

---

[41] Sally Picciotto: " After the 16th time, I recognized that Kevin performed a particular type of masculinity when he played Claudius, and this, in combination with his age and actual maleness, is what made for such a disturbing and effective exploration of male abuse of power."

[42] Chard Nelson: " I had the unique opportunity to observe this effect up close, and I'm clear that this was a conscious acting choice on Kevin's part. You see, after the season ended, Shotgun did a staged reading of Tom Stoppard's *Rosencrantz and Guildenstern Are Dead* in which Kevin reprised his role as Claudius, Cathleen was Gertrude, and I got to follow them around in a bit part as Polonius. So I literally got to stand behind the curtain with Kevin and watch how he consciously and with intention put on the blustering and dominating role of Claudius."

[43] Carolyn Jones: " As the season ripened so too did the various power shifts become more completely realized by all the actors. This was particularly true of Claudius and Gertrude but also between Ophelia and Polonius, and even between the hilarious Rosencrantz and Guildenstern."

44

Claudius-Gertrude relationship developed so palpably in this performance at least in part because it was the second time in a row that the same two actors played those parts.[45]

Indeed, from the ninth time on, much of what I was noticing in each performance was the variety in different actors' portrayals of the characters and the chemistry resulting from different combinations of actors in roles, as well as how these interpretations developed over time. I gradually stopped having "favorite" roles for each actor, because I started to appreciate the diversity in what each actor brought to each role. For example, I noticed different qualities in Ophelia depending on who played her: disappointment in the lack of emotional support from her father (David), vulnerability (Kevin), distress (Nick), vengeful defiance (Megan), rebelliousness (Beth), rage (El), youth and powerlessness (Cathleen)—all of which are important aspects of Ophelia's character and situation.[46] Once I had seen enough actors play a role, I projected echoes of all of the interpretations I'd seen onto whomever I was watching, so that these qualities might be in different proportions, but they were all present. If "we are all Hamlet," then we are

[45] Chard Nelson: " I often wondered during the course of the season what the play would have looked like with fixed casting, with the actors able to really invest in a single role, develop it, and hone the interactions with each other. I know it would have been good, and with the way the play was cut and re-formed, it would still have provided some unique insights into the story and characters. But no matter how good, it would ultimately be just another *Hamlet*. We would have lost all the insights gained from watching how seven different *Hamlets* play against seven different Claudiuses with seven different Ophelias, etc. It's a cliché that every performance of every show is unique, but the differences are usually subtler. In the *Hamlet* roulette, everything was different, all the time, with always something new to discern."

[46] Chard Nelson: " Early on, I think everyone was naturally focused on the role of *Hamlet*, who was playing it and how they differed. This is where I think I was particularly fortunate to have seen seven *Hamlets* in my first seven viewings. Having seen everyone's take on that role, I was free to think about the other characters and the nuances that each actor brought to them. I particularly enjoyed watching the range the actors brought to Claudius, where Kevin tended to rage and get rather physical, while Megan was very physically intimidating in a very different way, leaning in close rather than being loud and dominating. And in a whole different mien, Beth's Claudius was a stoic, calculating character, menacing in the suppression of the emotions you knew were roiling inside."

also all Ophelia.[47]

Tenth time

This was the first time I saw a man (Kevin) play Gertrude, and it proved again that even when a man played a female character it could resonate powerfully with me.

Eleventh time

The eleventh time I saw it, everyone except Kevin played a character of a different gender from their own:

Polonius/Priest/Osric:	Beth
Ghost/Gravedigger:	Kevin
Laertes:	Megan
Gertrude/Guildenstern:	Nick
Ophelia/Horatio:	David
Claudius/Rosencrantz:	Cathleen
Hamlet:	El

This configuration reinforced some of my previous observations about gender and age. For example, it's exciting to see a young woman express

[47] Chard Nelson: "To me, this might be the ultimate lesson of this exercise: All the combinations work, on some level. You can literally cast any actor in any of the roles. Some might provide more insights or more interesting insights, but until you see them, you'll never know. I don't think I was conscious before of just how much a director's casting decisions influence the audience's impression of a play. It's obvious that casting a Hamlet of a different gender changes a lot of the dynamics of the play. If you're committing to that casting for a whole season, you're unlikely to do it unless there is a very particular point you want to make. On the other hand, not making that choice also makes a point, but one that is probably not so obvious or controversial. The ability to explore all those dynamics, even briefly, was a huge boon, and if any of them didn't work, well, it was just one performance. Of course, the triumphs were equally fleeting."
48

rage physically as Hamlet. However, I also noticed that, due to societal expectations around gender, "subversive" casting could somewhat subvert the subversiveness of the staging. For example, having Ophelia echo Hamlet's staging during her "mad" scene, having her embody rage in the same way, could end up feeling less transgressive if an older man was playing her against a woman as Claudius.[49]

Twelfth and thirteenth times

After the twelfth viewing, I felt that although I liked aspects of the male actors' portrayals of Ophelia, her rage was only apparent to me in her mad scene when played by a woman. Nevertheless, during the first Act of my thirteenth viewing I briefly forgot the actor playing her (Nick) was male.

Fourteenth time

Polonius (played by Nick) seemed more obviously misogynistic than usual— not just in how he used his daughter as a pawn, but also in how he dominated conversations in which Gertrude ought to have been able to participate. Kevin-as-Gertrude's nonverbal reactions to this were strikingly real—I really believed that she was seething internally while projecting a calm exterior. This is a very common female experience, and I was pleased to see a man portray it with such delicacy and authenticity. It made me reflect on how subtle but effective some of the performances of gender are, especially given the important decision not to have the men exaggerate stereotypical

---

[49] K.M. Soehnlein: "This was also true when one of the two female actors of color, Cathleen and El, played Ophelia against white male actors playing Claudius (or Hamlet). The male punishing of the female read as extra cruel because not only was male privilege being abused, white privilege was as well, at least in the visual representation being presented. Thus 'color-blind casting' unexpectedly revealed the myth of color-blindness, which some white people like to claim regarding race ('I don't see color'). Context asserts itself, often painfully. As a white male, I felt implicated."
50

femininity when playing female roles in this production.[51] Performance of gender is, of course, most noticeable when an actor is cast against type—*e.g.*, Kevin's Gertrude, or how El takes up space as Hamlet—but not *exclusively* then: Kevin's Claudius and Nick's Polonius both involved performances of masculinity, and Megan's regal Gertrude gave the impression that the character was performing queenliness—a certain type of femininity, again connected with projecting a calm exterior.[52]

Sixteenth time

This was the first time I saw two men playing the King and Queen. Nick's Gertrude seemed to chafe more under the dominance of Kevin's Claudius— as if she was unable to swallow her anger. I couldn't tell how much of my reading it that way was because of choices Nick made and how much was just because he is also male. Regardless, it was exciting to watch their relationship deteriorate, because Gertrude's emotions were so close to the surface.[53]

I enjoyed watching the actors' interpretations of the roles deepen over time, providing insight into the acting *process*. Normally I would see a play once and think of it as a static thing, but this production, and my repeated viewings, reminded me that live theatre is dynamic. In some cases I saw actors pick up ideas from one another's interpretations. It was like a window into the rehearsal process, only better, because it felt more like

---

[51] Chard Nelson: " I was impressed early on with the subtlety of the male actors in the female roles. I know I saw David as Ophelia and Nick as Gertrude quite early in the run, and realized in both cases that without doing much overt stuff, David managed to be convincingly both young and female, and Nick both female and regal."

[52] Carolyn Jones: " At about this number of viewings I was very much aware of the constraints placed on the actors by the very singular staging, and to produce this 'queenliness' while making precisely the same moves made by all the actors came from somewhere deep inside."

[53] Carolyn Jones: " It was at about this time that I noticed all the actors relating to each other more in whatever parts they were playing. The power shift between Claudius and Gertrude is a great example, the actors now taking ownership of the play leaps and bounds beyond simply getting through it. You could count on a great variety of interactions. Characters really developed. David's Gravedigger felt epic. As Gertrude, Nick's scowl at the poison cup. The various Rosencrantzes and Guildensterns' subtle glances to one another."

meta-commentary.[54]

Part of the fun of returning to see the show so many times was making friends with the other people who attended nearly all of the repertory performances. Chatting during intermission, we bonded over how much we were enjoying repeated viewings and exchanged notes on what we were learning about the play by seeing it so many times. Hearing the perspectives of other, similarly addicted audience members also reminded me that my preferences were subjective.[55]

The fifteenth and sixteenth times, I marveled a bit at the fact that I still found it both interesting and funny, and I continued thinking about the play—and talking everyone's ear off about it—even when it went on hiatus.

Thoughts during the hiatus (August 19 to November 24, 2016)

If the production was conceived as a commentary on and rejection of typecasting, it certainly succeeded. Multiple viewings made me think about how much societal conditioning and expectations can affect my own responses to actors in certain parts, particularly in relation to the social status of the actors and their roles. However, I had some embryonic thoughts on this even the first time I saw one of the performances, and I also enjoyed seeing how many possibilities are opened up by casting against type.

In retrospect, I noticed that my initial thoughts on this experiment had

---

[54] K.M. Soehnlein: " When I see a production multiple times, I inevitably find it true that a second or third viewing reveals a cast relaxing into its roles so that the entire production seems to run like a well-oiled machine. But here there was no advancement toward 'relaxing' or 'well-oiled' because no two components were ever exactly the same."

[55] Chard Nelson: " This is a great point. Not only were we seeing a different play every night, but we were also often seeing it from different angles, perhaps sitting with different friends, and bringing in whatever mental detritus from our day might be lingering. There were definitely times when I was surprised by a reaction or an insight from one of my fellow addicts during intermission or when we'd cross-check our thoughts after the show. But as time went on I grew to realize that, like the cast, we were also different every night, so variation was to be expected and explored."

56

been entirely about what possibilities it offered for a single viewing. However, randomization actually implies multiplicity. This wasn't a production of *Hamlet* with traditional casting, nor was it a production with non-traditional casting. It was a production with a vast multiplicity of casting, offering unprecedented complexity and possibility. Only with multiple viewings could an audience member have a thorough appreciation for this project and for what randomized casting really means.[57]

Seventeenth to thirty-first times: Thoughts during the final run of repertory performances (November 25, 2016, to January 22, 2017)[59]

Any show that is performed live will have some variability in the quality of different performances, but for obvious reasons that variability was greater for the *Hamlet* roulette than for most other professional productions. The first performance after the three-month hiatus was pretty rusty. But it didn't take long for them to get back into the swing of it. Although most of these performances were still much messier than those over the summer, that didn't usually make it painful to watch. During this period, more of my recorded observations were about details and specific moments that distinguished the performances rather than the larger concepts I'd thought about earlier. For example:

Cathleen, one of the older actors, played Ophelia so youthfully that her furious, powerless, entirely nonverbal response to being scolded by her father reminded me of how I felt as a teenager when my father scolded me.

In this production, Polonius made some noise behind the curtain when he and the King and Queen were eavesdropping on Hamlet and Ophelia's conversation during the "get thee to a nunnery" scene. This is what prompted Hamlet to ask "Where is your father?" Megan performed Ophelia's response by pausing before saying "At home, my lord" with a significant look at

---

[57] Chard Nelson: "I will likely never see as many different interpretations of a single play as I did of *Hamlet* during this year. I saw about eighteen different shows, and although I'm sure I could find and attend eighteen different *Hamlets* in a single year, I doubt they would differ as much or in as interesting ways as these roulette versions did."
58

[59] Mark Jackson: "By this point, all five productions in the season were in repertory together, with the *Hamlet* actors each also playing in one to three others."

Hamlet. That look seemed to be an attempt to communicate to him that yes, she knew Polonius was there but that she had not volunteered for this, she was still on Hamlet's side. She could not say anything explicitly, precisely *because* Polonius was listening. It really reinforced that Ophelia was in an impossible situation, attempting a performance that could convey different things to her two audiences—not to mention the actual audience!

When I finally saw her play Claudius, El's performance of masculinity and authority was worth the wait. Her interpretation had fear simmering under the surface of every interaction with Hamlet, and selfishness informing nearly every decision. Her performance of masculine fury was uncontainable. I will forever feel sad that I never got to see her play that role opposite Kevin as Gertrude!

I noticed that Nick's Gertrude reacted to the poison (Act 5 Scene 2) immediately—making a face that showed that it tasted bad, so that it made sense for her to know why she was dying. I don't know whether other actors did that too. There were so many things happening on stage at the same time in that scene that I might not have caught it even if they did.

After the hiatus, I was surprised to notice that some of the audience giggled at Claudius' line, "Our sometime sister, now our queen" (Act 1 Scene 2), if Gertrude was played by a man. I didn't remember that happening before the hiatus, but afterwards it happened fairly consistently, despite the fact that this possibility was always present. This line occurs so early in the play that it was not yet obvious to a new audience member that the male actors would not exaggerate their performances of femininity. But I was still mildly nonplussed that people would find this particular against-type casting funny in and of itself, in a production known for its randomized casting.[60]

Twentieth time

This was the night I filled in the last two squares on my bingo card: I had finally seen everyone play every role!

Twenty-first time

I started to doubt my interpretation of Ophelia (played by Nick that night): was she really only pretending to be mad? I began to wonder if that might be a choice each actor made. For example, Megan's Ophelia very clearly

---

[60] K.M. Soehnlein: "Yes—this happened from the start, but only here, at this first direct acknowledgement of the switched-gender casting. It was as though the audience had to get this childish giggle out of its system and then grow up fast."
61

performed madness—she even winked at the audience before messing up her hair and makeup—while for some of the others this was a little bit ambiguous. I reflected on my blog at the time:

> I can't think why they would have her dishevel herself on stage, ask us if she looks mad, and enlist our assistance in calling the Queen onto the stage, if not to make clear that her "madness" is an act. But that's the only evidence I have, really, and the rest of her "mad" scene does not make it clear whether she knows what she is doing. I suppose it doesn't matter, in that this staging still gives her more agency than most productions do.[62]

Twenty-third time

This performance featured the best request for a line prompt that I've ever witnessed. After Hamlet, played this time by Megan, chased Rosencrantz and Guildenstern from the stage before going to his mother's closet, there was a particularly dramatic moment with a sound and light cue. At that point, Megan whirled around, faced the audience, and shouted out—fully in character—"LINE!" in order to be reminded of the beginning of Hamlet's speech: "Now is the very witching time of night…" I loved that she had no shame! She was fully committed to admitting that she couldn't remember what to say, and to getting the words right by asking for a reminder.[63] This fit

---

[62] K.M. Soehnlein: "The question Sally raises here strikes me as this production's true wildcard, alternately clarifying and tangled in knots. Giving Ophelia agency was a stated goal of the production during its initial workshopping of the text, I was told. But such a contemporary feminist intention inevitably bumps up against Shakespeare's inherent sexism, as he at different moments privileges the murderous Hamlet to condemn both Ophelia ('God has given you one face and you make yourself another') and Gertrude ('Frailty, thy name is woman') for lesser offenses. This modernizing interpretation never fully felt resolved by the production, its text, staging, or actors, even though I eventually reached my own personal understanding of it."

[63] Chard Nelson: "I remember talking with some of the actors early in the season about how it was going, and what they were finding hard. All of them mentioned that the single hardest thing was learning to call for a line during performance, something they would ordinarily rather die than do. But they all realized the necessity of having that lifeline. Seeing them all learning to overcome years of conditioning was impressive."

in perfectly with her interpretation of Hamlet: after having seen the ghost, she played him as being entirely in control of every conversation. Her confidence in asking for the prompt made it feel like nothing had gone wrong.

Twenty-fourth time

Four actors were cast in the same roles they had played two nights earlier. I enjoyed seeing the development of the relationship between Megan's Hamlet and El's Ophelia for the second performance in a row. I especially loved the long pause after Polonius' noise behind the curtain during the "get thee to a nunnery" scene. The eye contact between the two was intense, as Ophelia watched it dawn on Hamlet that they were being watched, his anger flared, and she desperately tried to communicate with him without speaking.[65]

Twenty-eighth time

Around this time, I started feeling like every performance was the best it'd ever been.

Twenty-ninth time

For the first time, I finally noticed that Ophelia was just as delighted as Hamlet was to have gotten a reaction out of Claudius in the play-within-the-play. Also in that performance, which was the first time Nick had played Hamlet in over six months, the scene between Osric and Hamlet was even

---

64

[65] Chard Nelson: " Over the last month or so of the repertory season, I could really sense the cast getting into a groove. (This was true for the other shows in the rep as well.) There was a level of comfort, perhaps because they were no longer learning more new shows, and in fact were eventually shedding shows and could now focus on only one or two. I saw this reflected both in the level of non-verbal communication between the actors and the reduced frequency of calling for lines. Even when a line was dropped or flubbed, they were much more confident in just plowing through. Perhaps most thrilling was seeing the actors, often assuming that this might be the last opportunity to play a given role, clearly trying out new things they'd been wanting to do."

funnier than usual. Kevin's hair as Osric always cracked me up before he even said anything, and he spoke the lines in a distinctive and amusing way. That night, Nick made it even funnier by having Hamlet mimic Osric's affected speech mannerisms, which I think was a new idea.[66] Playing up the comedy so much in the penultimate scene in the play made Hamlet's death feel even more tragic.

Thirtieth time

I reflected that how I felt about a performance depended less on who played Hamlet—all of them were very good, though not necessarily in the same way—and more on who played the other roles. Mark succeeded in his goal of broadening the focus beyond the title character to the whole play, but perhaps it required multiple viewings for an audience member to reach that point.[67]

That night, the other regulars and I were already feeling sad about the fact that there was only one performance left.[68]

---

[66] Chard Nelson: " I was also there that night, and that exchange was one of my favorite moments of the whole season. I talked to Kevin about it after the show, and he said it was spontaneous. He said he heard Nick's mimicking tone and thought ' Is he flirting with me? Well, OK!' and they both just ratcheted it up with each line. It was brilliant and funny and could really only happen at that stage of the season."

[67] Chard Nelson: " Agreed. I brought several friends to see performances of *Hamlet* during the year, and although all said it was good, most did not return. Looking back over such a long, full season, it's hard to imagine the poverty of seeing it only once or twice!"

[68] Chard Nelson: " As an audience member, I'm not used to the highs and lows that upon reflection I realize must come for actors during the run of any show. Those of us who saw it so much definitely had a roller coaster ride of our own: the fun of watching it all come together early on, seeing each actor feeling for a way through each of the parts and dealing with long droughts between performing a given role, realizing how much we'd miss it during the hiatus, and not wanting it ever to end even though it must. And bonding with our fellow addicts. It's not quite the same as the way a cast bonds, but certainly deeper than just a shared performance or two."

69

Thirty-first time

Alas, it was the final performance. Beth gave her strongest, most confident, most playful performance as Hamlet, except for the "O, what a rogue and peasant slave am I" soliloquy, where she blanked out and needed repeated prompting.[70] As another regular pointed out, it was a fittingly self-referential scene for that to happen in.

Thoughts after the closing performance

On gender: There was a sort of spectrum of approaches that the actors took in dealing with gender. Nick and Beth, for example, basically seemed to play each character without specifically performing the gender even if it was different from their own. At least, that's how it seemed to me; maybe they were just very understated performances of gender. Toward the other end of the spectrum, El performed masculinity when playing Hamlet or Claudius, while Kevin not only performed femininity as Gertrude but also masculinity as Claudius. All of these approaches worked, but if you think about it, they were also all rather radical. To say that these characters essentially exist as *characters without genders*—that's radical. And it conflicts a little for Ophelia, because her character's situation is very gendered. But this approach just brings that fact into relief. Also, having a woman swaggering around in a way that is convincingly masculine—that's radical. Having a man portray a woman having to endure misogynistic treatment—that's radical. And in this context, in which there were opportunities to see all the other choices, it was even radical to see a man performing masculinity rather than just assuming his own effortless maleness would do that job for him.

On meta: I started thinking about the prelude to the show. The director— or some other member of the company—introduced the show, called the actors to come on stage, and had the audience pull actors' names out of

---

[70] Chard Nelson: "This was a very satisfying ending for me. Having started my run seeing Beth as Hamlet in the dress rehearsal where I left feeling like the whole thing might be a disastrous mistake, I didn't see her in that role again until New Year's Eve, and she was very good. But closing night was truly special. Beth embraced the role, taking it in a quite different direction than she had before. As hard as it was to say good-bye to the production that had been such a huge part of my year, it was most pleasing to see such a successful performance from an actor who struggled so much at the start."
71

Yorick's skull to determine who would play which role. The actors came running out on stage, not in costume, ostensibly as themselves. But… were they *performing* themselves? They weren't in costume as their characters, since they didn't yet know whom they would play. But they *were* in *a* costume: a white shirt and white trousers, with black boots. And they knew they had an audience. They ran onto the stage with very high energy. Of course, they were probably more nervous than before performing other plays, just because of the uncertainty of what they would have to do. But how much effort was involved in their jocularity and excitement? Were their reactions to their names being pulled spontaneous and genuine? Were they ever disappointed with the roles they got? They never acted like it. So, yes, of course they were performing as "themselves" as soon as they were on stage, which adds an additional layer of meta: I've mentioned that the illusion was thin in this production, but even the thinness of the illusion was sort of an illusion: we only *thought* we saw the actors "not performing" before the roles were drawn.

On math: the distribution of who played what is what mathematicians call "asymptotically uniform." That is, theoretically, if there were a very large number of performances, each actor would play each role approximately the same number of times, and each role would be played by each actor approximately the same number of times. In reality, things were slightly complicated by there being an understudy, Caleb Cabrera, who only played Laertes, and by Cathleen's injury constraining her to play only the Ghost and Gravedigger for the final few weeks. But even if I don't consider Cathleen or the character Laertes, the role distribution was pretty uneven among the performances I saw. For example, I only saw Megan as Gertrude twice, while I saw Nick as Gertrude eight times. So, basically, thirty-one performances is not a "very large" number.[72]

Mark mentioned that he thought a theatre audience could have the same relationship to a theatre company as a sports fan has to a team.[73]

---

[72] Chard Nelson: " I ' only' saw about a third of the performances, and as Sally notes, that's not statistically all that comprehensive. Indeed, I found myself feeling jealous of those who got to see even more performances than I did, and even jealous of those who saw fewer, but who got to see some shows that I missed. It was very personal."

[73] Chard Nelson: " As a sports fan, I totally get this. I'm sure I am a rare individual who is an ardent season ticket holder for a baseball team, a college basketball team, and at least a handful of different local theatre companies. And if I saw about a third of the *Hamlet* performances, that's about in line with the percentage of baseball games I get to in the season. The biggest difference, really, is that the theatre experience is much more intimate, and I now personally know all of the *Hamlet* cast and crew and

That is indeed how I ended up feeling.[74] This production was a living, growing, developing thing, and I felt that being an external witness to it was an important role, almost a form of participation.[75] Players need an audience, after all. Mark also said that this show was about the journey, not the destination. This turned out to be true not only for the company, but for the returning audience members, too. I was lucky to have had the privilege of tagging along on this journey with them.

---

felt like they actually valued chatting and getting reactions after the shows. But I think it's safe to say that my relationship with the Shotgun Players is emotionally quite similar to my relationship with my Giants. Coincidentally, one of the friends who consistently joshed me about how much I watched *Hamlet* is an even bigger baseball fan than I am, and when I was at the theatre, he was often watching a ballgame."

[74] K.M. Soehnlein: "As a repeat member of the audience, but also as a spouse to one of the actors and a friend to many members of the cast and production team—I've known Mark and Beth nearly as long as I've known Kevin—my own reactions were deeply personal, less like watching a favorite sports team and more like returning to a family Thanksgiving dinner, where we eat the same food but don't all sit at the same seats around the table, altering the dynamics and the conversations and who slips into which role. Someone's going to be generously helpful to Grandma while someone else gets too drunk and upends the peace, but from one occasion to the next, it might not be the person you expect."

[75] Chard Nelson: "I find it amusing that neither my baseball buddies nor my theatre friends generally understand why I like both activities so much. But ultimately I'm there for the same reasons: I'm watching people do things I can imagine doing, but have neither the time nor talent to get to that level. Every game/performance is different, for all kinds of reasons (weather, timing, practice, experience, injuries, etc.). And you never know how it's going to turn out. But you develop attachments to the players, individually and collectively, and you share that with the audience around you. It's all about community, as expressed by the writer Spider Robinson: 'Shared pain is lessened; shared joy is increased.' True at the ballpark, true at the theatre."

Questions

What is the audience's job, as opposed to their role or their personal reason for being there?

How is this job done well? How is it done not well?

What is the difference—if there is one—between being an audience to Shakespeare versus other writers or performance genres?

Conclusion(s)
The Reader

Afterword
Clark Morgan[1]

This whole thing started many years ago when a friend and I saw a bad production of *Hamlet* in London. Laertes pissed in a basin and washed his face with it, Ophelia was a junkie who OD'd on heroine, and Hamlet did the "To be or not to be" while an off-stage firing squad massacred political prisoners at the end of each line. All this was meant to make the play more relevant or politically engaged or socially aware or something like that. I can't remember even though the director had provided a lengthy explanation of her intentions in the program.

The curtain finally fell and we fled to a nearby pub. Recovering the power of speech, my friend declared *Hamlet* was dead. It had become a vehicle for the director, he said. It had become a showcase for the actor playing The Dane. It was too famous, too much of a career move. The endless flood of productions, including big money Hollywood films, meant audiences would not be happy with just plain old *Hamlet*. They expected a new take, some flashy twist of setting or casting, preferably both. You couldn't just do *Hamlet*, you had to do something to it. "*Hamlet's* over," my friend concluded. "You can't put it on any more. You can only read it."

I mulled this over for the next few days, trying to think up some way of resuscitating the play—partly out of love for it, but also, you should one-up your friends whenever you can. How to stop directors and producers from decorating the play? How to stage it without aggrandizing the actor playing Hamlet? How to sidestep the Hamlet Show and get back to the tragedy?

An evil thought occurred: what if all the actors learned all the lines and could play every role and roles were assigned every night by chance? In a *Hamlet* where there was no one person playing Hamlet, everyone would have to focus on playing the play, beat by beat, scene by scene. The Herculean task of rehearsing and staging it would demand minimalism and squelch directorial tomfoolery. The roulette device would seem novel enough to make the register ring. The audience's attention would shift from performance to story, and the play would rise from the dead. Brilliant.

But impossible.

---

[1] All footnotes in this chapter are by Clark Morgan.

2

As has already been noted at the front of this book, one afternoon years later, after several ales, I mentioned this idea to Mark Jackson. An odd glint came into his eye, and he fell—by a certain declension—into the madness that became the *Hamlet* roulette.

I read *Hamlet* for the first time when I was sixteen sitting under a tree on my lunch break. It changed everything. Before, the world had been flat, black and white, and no more than exactly what it seemed, if not a little less. But now it seemed alive with possibility—ideas I never imagined, feelings that seemed to come from my own heart, but that I could never have articulated. I was amazed: the same language I spoke could do this? Clearly, the world was a marvel and I had been asleep. Even the country-fried Dudsville where I grew up was suddenly full of depth, music, color, love, and danger. Full of possibility. It was almost a physical sensation, a delight and a wound—like being in love.

Since then I've seen it performed countless times, but only rarely, and just for a moment or two, have I felt anything like that sense of the world opening up, of love and awe. Why was reading it a wonder and watching it always a disappointment and often a chore?

I blame Interpretation. That summer when I read *Hamlet* I'd never seen it on stage. There was nothing between me and the play—no director or actors or dramaturge or sets or costumes—just Shakespeare's words and my imagination. The power of the play comes from the story, the characters, their puzzling and contradictory intentions and actions, and of course the language. But this all gets obscured when theatre makers set to interpreting it, when they make a "version"—gussying it up with accents, and basins of piss and antebellum balls, and swastikas and jodhpurs and so forth.

Imagine if the world's greatest culinary genius had left us the ingredients and instructions for making the world's greatest soufflé, but the only thing chefs, cooks, waiters, and diners could think about is the raspberry sauce that's going to go on top.

Does *Hamlet* need any sauce?

The roulette device, I hoped, would get actors and directors to skip the sauce and focus on story and language. It would allow them to simply act out the script, to do just enough to activate the spectator and then, with Taoistic grace, get out of the way. Not to add but to subtract. Not to portray, but to *enact*.

3

And yes, of course, all performance is interpretation. And of course nobody can just do *Hamlet*, because of course there is no *Hamlet* per se, only one's reading of it. To stage it is to make choices both conscious and unconscious, to assume, to construe, etcetera. Of course. But why not leave the bulk of the interpreting to the semiotician who paid for the seat? Theatre happens only superficially on stage, mostly it happens in the mind.

Maybe one root of the problem is a misunderstanding of what art is supposed to be doing. Art has no obligation to be "relevant." It has no obligation either to challenge or affirm political views. It has no obligation to take a position, to fight for justice, incite activism or give a voice to the underrepresented. It's not something we ought to take because it's good for us like broccoli and church. "The allotted function of art is not, as is often assumed, to put across ideas, to propagate thoughts, to serve as an example," wrote the Russian filmmaker, Andrei Tarkovsky. "The aim of art is to plow and harrow the soul, and render it capable of turning to good" (1986: 43). Note Tarkovsky doesn't say it's the job of art to tell us what is good, nor to teach us anything at all, only to plow and harrow.

A good play plunges us into a dilemma which has no rational solution but which nevertheless requires the protagonist (who is the spectator's doppelganger) to choose, to act, and then to bear the consequences. These consequences are unforeseen, unfair, and monstrous, yet inevitable. If we identify with the protagonist, watching this unfold is shattering—"a sublime trauma" in Tarkovsky's phrase (Ibid). A play is a crucible where our belief systems go up in flames. A play dismantles our convictions—be they progressive or retrograde—sabotages ideology, undermines all categories and leaves us naked, shivering, and bereft of certainty. Stripped of our protective coating of ready answers, we become capable of looking at the truth of being human—a truth so hard we break down into tears or laughter. "A book must be the axe for the frozen sea inside us," wrote Kafka (1977: 32).

When *Hamlet* becomes a platform for a position, a religion, an ideology, or for comment on current affairs, it stops being the axe and starts making more ice. Suppose we set the play in the White House, for example, and we make it a commentary on Trump's America. No doubt we could rustle up some clever parallels, some of the speeches would have an arch double-entendre clang, and it would be fun to spray-tan Claudius. But to what end? Some people would have their opinions confirmed, others would feel attacked—just like in the world of politics. In other words, no change. Just

---

4

more ice.[5]

This kind of theatre is doomed to impotence because it operates on the level of rational discourse. It confuses *logos* and *mythos*. Rational discourse, *logos*, makes an appeal to the intellect. It can be weighed and debated on the merits. People either agree or disagree. But as Ivan notes at the end of Yasmina Reza's play, *Art*, "Nothing formative in the world, nothing great or beautiful in the world has ever been born of rational argument" (1996: 47).

Logos lacks the power to crack the individual on the deepest level, for one thing, because it poses an artificial choice, an oversimplification: left wing or right wing, just or unjust, right or wrong. But of course this boneheaded binary fib runs counter to our actual experience of the world where things are appallingly complex and appallingly mixed, and of our own hearts, given to both goodness and perfidy. To put it another way, art isn't on the side of the orthodox or the heterodox; it's on the side of the paradox.

Theatre gathers these contradictions and binds them into *mythos*, into inscrutable predicaments, which, like our own lives, offer no easy way out. Like all art, theatre operates on a spiritual level—beyond the rational. No one can disagree with Bach's *Air on the G String*, for instance. You can be moved or bored maybe, but you can't argue with it. In the same way, *Hamlet* presents a situation beyond argument, beyond explanation, ultimately beyond words. "The rest is silence."

What Milan Kundera observes of fiction is equally true of the drama: "The stupidity of people comes from having an answer for everything, the wisdom of the novel comes from having a question for everything" (1980: 237). The idea that became the *Hamlet* roulette was—for me anyway—a way of preventing the play from careening into the answer ditch and keeping it pointed down the road of the question.

So much for theory. What about practice? By the time the *Hamlet* roulette had moved from daydream to deadly earnest, I had moved to New York City.

---

[5] In this regard, Brecht's division of theatre into "epic" and "dramatic" is a bum steer. The point of theatre is neither to keep us remote and objective, nor is it to let us have a little cry and then go off for oysters and champagne. Both of those options suppose a contained theatre experience that comes to an end, and then we move on to something else: either storming City Hall or passing out in a recliner. The point of theatre is that it shouldn't ever come to an end, that we can't forget it, that we press on with *Hamlet* ever deeper inward.

6

I wasn't involved in editing, casting, or rehearsal and hadn't even talked to Mark about how the show was going. So I entered the foyer of the Ashby Stage like a vagabond uncle about to meet his adult nephew for the first time—full of extravagant hopes and total ignorance. Happy to relate, the nephew turned out to be much bigger and more interesting than hypothesized.

Sitting in the auditorium waiting for the show to begin, the reality of what was about to happen started to sink in. I noticed a nervousness bubbling up in the crowd, and myself as well. The anxiety increased when the actors came out and stood there before us visibly jittery. It hit a crescendo as the luck of the draw decided the roles. Clearly everything was not under control.

That little ritual of picking the roles had a massive effect on the rest of the play that I had not foreseen. At a conventional performance where the curtain rises with actors already in character, the audience is forced into the passive role of judge, deciding whether the illusion is compelling enough to sweep them along. But seeing the actors for the first time as themselves, not as characters, scuttled any pre-fab illusion that they "were" Hamlet or Ophelia or the Gravedigger. They were people. And they were going to unfold a tale for us. But that unfolding would need our indulgence, our complicity, and our powers of imagination. The audience assigning the roles by lot was the visible symbol that this *Hamlet* would be a joint undertaking. It instantly bound actors and audience together. The mimed swordfights might have been the most striking example of this actor-audience collaboration, but it shot through every moment of the play.

When the actors returned a few minutes later, already known to us but now in costume, it emphasized theatre's underlying playfulness, but also its seriousness. We were crossing over from the ordinary to the mythic. Something extraordinary was about to happen, something worth our total attention. A magician's art depends on the spectator not seeing how it's done. But in the *Hamlet* roulette, letting the audience in on it created a feeling ten times more magical, because it explicitly called to the spectator's imagination. And the spectator consciously answered back.

This is part of the reason why the actors calling for a forgotten line was so exciting. Usually when an actor dries onstage you get a sick feeling, as when someone has pulled the chair out from under you and your bottom searches in vain for something to rely on. But in the *Hamlet* roulette, calling for a line was almost an act of triumph. Far from a shameful defeat, it revealed the actor's pluck. It reaffirmed the solidarity of actor and spectator. It didn't feel like a break in the illusion, because there had been no illusion. We weren't watching some simulation of a boob tube simulation, but live, uncanned

7

performance. Honesty is electrifying.

If the goal of the roulette device was to take the focus off the actor playing Hamlet, it only partially succeeded. Playing Hamlet is still a feat, even if everyone else onstage can do it too. And I still found myself wondering how the actor would tackle the soliloquies. Nevertheless, I think it did chip away at the tyranny of the "The Dane." For one thing, nobody could come to the play to see a particular actor's version of Hamlet; they could only come to see the ensemble play *Hamlet*. That de-emphasized the title role and made me more aware of all the others. I wasn't tapping my foot waiting for the heavies to come out and do the set pieces. I found myself much more involved in each moment and each line and more interested in the interactions of the characters/actors.

Rather than watching and evaluating any one actor's interpretation of a particular role, I felt I was seeing the total work of all the actors in concert, whether speaking or silent, onstage or off. The main character was the *Hamlet* roulette. Could we call this collective style of acting polyphonic? In Renaissance polyphony, no one voice sings the dominant melody. Instead every voice sings the lead for a few notes before it passes imperceptibly to the next voice, each voice contributing to the overall sound—even during the rests. Melody and harmony become irrelevant, lost in the totality of the piece. In the same way lead role and supporting role were swallowed up in the totality of the *Hamlet* roulette. Maybe I was seeing *Hamlet* for the first time ever—the story, the schemes and desires of the characters, the language, and the performances of the actors all as a unified whole.

Back when the roulette idea was just a concept, I wanted to concentrate all focus, like a laser beam, on the story. I had supposed making the actors interchangeable would make them pretty much disappear. It did exactly the opposite. It made the spectator intensely aware of the actors and their effort. Each one was performing a jaw-dropping feat of virtuosity and it was impossible not to think of that again and again, and impossible not to feel their exertion.

But, paradoxically again, this had the effect of concentrating the audience's attention on each moment of the play. Nothing was rote. Nothing was in passing. Nothing was a given. Everything was for keeps. The actors had not become invisible; they had become transparent. You could see the actors telling us the story, and the play became visible through them.

Which brings us to casting. Diversity in casting should be a given. It makes the work stronger, and it's more fun. Actors from differing backgrounds bring a richness to a production that actors from the same

---

8

background cannot. Yet the genius of this production was not only that it featured a diverse cast, but that the audience then assigned the roles by chance. Thus all the actors, regardless of age, gender, or race, had an equal shot at any role. Such an egalitarian ideal can prevail in the theatre, though not yet as readily in the office or street or halls of justice. Theatre is a spiritual space reserved for the irrational and unsolvable. It cannot change beliefs or policy. But it can create that sublime trauma that leaves us capable of changing ourselves.

Sometimes I think theatre makers suffer from an inferiority complex. Here we are cavorting around onstage while the people we went to university with are analyzing currency markets or firming up third-stage funding for their app, or teaching in inner-city schools. We secretly fear theatre is inherently unserious, and we look for some cover for having this much fun.[9] This notion seems but a modern variation of the old Puritanical insistence that theatre must have some utility. But what exactly do we mean by utility? As Dostoyevsky asked, "How can you determine, measure and weigh the benefit that the *Iliad* has brought to the whole of humanity? Where, when, in what cases has it been useful and in which way?" (1997: 126).

Watching a woman play Hamlet, or two men play the married couple Claudius and Gertrude, or a queer person of color play Laertes, upended my rational expectations in a way that drove me further into something—in this case a play—that I already thought I knew. Breaking conventional notions of who plays Hamlet or Gertrude or Laertes made me think more deeply and feel more intensely about these characters.

Hamlet is not a person or a type of person. Hamlet is an existential predicament. The human situation we call "Hamlet" can contain all the identities of any Hamlet actor past present or future—and, not only contain, but be enriched by the differing personal experiences of the actors. The role is like a gem. Each actor is a blade striking a beautiful new facet, yet it's one single stone. And so Hamlet can at once unite us and maintain our differences. Is this rational? It's certainly not policy. But it's undoubtedly precious.

In short, the reality of the *Hamlet* roulette far outstripped its conception. It may not have been the most brilliantly acted production I've ever seen, but it

---

[9] As Roland Barthes put it, "No sooner has a word been said about the pleasure of the text than two policemen are ready to jump on you: the political policeman and the psychoanalytical policeman: pleasure is either idle or vain, a class notion or an illusion" (1975: 57).

10

was by far the clearest and most thrilling. It gave me that feeling of wonder, that sense of love and danger and new possibility that I'd felt reading the play for the very first time. That power came directly from its departures from conventional theatre: simplicity, honesty, polyphonic acting, audience complicity, and greatest of all, audacity.

When I walked into the theatre that night and read the production's motto, my heart beat a little faster: The play's the thing. Amen. But it might just as well have been: The readiness is all.

11

The Tragedy of
HAMLET
Prince of Denmark

Edited by the Director & Cast
For the 2016 Shotgun Players Production

Annotated by Nick Medina[1]

Character Tracks:

1. Polonius / Priest / Osric
2. Ghost / Gravedigger
3. Laertes
4. Ophelia / Horatio
5. Gertrude / Guildenstern
6. Claudius / Rosenkrantz
7. Hamlet

---

[1] Mark Jackson:" This first footnote excepted, all others in this chapter are by actor Nick Medina. I asked Nick to annotate our script because I thought he would enjoy the task, being an exceptionally well-studied Shakespeare devotee. But even more so, I asked him because he did not particularly care for our edit of the text. This made the prospect of his commentary far more interesting than that of anyone who did like the edit. I am indeed grateful Nick took up the task. Though I don't personally share his scholarly, more traditional approach to Shakespeare as it translates into performance, I greatly appreciate the insights his attention to textual detail can illuminate. Nick was an asset to our production in this, in addition to as an actor. As with other chapters, empty footnotes dot this one too and the reader is invited to add to Nick's commentary."

2

PRESHOW

> *The character tracks are selected in the above order. The*
> *audience draws the actors' names out of Yorick's skull. Once an*
> *actor is selected, they go immediately backstage to get ready.*
> *When casting is complete, a short song plays. When the song is*
> *done, the play begins.*

ACT I
SCENE II [3]

Enter CLAUDIUS, GERTRUDE, HAMLET, POLONIUS, LAERTES,
and OPHELIA.[5]

CLAUDIUS
Though yet of Hamlet our dear brother's death
The memory be green, and that it us befitted
To bear our hearts in grief and our whole kingdom
To be contracted in one brow of woe,
Yet so far hath discretion fought with nature
That we with wisest sorrow think on him,

---

[3] The Careful Reader will note the omission of the first scene of the play: Opening just past midnight on Elsinore's Battlements, a cadre of spooked sentries interact with a mute ghost. While rich in atmosphere, this opening tableau includes three characters who never reappear after the first act, and a hefty dose of political exposition.
[4]

[5] Act 1 Scene 2 commonly replaces the first scene of the play. Opening with Claudius' smooth-as-silk oratory, the play leaps into action. In our production, the stage had another level, a stage within a stage. Atop this meta-theatrical platform Gertrude and Claudius, almost indistinguishable in their matching white suits, look down on both the court and the audience. Yet, while their lofty position gives them some power, they are also on display. This is Claudius' first public appearance as King, and it can't go wrong.

Together with remembrance of ourselves.
Therefore our sometime sister, now our queen,
Have we, as 'twere with a defeated joy,
With mirth in funeral and with dirge in marriage,
In equal scale weighing delight and dole,[6]
Taken to wife: nor have we herein barr'd
Your better wisdoms, which have freely gone
With this affair along. For all, our thanks.[7]
And now, Laertes, what's the news with you?
You told us of some suit, Laertes; and that
The head is not more native to the heart
Than is the throne of Denmark to thy father,
What wouldst thou have, Laertes?

LAERTES
My dread lord,
Your leave and favor to return to France;
From whence, though willingly, I came to Denmark
To show my duty in your coronation.

CLAUDIUS
Have you your father's leave? What says Polonius?

POLONIUS
He hath, my lord, wrung from me my slow leave
By laborsome petition, and at last
Upon his will I seal'd my hard consent.

---

[6] A crystalline example of antithesis, Shakespeare's guiding formal principle. Throughout his work, he juxtaposes words and images with their opposite, creating a potent synthesis stronger than the individual parts. The careful actor finds these opposites and plays them up.

[7] So much for the diplomats, Cornelius and Voltemand, cut from our production. Also excised is any mention of Fortinbras. Apart from necessitating the loss of one of Hamlet's best soliloquies, in Act 4, the play works just as well without the Scandinavian political intrigue.

8

CLAUDIUS
Take thy fair hour, Laertes; time be thine,[9]
And thy best graces spend it at thy will!
But now, my cousin Hamlet, and my son,–

HAMLET
[*Aside*] A little more than kin, and less than kind.

CLAUDIUS
How is it that the clouds still hang on you?

HAMLET
Not so, my lord; I am too much i' the sun.

GERTRUDE
Good Hamlet, cast thy nighted color off,[10]
And let thine eye look like a friend on Denmark.
Do not forever with thy veiled lids
Seek for thy noble father in the dust:
Thou know'st 'tis common; all that lives must die,
Passing through nature to eternity.

HAMLET
Ay, madam, it is common.

GERTRUDE
If it be,[11]
Why seems it so particular with thee?

---

[9] One commentator opined that Claudius sent the wrong son away: he should have kept Laertes, the hotheaded yet tractable man of action, close at hand, and sent the unpredictable Hamlet back to Wittenberg (Pennington, 2000).

[10] Gertrude always uses "thou," the informal second person pronoun, when speaking to her son. Hamlet always returns her the formal pronoun "you." We have lost this distinction today, but an Elizabethan audience would be alive to the shift in meaning. In using the formal "you," Hamlet puts a chilly distance between himself and his mother.

[11] This is an example of a shared line: Hamlet speaks seven of the line's ten syllables, and Gertrude picks up the last three. Shakespeare directs from the page: here he is telling the actor playing Gertrude to pick up the cue by carrying on Hamlet's rhythm.

HAMLET
Seems, madam! nay it is; I know not 'seems.'[12]
'Tis not alone my inky cloak, good[14] mother,
Nor customary suits of solemn black,
Nor windy suspiration of forced breath,
No, nor the fruitful river in the eye,
Together with all forms, moods, shapes of grief,
That can denote me truly: these indeed seem,
For they are actions that a man might play:
But I have that within which passeth show;
These but the trappings and the suits of woe.

---

[12] The meta-theatrical theme raises its head: Hamlet employs a dialectic of being and seeming, inner woe and outer show, authenticity and play. Also note the preponderance of monosyllables, another example of Shakespeare's direction. Nearly fifty percent of all of Shakespeare's plays are monosyllabic, signaling the actor to slow down. Try to say this line quickly, and you will have a jumble on your hands.

[13]

[14] There are three versions of *Hamlet*: The so called "Bad Quarto," a good Quarto, and the Folio. The Bad Quarto is a pirated edition with substantial changes in the dialogue, names, and placement of events (For example, Polonius is called Corambis, the Nunnery scene takes place before the arrival of the players, and "O what a rogue and peasant slave am I" reads "Why what a dunghill idiot slave am I.") Some scholars believe this text is an earlier version of Shakespeare's play. Others argue that a cash-strapped actor—probably the bit player who acted the sentry Marcellus—reconstructed the play by memory and sold it to a printer. The Quarto was an official version published in Shakespeare's lifetime, the Folio shortly after his death. The differences are both small and large: both feature whole sections of text not present in the other, and there are innumerable word substitutions. I have marked my favorite textual variants. In this line, the Quarto reads "cold mother," further estranging this tense mother/son relationship.

CLAUDIUS
'Tis sweet and commendable in your nature, Hamlet,[15]

---

[15] A note on verse: Most actors can easily define Iambic Pentameter as a line of five feet alternating between a slack and a stressed syllable (di-DUM-di-DUM-di-DUM-di-DUM-di-DUM). We learn it early on, and then forget it. However, speaking in this strict pattern turns Shakespeare verse into deadly monotony, missing its natural rhythms. The Elizabethans never referred to their meter as Iambic Pentameter: they called it Blank Verse. The verse line is the poet's blank canvas, a neutral pattern from which the author deviates to create both naturalistic and artificial rhythms. Blank Verse tells an actor when to speed up and slow down, when to take a beat or pick up a cue, when to pause and for how long, and which words are most important. The syncopation of the line subconsciously communicates intention to the actor, and delivers aural variety to the audience. It predigests information, breaking complex grammatical structures and extended metaphors into manageable chunks. To unlock the rhythms and thoughts underneath the text, the actor must make peace with the Blank Verse line. If we ignore it, we lose both rhythmic energy and meaning, but how do we honor the line? The answer lies in the breath... Public Poets (those who wrote for the open stage) tried many different meters before they settled on Blank Verse sometime in the 1580's and there are several good reasons it took hold: the di-DUM of the Iambic foot mimics the pitter pat of the human heart; the human mind can comprehend about five to seven English words at a time; we form memories in three to five-second bursts, about the time it takes to speak a verse line; Most importantly, we optimally breathe every nine to eleven syllables. Shakespeare's actors—un-mic'ed and projecting to dense crowds of 2000 people—refilled their lungs on every single line. Even footed meter (tetrameter with four feet or hexameter with six) tends to push the reader or speaker forward while odd footed meters cause us to subconsciously pause on the missing last even foot. The odd footed Blank Verse line allows the actor time to breathe at a natural spot. The players share in both the iambic heartbeat, and in the mindful breaths every three to five seconds. The pause for breath—ideally brief, almost imperceptible—allows the audience just enough time to digest what has happened or anticipate what will come next, and forces the actor to take each line as its own unit of thought. With each line separated by a breath, the structure—and structural deviations—

To give these mourning duties to your father:
But, you must know, your father lost a father;
That father lost, lost his. And to persever
In obstinate condolement is a course
Of impious stubbornness; 'tis unmanly grief;
'tis a fault to heaven, a fault to nature,
To reason most absurd, whose common theme
Is death of fathers.[16] Pray you, throw to earth
This unprevailing woe, and think of us
As of a father:[17] for let the world take note,
You are the most immediate to our throne;
And with no less nobility of love
Than that which dearest father bears his son,
Do I impart toward you. For your intent
In going back to school in Wittenberg,
It is most retrograde to our desire:
And we beseech you, bend you to remain
Here, in the cheer and comfort of our eye,
Our chiefest courtier, cousin, and our son.

GERTRUDE
Let not thy mother lose her prayers, Hamlet:
I pray thee, stay with us; go not to Wittenberg.[19]

HAMLET
I shall in all my best obey you, madam.

---

becomes much clearer, and the thoughts expressed in the text are carved into manageable units.

[16] Much ink has been spilled in linking this play with the death of John Shakespeare in September of 1601. In addition to his father's death, Shakespeare's son, Hamnet, died in 1596. Half of a pair of twins, the theme of familial loss and mourning pervades Shakespeare's plays of this era, including the twins-in-mourning farce, *Twelfth Night*, written directly after *Hamlet*.

[17] My pet theory has always been that Claudius and Gertrude's affair stretches far back in time, and Hamlet really is Claudius' son. This line takes on an ironic honesty in this reading.

18

[19] Gertrude is the Queen of Monosyllables.

CLAUDIUS
Why, 'tis a loving and a fair reply:
Be as ourself in Denmark. Madam, come;
This gentle and unforced accord of Hamlet
Sits smiling to my heart: in grace whereof,
No jocund health that Denmark drinks to-day,
But the great cannon to the clouds shall tell,
Come away.

Exeunt all but HAMLET.

HAMLET[20]
O, that this too too solid flesh would melt
Thaw and resolve itself into a dew!
Or that the Everlasting had not fix'd
His canon 'gainst self-slaughter! O God! God!
How weary, stale, flat and unprofitable,
Seem to me all the uses of this world!
Fie on't! ah fie! 'tis an unweeded garden
That grows to seed; things rank and gross in nature
Possess it merely. That it should come to this!
But two months dead: nay, not so much, not two.
So excellent a king;[21] so loving to my mother
That he might not beteem the winds of heaven
Visit her face too roughly. Heaven and earth,
Must I remember? Why, she would hang on him
As if increase of appetite had grown
By what it fed on: and yet, within a month–
Let me not think on't–Frailty, thy name is woman![22]–

---

[20] The first speech explored in the workshop phase, Mark decided on a very strict interpretation: a torrent of pent up words, spoken with arms raised above the head in a stylized gesture of disgust originated by Beth Wilmurt. Certainly, there are outbursts of disgust, but there is also grief carefully expressed through rich metaphor. The persistent monosyllables and frequent enjambment tell the actor to slow down, playing the mid-line punctuation as beat shifts. Mark wanted this speech to be all of a piece, a machine gun blast of feeling, but Shakespeare indicates a mind looking for the right words to express the ineffability of his mourning, anger, and betrayal.
[21] The cuts in this speech are largely classical allusions and several complex images of Gertrude's swift remarriage.
[22] Hamlet's persistent misogyny is front and center whenever he thinks of his mother.

A little month; a beast that wants discourse of reason
Would have mourn'd longer–married with my uncle,
My father's brother, but no more like my father
Than I to Hercules; within a month
She married. O, most wicked speed, to post
With such dexterity to incestuous sheets!
It is not nor it cannot come to good.
But break, my heart; for I must hold my tongue.

Enter HORATIO.

HORATIO
Hail to your lordship!

HAMLET
Horatio, or I do forget myself.

HORATIO
The same, my lord, and your poor servant ever.

HAMLET
My good friend; I'll change that name with you.
But what in faith make you from Wittenberg?

HORATIO
A truant disposition, good my lord.

HAMLET
I would not hear your enemy say so.
And what is your affair in Elsinore?

HORATIO
My lord, I came to see your father's funeral.

HAMLET
I pray thee, do not mock me, fellow-student;
I think it was to see my mother's wedding.

HORATIO
Indeed, my lord, it follow'd hard upon.

HAMLET
Thrift, thrift, Horatio! the funeral baked meats
Did coldly furnish forth the marriage tables.
Would I had met my dearest foe in heaven
Or ever I had seen that day, Horatio!
My father!–methinks I see my father.

HORATIO
Where, my lord?

HAMLET
In my mind's eye, Horatio.

HORATIO
I saw him once; he was a goodly king.

HAMLET
He was a man, take him for all in all;
I shall not look upon his like again.

HORATIO
My lord, I think I saw him yesternight.

HAMLET
Saw? who?

HORATIO
My lord, the king your father.

HAMLET
The king my father!

HORATIO
Season your admiration for awhile
With an attent ear, till I may deliver
This marvel to you.

HAMLET
For God's love, let me hear.

HORATIO
In the dead vast[25] and middle of the night,
A figure like your father,
Armed at point exactly,[27]
Appeared before me, and with solemn march
Went slow and stately by: twice he walk'd
By my oppress'd and fear-surprised eyes,
whilst I, distilled almost to jelly,
Stood dumb and spake not to him.
I knew your father;
These hands are not more like.

HAMLET
But where was this?

HORATIO
Upon the platform where I watch'd.

HAMLET
Did you not speak to it?

HORATIO
My lord, I did;
But answer made it none:
the morning cock crew loud
And at the sound it vanish'd from my sight.

HAMLET
'Tis very strange.[28]

HORATIO
As I do live, my honor'd lord, 'tis true.

---

[25] Quarto reads " dead waste."

[26]

[27] The verse is particularly choppy here because this dialogue originally included the Danish sentries Marcellus and Bernardo, both cut from this production.

[28] The following short lines are clearly meant to be shared, creating a rapid-fire patter between the two old friends.

HAMLET
Arm'd, say you?

HORATIO
Arm'd, my lord.

HAMLET
And look'd he frowningly?

HORATIO
A countenance more in sorrow than in anger.

HAMLET
And fix'd his eyes upon you?

HORATIO
Most constantly.

HAMLET
I would I had been there.

HORATIO
It would have much amazed you.

HAMLET
Very like, very like.
I will watch tonight;
Perchance 'twill walk again.
If it assume my noble father's person,
I'll speak to it, though hell itself should gape.
If you have hitherto conceal'd this sight,
Let it be tenable in your silence still;
And whatsoever else shall hap tonight,
Give it an understanding, but no tongue:
So, fare you well:
Upon the platform, 'twixt eleven and twelve,
I'll visit you.

HORATIO
My duty to your honor.

HAMLET
Farewell.

Exit HORATIO.

HAMLET
My father's spirit–in arms! all is not well;
I doubt some foul play. Would the night were come!
Till then sit still, my soul: foul deeds will rise,[30]
Though all the earth o'erwhelm them, to men's eyes.

Exit.

ACT I
SCENE III

Enter LAERTES and OPHELIA.

LAERTES
My necessaries are embark'd.[32]
And, sister, as the winds give benefit
And convoy is assistant, do not sleep,
But let me hear from you.

OPHELIA
Do you doubt that?

---

[30] Note the three lines with punctuation in the middle;
These are called caesurae. A caesura (non-breath pause)
occurs when punctuation falls in the middle of the line;
Shakespeare uses it to mark a beat shift. The actor must
slow down the entire line to take the curve in thought.
Characters often make decisions or reach realization
in these punctuated lines. This technique also adds
naturalistic rhythmic variety.
31

[32] I don't recall why Laertes' "farewell" was cut from
the end of this line, but I always kept it in. Not only to
regularize the meter, but also to establish his imminent
exit.

LAERTES
For Hamlet and the trifling of his favor,
Hold it a fashion and a toy in blood,
The perfume and suppliance of a minute; No more.

OPHELIA
No more but so?

LAERTES
Think it no more; Perhaps he loves you now–

OPHELIA
–And, now, no soil nor deceit[33] doth besmirch
The virtue of his will.[34]

LAERTES
–His greatness weigh'd, his will is not his own;
For he himself is subject to his birth:
He may not, as unvalued persons do,
Carve for himself; for on his choice depends
The safety and health of this whole state.

OPHELIA
If he says he loves me
It fits your wisdom so far to believe it
As he in his particular act and place
Doth give his saying deed.

LAETRES
Fear it, Ophelia, fear it, my dear sister,
And keep you in the rear of your affection,

---

[33] One of the handful of word substitutions throughout the cut; the word in the original text is "cautel" meaning deceit or caution.

[34] In an attempt to give Ophelia more agency, we made several major departures from the original text. Here is an example of one of the more successful alterations. In the original text, Laertes speaks this entire dialogue to his sister. Here, Ophelia gets to push back against her brother's patriarchal sermonizing.

35

Out of the shot and danger of desire.
Be wary then: best safety lies in fear.

OPHELIA
But, good my brother,
Do not, as some ungracious pastors do,
Show me the steep and thorny way to heaven;
Whiles, like a puff'd and reckless libertine,
Himself the primrose path of dalliance treads,
And recks not his own rede.

LAERTES
O, fear me not.

Enter POLONIUS.

POLONIUS
Yet here, Laertes! aboard, aboard, for shame!
The wind sits in the shoulder of your sail,
And you are stay'd for. There; my blessing with thee!
And these few precepts in thy memory
See thou character. Give thy thoughts no tongue,
Nor any unproportioned thought his act.
Be thou familiar, but by no means vulgar.
Beware of entrance to a quarrel, but being in,
Bear't that the opposed may beware of thee.
Neither a borrower nor a lender be;
For loan oft loses both itself and friend,
And borrowing dulls the edge of husbandry.
This above all: to thine ownself be true,
And it must follow, as the night the day,
Thou canst not then be false to any man.
Farewell: my blessing season this in thee![36]

LAERTES
Most humbly do I take my leave, my lord.

---

[36] Although we made some hefty cuts to this famous speech, no audience members ever seemed to notice. Kevin Clarke was very sad to lose Polonius' fashion advice: " Costly thy habit as thy purse can buy/ But not express'd in fancy; rich, not gaudy.
37

POLONIUS
The time invites you; go.

LAERTES
Farewell, Ophelia; and remember well
What I have said to you.

OPHELIA
'Tis in my memory lock'd,
And you yourself shall keep the key of it.

LAERTES
Farewell.

Exit LAERTES.

POLONIUS
What is't, Ophelia, he hath said to you?

OPHELIA
So please you, something touching the Lord Hamlet.

POLONIUS
Marry, well bethought:[38]
'Tis told me, he hath very oft of late
Given private time to you; and you yourself
Have of your audience been most free and bounteous:
If it be so, I must tell you,
You do not understand yourself so clearly
As it behoves my daughter and your honour.
What is between you? give me up the truth.

OPHELIA
He hath, my lord, of late made many tenders
Of his affection to me.

POLONIUS
Affection! pooh! you speak like a green girl.
Do you believe his tenders, as you call them?

---

[38] A short line, suggesting a meaningful pause.
[39]

OPHELIA
I do not know, my lord, what I should think.

POLONIUS
Marry, I'll teach you: think yourself a baby
That you have ta'en these tenders for true pay,
Which are not sterling. Tender yourself more dearly;
Or you'll tender me a fool.

OPHELIA
My lord, he hath importuned me with love
In honorable fashion.

POLONIUS
Ay, fashion you may call it.

OPHELIA
And hath given countenance to his speech, my lord,
With almost all the holy vows of heaven.

POLONIUS
Ay, springes to catch woodcocks. I do know,
When the blood burns, how prodigal the soul
Lends the tongue vows: these blazes, daughter,
Giving more light than heat,
You must not take for fire. For Lord Hamlet:
Believe so much in him, that he is young
And with a larger tether may he walk
Than may be given you. In few, Ophelia:
I would not, in plain terms, from this time forth,
Have you so slander any moment leisure,
As to give words or talk with the Lord Hamlet.
Look to't, I charge you: come your ways.

Exeunt.

40

ACT I
SCENE IV[41]

Enter HAMLET and HORATIO.

HAMLET
What hour now?

HORATIO
I think it lacks of twelve.

HAMLET
No, it is struck.

HORATIO
Indeed? I heard it not: then it draws near the season
Wherein the spirit held his wont to walk.

An explosion of fireworks in the distance.

HORATIO
What does this mean, my lord?

HAMLET
The king doth wake to-night and takes his rouse,
And, as he drains his draughts of Rhenish down,
Thus brays the triumph of his pledge.

HORATIO
Is it a custom?

HAMLET
Ay, marry, is't:
But to my mind, it is a custom
More honor'd in the breach than the observance.
This heavy-headed revel east and west
Makes us traduced and tax'd of other nations:

---

[41] This scene compresses two scenes from the original text, and once again cuts the Danish Sentries.
42

They clepe us drunkards, and with swinish phrase
Soil our achievements.

Enter GHOST.

HORATIO
Look, my lord, it comes!

HAMLET
Angels and ministers of grace defend us!
Be thou a spirit of health or goblin damn'd?
Bring with thee airs from heaven or blasts from hell?
King, father, royal Dane: O, answer me!
Let me not burst in ignorance;
What may this mean,
That thou, dead corpse,
Revisit thus the glimpses of the moon,
Making night hideous?
Say, why is this? What should we do?

GHOST beckons HAMLET.

HORATIO
It waves you to a more removed ground:
But do not go with it.

HAMLET
Why, what should be the fear?
I do not set my life at a pin's fee;
And for my soul, what can it do to that,
Being a thing immortal as itself?

HORATIO
What if it tempt you toward the cliff, my lord,
And there assume some other horrible form,
Which might deprive your sovereignty of reason
And draw you into madness? think of it.

HAMLET
It waves me still.

HORATIO
You shall not go, my lord.

HAMLET
Hold off your hands.

HORATIO
Be ruled; you shall not go.
HAMLET
My fate cries out! Unhand me, Horatio.
By heaven, I'll make a ghost of him that stays me!
I say, Away!

Exit HORATIO.

HAMLET
Where wilt thou lead me? speak.

GHOST
Mark me.

HAMLET
I will.

GHOST[45]
My hour is almost come,
When I to sulfurous and tormenting flames
Must render up myself.

HAMLET
Alas, poor ghost!

44

[45] For at least the first month of performance, there was a fifty-fifty chance of these lines being dropped. Perhaps we so consistently dropped these lines because of the precise movements required for the Ghost's entrance; perhaps because we were eager to get to the meat of the scene.

GHOST
Pity me not, but lend thy serious hearing
To what I shall unfold.

HAMLET
Speak; I am bound to hear.

GHOST
So art thou to revenge, when thou shalt hear.

HAMLET
What?

GHOST
I am thy father's spirit,
Doom'd for a certain term to walk the night
And for the day confined to fast in fires
Till the foul crimes done in my days of nature
Are burnt and purged away. But that I am forbid
To tell the secrets of my prison-house,
I could a tale unfold whose lightest word
Would harrow up thy soul. List, list, O, list!
If thou didst ever thy dear father love—

HAMLET
O God!

GHOST
Revenge his foul and most unnatural murder.

HAMLET
Murder!

GHOST
Murder most foul, strange, and unnatural.

HAMLET
Haste me to know't, that I, with wings as swift
As meditation or the thoughts of love,
May sweep to my revenge.

GHOST

'Tis given out that, sleeping in my orchard,
A serpent stung me; so the whole ear of Denmark
Is by a forged process of my death
Rankly abused: but know, thou noble youth,
The serpent that did sting thy father's life
Now wears his crown.

HAMLET

O my prophetic soul! My uncle!

GHOST

Ay, that incestuous, that adulterate beast,
With witchcraft of his wit, with traitorous gifts,–
won to his shameful lust
The will of my most seeming-virtuous queen:
O Hamlet, what a falling-off was there;
From me, whose love was of that dignity
That it went hand in hand even with the vow
I made to her in marriage, and to decline
Upon a wretch, whose natural gifts were poor
To those of mine, and prey on garbage!
But, soft! methinks I scent the morning air;
Brief let me be. Sleeping within my orchard,
Upon my secure hour thy uncle stole,
And in the porches of my ears did pour
A leperous distilment; whose effect
Holds such an enmity with blood of man
That swift as quicksilver it courses through
The natural gates and alleys of the body,
And with a sudden vigor doth posset
And curd, like eager droppings into milk,
The thin and wholesome blood; so did it mine.
Thus was I, sleeping, by a brother's hand,
Of life, of crown, of queen, at once dispatch'd:
No reckoning made, but sent to my account
With all my imperfections on my head:
O, horrible! O, horrible! most horrible!
If thou hast nature in thee, bear it not;

47

Let not the royal bed of Denmark be
A couch for luxury and damned incest.
Adieu, adieu! Hamlet, remember me.

Exit GHOST.

HAMLET
O all you host of heaven! O earth! what else?
And shall I couple hell? O, fie! Hold, my heart;
And you, my sinews, grow not instant old,
But bear me stiffly up. Remember thee!
Ay, from the table of my memory
I'll wipe away all trivial fond records,
All saws of books, all forms, all pressures past,
And thy commandment all alone shall live
Within the book and volume of my brain,
Unmix'd with baser matter: yes, by heaven!
O most pernicious woman!
O villain, villain, smiling, damned villain!
That one may smile, and smile, and be a villain;
At least I'm sure it may be so in Denmark:
So, uncle, there you are. Now to my word;
I have sworn it–

HORATIO
[*Off*] –My lord—

HAMLET
–So be it!

Enter HORATIO.

HORATIO
How is't, my noble lord? What news?

HAMLET
O, wonderful!

HORATIO
Good my lord, tell it.

HAMLET
No; you'll reveal it.

HORATIO
Not I, by heaven.

HAMLET
I hold it fit that we shake hands and part:
You, as your business and desire shall point you;
For every man has business and desire,
Such as it is; and for mine own poor part,
Look you, I'll go pray.

HORATIO
These are but wild and whirling words, my lord.

HAMLET
I'm sorry they offend you.

HORATIO
There's no offence, my lord.

HAMLET
Yes, by Saint Patrick, but there is, Horatio,
And much offence too!
It is an honest ghost, that let me tell you!
And now, good friend,
As you are friend, scholar and soldier,
Give me one poor request.

HORATIO
What is't, my lord? I will.

HAMLET
Never make known what you have seen tonight.

HORATIO
I will not.

HAMLET
Nay, but swear't.

HORATIO
I have sworn already.

Enter GHOST.

GHOST
Swear.

HAMLET
Come on–you hear this fellow–
Consent to swear.

HORATIO
O day and night, but this is wondrous strange!

HAMLET
And therefore as a stranger give it welcome.
There are more things in heaven and earth, Horatio,
Than are dreamt of in your philosophy. But come;
Here, as before, never, so help you mercy,
How strange or odd soe'er I bear myself–
As I perchance hereafter shall think meet
To put an antic disposition on–
That you, at such times seeing me, never shall
give out that you know aught of me:

GHOST
Swear!

HAMLET
Swear.

HORATIO
I swear.

HAMLET
Rest, rest, perturbed spirit!

Exit GHOST.

HAMLET
So, Horatio,
With all my love I do commend me to you:
Let us go in together;
The time is out of joint: O cursed spite,
That ever I was born to set it right!

Exeunt.

ACT II
SCENE I

HAMLET whispers instructions hurriedly to OPHELIA. HAMLET hides to the side as:[52]

Enter POLONIUS.[53]

OPHELIA
O, my lord, my lord, I have been so affrighted!

POLONIUS
How now, Ophelia! what's the matter?

OPHELIA
My lord, as I was sitting in my closet,
Lord Hamlet,

51

[52] The next step in the attempt to give Ophelia agency: An elaborate pantomime in which Ophelia is "in" on Hamlet's plan, and agrees to fool her father regarding Hamlet's mental state.

[53] Logically cut in many productions, here Polonius originally dispatches a servant to spy on his son in Paris. It's funny, and it sets up Polonius' clever scheming so well, but I don't expect it in most productions.

Pale as his shirt; his knees knocking each other;
And with a look so piteous in purport
As if he had been loosed out of hell
To speak of horrors,–he comes before me.

POLONIUS
Mad for thy love?

OPHELIA
My lord, I do not know;
But truly, I do fear it.

POLONIUS
What said he?

OPHELIA
He took me by the wrist and held me hard;
Then goes he to the length of all his arm;
And, with his other hand thus o'er his brow,
He falls to such perusal of my face
As he would draw it. Long stay'd he so;
At last, a little shaking of mine arm
And thrice his head thus waving up and down,
He raised a sigh so piteous and profound
As it did seem to shatter all his bulk
And end his being: that done, he lets me go:
And, with his head over his shoulder turn'd,
He seem'd to find his way without his eyes;
For out o' doors he went without their helps,
And, to the last, bended their light on me.

POLONIUS
This is the very ecstasy of love,
What, have you given him any hard words of late?

OPHELIA
No, my good lord, but, as you did command,
I did repel his letters and denied
His access to me.

POLONIUS
That hath made him mad.
I am sorry that with better heed and judgment
I had not quoted him: I fear'd he did but trifle,
And meant to wreck thee; but, beshrew my jealousy!
Come, go we to the king:
This must be known; which, being kept close, might move
More grief to hide than hate to utter love.

Exeunt. HAMLET and OPHELIA exchange a look as she goes.[55]

ACT II
SCENE II

Enter CLAUDIUS, GERTRUDE, POLONIUS, and OPHELIA.[56]

CLAUDIUS
Art thou the father of good news?

POLONIUS
My liege,
I hold my duty, as I hold my soul,
And I do think that I have found
The very cause of Hamlet's lunacy.

CLAUDIUS
O, speak of that; that do I long to hear.

POLONIUS
My liege, and madam, to expostulate
What majesty should be, what duty is,
Why day is day, night night, and time is time,
Were nothing but to waste night, day and time.
Therefore, since brevity is the soul of wit,
And tediousness the limbs and outward flourishes,

---

[55] I believe Hamlet often gave Ophelia a thumbs-up.
[56] Although not present in the original stage directions, a silent Ophelia was very effectively stationed downstage-left for the humiliating reading of her private love letters.
[57]

I will be brief: your noble son is mad:
Mad call I it; for, to define true madness,
What is't but to be nothing else but mad?

GERTRUDE
More matter, with less art.

POLONIUS
Madam, I swear I use no art at all.
That he is mad, 'tis true: 'tis true 'tis pity;
And pity 'tis 'tis true: a foolish figure,
But farewell it, for I will use no art.
Mad let us grant him then: and now remains
That we find out the cause of this effect,
Or rather say, the cause of this defect,
For this effect defective comes by cause:
Thus it remains, and the remainder thus. Perpend:
I have a daughter–have while she is mine–
Who, in her duty and obedience, mark,
Hath given me these: now gather, and surmise.

Reads from one in a stack of letters:

'To the celestial and my soul's idol, the most
beautified Ophelia,'–
That's an ill phrase, a vile phrase; 'beautified' is
a vile phrase: but you shall hear. Thus:

Reads again:

'In her excellent white bosom–

GERTRUDE
Came this from Hamlet to her?

Takes letter from POLONIUS and reads.

POLONIUS
Good madam, stay awhile.

GERTRUDE[59]
'Doubt thou the stars are fire;
Doubt that the sun doth move;
Doubt truth to be a liar;
But never doubt I love.
O dear Ophelia, I am ill at these numbers;
I have not art to reckon my groans: but that
I love thee best, O most best, believe it. Adieu.
Thine evermore most dear lady, whilst
this machine is to him, Hamlet.'

GERTRUDE continues to leaf through the various letters as the men continue:

POLONIUS
This, in obedience, hath my daughter shown me,
And more above, hath his solicitings,
As they fell out by time, by means and place,
All given to mine ear.

CLAUDIUS
But how hath she received his love?

POLONIUS
What do you think of me?

CLAUDIUS
As of a man faithful and honorable.

POLONIUS
I would fain prove so. But what might you think,
Or my dear majesty your queen here, think,
If I had look'd upon this love with idle sight;
What might you think? No, I went round to work,
And my young mistress thus I did bespeak:
'Lord Hamlet is a prince, out of thy star;
This must not be:' and then I precepts gave her,
That she should lock herself from his resort,

---

[59] This text is spoken by Polonius in the original text.
[60]

Which done, she took the fruits of my advice;
And he, repulsed–a short tale to make–
Fell into a sadness, then into a fast,
Thence to a watch, thence into a weakness,
Thence to a lightness, and, by this declension,
Into the madness wherein now he raves,
And all we mourn for.

CLAUDIUS
[*To Gertrude*] Do you think 'tis this?

POLONIUS
Take this from this if this be otherwise.

GERTRUDE
[*To Claudius*] It may be, very likely.

CLAUDIUS
How may we try it further?

POLONIUS
You know, sometimes he walks four hours together
Here in the lobby.

GERTRUDE
So he does indeed.

POLONIUS
At such a time I'll loose my daughter to him:
Be you and I behind an arras then;
Mark the encounter: if he love her not
And be not from his reason fall'n thereon,
Let me be no assistant for a state,
But keep a farm and carters.

CLAUDIUS
We will try it.

POLONIUS
But, look,
Away, I do beseech you, come, away:
I'll board him presently.

Exeunt CLAUDIUS, GERTRUDE, and OPHELIA.

Enter HAMLET, reading.

POLONIUS
How does my good Lord Hamlet?

HAMLET
Well, God-a-mercy.

POLONIUS
Do you know me, my lord?

HAMLET
Excellent well; you are a fishmonger.

POLONIUS
Not I, my lord.

HAMLET
Then I would you were so honest a man.

POLONIUS
Honest, my lord!

HAMLET
Ay, sir; to be honest, as this world goes, is to be
one man picked out of ten thousand.

POLONIUS
That's very true, my lord.

62

HAMLET
For if the sun breed maggots in a dead dog, being a
Good kissing carrion,[64] –Have you a daughter?

POLONIUS
I have, my lord.

HAMLET
Let her not walk i' the sun: conception is a
blessing: but not as your daughter may conceive.
Friend, look to 't.

POLONIUS
[*Aside*] Still harping on my daughter:
he is far gone, far gone.
What do you read, my lord?

HAMLET
Words, words, words.

POLONIUS
What is the matter, my lord?

HAMLET
Between who?

POLONIUS
I mean, the matter that you read, my lord.

HAMLET
Slanders, sir: for the satirical rogue says here
that old men have[65] eyes purging thick amber and
plum-tree gum and that they have a plentiful lack of
wit, together with most weak hams: all which, sir,
though I most powerfully and potently believe, yet

63

[64] There is no scholarly consensus as to the meaning of this line. Early editors changed "good" to "god."
[65] The original list of Old Man attributes begins with "grey beards." All references to beards have been excised.

yourself, sir, should be old as I am, if like a crab
you could go backward.

POLONIUS
[*Aside*] Though this be madness, yet there is method
in 't. Will you walk out of the air, my lord?

HAMLET
Into my grave.

POLONIUS
Indeed, that is out o' the air.
[*Aside*] How pregnant sometimes his replies are! I will
leave him, and presently contrive the means of
meeting between him and my daughter.–My honorable
lord, I will most humbly take my leave of you.

HAMLET
You cannot, sir, take from me any thing that I will
more willingly part withal: except my life. Except
my life. Except my life.

POLONIUS
Fare you well, my lord.

HAMLET
These tedious old fools!

Enter ROSENCRANTZ and GUILDENSTERN.[66]

---

[66] During the cutting process, I worried very much about the treatment of these two characters. Doubled with Claudius and Gertrude, with whom they normally share the stage for most of their stage time, Rosencrantz and Guildenstern appear and disappear twice, and are never mentioned after their second appearance. The audience never had a problem with the cuts, and they routinely found R&G weirdly funny. Many people say these two minor characters are their favorite characters in Shakespeare; I can only assume they mean they are their favorite characters in *Rosencrantz and Guildenstern Are Dead*, Tom Stoppard's fan fiction of Shakespeare.
67

POLONIUS
Welcome, dear Rosencrantz and Guildenstern.
You go to seek the Lord Hamlet; there he is.

ROSENCRANTZ
[*To POLONIUS*] God save you, sir!

Exit POLONIUS.

ROSENCRANTZ
My honored lord!

GUILDENSTERN
My most dear lord!

HAMLET
My excellent good friends. How dost thou,
Guildenstern? Rosencrantz. How do ye both?

ROSENCRANTZ
As the indifferent children of the earth.

GUILDENSTERN
Happy, in that we are not over-happy;
On fortune's cap we are not the very button.

HAMLET
Nor the soles of her shoe?

ROSENCRANTZ
Neither, my lord.

HAMLET
Then you live about her waist, or in the middle of
her favors?[69]

ROSENCRANTZ
'Faith, her privates we.

68

[69] Some actors in our production lewdly fingered their books on this line, to the glee of the actors playing R&G.

HAMLET
O, most true; she is a strumpet.
What's the news?

ROSENCRANTZ
None, my lord, but that the world's grown honest.

HAMLET
Then is doomsday near. But your news is not true.
Let me question more in particular: what have you,
my good friends, deserved at the hands of fortune,
that she sends you to prison hither?

ROSENCRANTZ
Prison, my lord!

HAMLET
Denmark's a prison.

GUILDENSTERN
Then is the world one.

HAMLET
A goodly one; in which there are many confines,
wards and dungeons, Denmark being one o' the worst.

GUILDENSTERN
We think not so, my lord.

HAMLET
Why, then, 'tis none to you; for there is nothing
either good or bad, but thinking makes it so: to me
it is a prison.

ROSENCRANTZ
Why then, your ambition makes it one; 'tis too
narrow for your mind.

HAMLET
O God, I could be bounded in a nut shell and count

myself a king of infinite space, were it not that I
have bad dreams…
But, in the beaten way of friendship,
what make you at Elsinore?

ROSENCRANTZ
To visit you, my lord; no other occasion.

HAMLET
Beggar that I am, I am even poor in thanks; but I
thank you. Were you not sent for? Is it
your own inclining? Is it a free visitation? Come,
deal justly with me: come, come; nay, speak.

GUILDENSTERN
What should we say?

HAMLET
Why, anything, but to the purpose. You were sent
for; and there is a kind of confession in your looks
which your modesties have not craft enough to color:
I know the good king and queen have sent for you.

ROSENCRANTZ
To what end, my lord?

HAMLET
That you must teach me. Be even and direct:
Whether you were sent for, or no.

ROSENCRANTZ
[*Aside to GUILDENSTERN*] What say you?

GUILDENSTERN
My lord, we were sent for.

HAMLET
I will tell you why; so your secrecy to the king
and queen molt no feather. I have of late–but
wherefore I know not–lost all my mirth, forgone all

custom of exercises; and indeed it goes so heavily
with my disposition that this goodly frame, the
earth, seems to me a sterile promontory, this most
excellent canopy, the air, look you, this brave
o'erhanging firmament, this majestical roof fretted
with golden fire, why, it appears no other thing to
me than a foul and pestilent congregation of vapors.
What a piece of work is a man. How noble in reason.
How infinite in faculty. In form and moving how
express and admirable. In action how like an angel.
In apprehension how like a god! the beauty of the
world! the paragon of animals! And yet, to me,
what is this quintessence of dust? Man delights not
me. No, nor woman neither, though by your smiling
you seem to say so.

ROSENCRANTZ
My lord, there was no such stuff in my thoughts.

HAMLET
Why did you laugh then, when I said 'man delights not me'?[73]
Good my friends, you are welcome to Elsinore: but my
uncle-father and aunt-mother are deceived.

GUILDENSTERN
In what, my dear lord?

HAMLET
I am but mad north-north-west: when the wind is
southerly I know a hawk from a handsaw.
You are welcome to Elsinore.

ROSENCRANTZ
Good my lord.

72

[73] In the original text, R&G inform Hamlet of the Players on route to Elsinore; here, they suffered a very humorous awkward pause.

HAMLET
Ay, so, God be with ye.

Exeunt ROSENCRANTZ and GUILDENSTERN.

HAMLET
Now I am alone.
O, what a rogue and peasant slave am I! [74]
Is it not monstrous that a player, here,

---

[74] A Shakespearean soliloquy usually follows a set pattern: a character in turmoil picks up on outside stimulus (e.g.; "Is this a dagger I see before me?" (*Macbeth*) or Why do all the dudes like Hermia more than me? (*Midsummer*)). The Speaker then uses the stimulus as a metaphor to work through their thicket of problems. Finally, the speaker decides on a plan of action, or decides there is nothing to be done ("But break my heart, for I must hold my tongue" (*Hamlet*)). In the uncut version of this play, this speech follows that pattern to a tee: the Player, capable of showing intense emotion and passion over the long dead Hecuba, provides the stimulus for Hamlet, still dealing with the gap between what he feels on the inside, and what he shows outside. Hamlet then compares his situation to the Player's performance before realizing he can use the Player to catch Claudius' conscience and reveal his guilt. There are a number of problems present in this cut of the text. For one, Hamlet's doubts as to the Ghost's veracity are all cut: In the original text of this speech, he worries the Ghost may be a "devil" who assumes a "pleasing shape" to damn him. Without this pressure to prove the Ghost correct, why should Hamlet stage his *Mousetrap* anyway? Further, no Player appears before the speech—or at all! That means Hamlet does not request the macabre recitation of the fall of Troy, and the Player does not shed any tears over Hecuba, and Hamlet has no one to compare his emotions to. The decision to stage a play-within-a-play without any Players further complicates matters, but I will address those in the coming scene. The excision of the Players was the most problematic cut in the entire production, and this *Hamlet Machine* largely broke down from this speech to after *The Mousetrap*.
75

But in a fiction, in a dream of passion,
Could force his soul so to his own conceit
That from her working all his visage wann'd,
Tears in his eyes, distraction in's aspect,
A broken voice, and his whole function suiting
With forms to his conceit? and all for nothing!
What would he do,
Had he the motive and the cue for passion
That I have? He would drown the stage with tears
And cleave the general ear with horrid speech,
Make mad the guilty and appall the free,
Confound the ignorant, and amaze indeed
The very faculties of eyes and ears. Yet I,
A dull and muddy-mettled rascal, do nothing;
Am I a coward?
Who calls me villain? breaks my pate across?
Tweaks me by the nose? who does me this?
Ha?
'Swounds, I should take it: for it cannot be,
But I am pigeon-liver'd and lack gall,
I should have fatted all the region kites
With this slave's offal! Bloody, bawdy villain!
Remorseless, treacherous, lecherous, kindless villain!
O, vengeance!
Why, what an ass am I! This is most brave,
That I, the son of a dear father murder'd,
Prompted to my revenge by heaven and hell,
Must, like a whore, unpack my heart with words!
Fie upon't! fie!
…I have heard
That guilty creatures sitting at a play
Have by the very cunning of the scene
Been struck so to the soul that presently
They have proclaim'd their malefactions;
For murder, though it have no tongue, will speak
With most miraculous organ. I'll
Play something like the murder of my father
Before mine uncle: I'll observe his looks;
I'll tent him to the quick: if he but blench,

76

I know my course. The play's the thing
Wherein I'll catch the conscience of the king.

Exit.

ACT III
SCENE I

Enter CLAUDIUS, GERTRUDE,[77] POLONIUS, and OPHELIA.

POLONIUS
Ophelia, walk you here. Gracious, so please you,
We will bestow ourselves.

GERTRUDE
Ophelia, I do wish
That your good beauties be the happy cause
Of Hamlet's wildness: so shall I hope your virtues
Will bring him to his wonted way again.

CLAUDIUS
I hear him coming: let's withdraw.

Exeunt CLAUDIUS, GERTRUDE, and POLONIUS.

Enter HAMLET. OPHELIA remains unseen to the side.

HAMLET
To be, or not to be: that is the question:[78]

---

[77] Gertrude has been added to this scene.
[78] Many actors are taught to find operative words; Blank Verse makes that search much easier. To keep the verse taut, the actor must lift the last word of every line. Carrying the end of each line up and forward creates energy for the discoveries in the next line. Take any speech in Shakespeare, and, looking at just the last word of each line, you will find all you need to know about the most important themes. For instance, this most famous of speeches: Question, Suffer, Fortune, Troubles, Sleep, End, Shocks, Consummation, Sleep, Rub, Come, Coil, Respect, Life, Time, Contumely, Delay, Spurns, Takes, Make, Bear, Life, Death, Bourn, Will, Have, Of, All, Resolution, Thought, Moment, Awry.

Whether 'tis nobler in the mind to suffer
The slings and arrows of outrageous fortune,
Or to take arms against a sea of troubles,
And by opposing end them? To die: to sleep;
No more; and by a sleep to say we end
The heartache and the thousand natural shocks
That flesh is heir to, 'tis a consummation
Devoutly to be wish'd. To die, to sleep;
To sleep: perchance to dream: ay, there's the rub;
For in that sleep of death what dreams may come,
When we have shuffled off this mortal coil,
Must give us pause: there's the respect
That makes calamity of so long life;
For who would bear the whips and scorns of time,
Th' oppressor's wrong, the proud man's contumely,
The pangs of despised love, the law's delay,
The insolence of office and the spurns
That patient merit of the unworthy takes,
When he himself might his quietus make
With a bare bodkin? who would fardels bear,
To grunt and sweat under a weary life,
But that the dread of something after death,
The undiscover'd country from whose bourn
No traveller returns, puzzles the will
And makes us rather bear those ills we have
Than fly to others that we know not of?
Thus conscience does make cowards of us all;
And thus the native hue of resolution
Is sicklied o'er with the pale cast of thought,
And enterprises of great pith and moment
With this regard their currents turn awry,
And lose the name of action.

OPHELIA
Good my lord.
How does your honor for this many a day?

HAMLET
I humbly thank you; well, well, well.

OPHELIA
My lord, I have remembrances of yours,
That I have longed long to re-deliver;
I pray you, now receive them.

HAMLET
No, not I;
I never gave you aught.

OPHELIA
My honor'd lord, you know right well you did;
And, with them, words of so sweet breath composed
As made the things more rich. Their perfume lost,
Take these again.

HAMLET
Ha, ha! Are you honest?

OPHELIA
My lord?

HAMLET
Are you fair?

OPHELIA
What means your lordship?

HAMLET
That if you be honest and fair, your honesty should
admit no discourse to your beauty.

OPHELIA
Could beauty, my lord, have better commerce than
with honesty?

HAMLET
Ay, truly; for the power of beauty will sooner
transform honesty from what it is to a bawd than the

force of honesty can translate beauty into his
likeness. I did love you once.

OPHELIA
Indeed, my lord, you made me believe so.

HAMLET
You should not have believed me; I loved you not.

OPHELIA
I was the more deceived.

HAMLET
Get thee to a nunnery: why wouldst thou be a
breeder of sinners? I am myself indifferent honest;
but yet I could accuse me of such things that it
were better my mother had not borne me.
What should such fellows as I do crawling
between earth and heaven? We are arrant knaves,
all; believe none of us. Go thy ways to a nunnery.
Where's your father?

OPHELIA
At home, my lord.

HAMLET
Let the doors be shut upon him, that he may play the
fool no where but in's own house. Farewell.
If thou dost marry, I'll give thee this plague for
thy dowry: be thou as chaste as ice, as pure as
snow, thou shalt not escape calumny. Get thee to a
nunnery, go: farewell. Or, if thou wilt needs
marry, marry a fool; for wise men know well enough
what monsters you make of them. To a nunnery, go,
and quickly too. Farewell.

OPHELIA
O heavenly powers, restore him!

HAMLET
I have heard of your paintings too, well enough; God
has given you one face, and you make yourselves
another: you jig, you amble, and you lisp, and
nick-name God's creatures, and make your wantonness
your ignorance. Go to, I'll no more on't; it hath
made me mad. I say, we will have no more marriages:
those that are married already, all but one, shall
live; the rest shall keep as they are. To a
nunnery, go.

Exit HAMLET.

OPHELIA
O, what a noble mind is here o'erthrown!
The courtier's, soldier's, scholar's, eye, tongue, sword;
The expectancy and rose of the fair state,
The glass of fashion and the mold of form,
The observed of all observers, quite, quite down!
And I, of ladies most deject and wretched,
That suck'd the honey of his music vows,
Now see that noble and most sovereign reason,
Like sweet bells jangled, out of tune and harsh;
Blasted with ecstasy: O, woe is me,
To have seen what I have seen, see what I see!

Re-enter CLAUDIUS, POLONIUS, and GERTRUDE.

CLAUDIUS
Love! his affections do not that way tend.

POLONIUS
How now, Ophelia!
You need not tell us what Lord Hamlet said;
We heard it all.

CLAUDIUS
Nor what he spake, though it lack'd form a little,
Was not like madness.

GERTRUDE
There's something in his soul,
O'er which his melancholy sits on brood.

CLAUDIUS
And I do doubt the hatch and the disclose
Will be some danger: which for to prevent,
I will in quick determination
Thus set it down: he shall with speed to England,
[*to GERTRUDE*] What think you on't?

POLONIUS
It shall do well: but yet do I believe
The origin and commencement of his grief
Sprung from neglected love. My lord, do as you please;
But, if you hold it fit,
Let his queen mother all alone entreat him
To show his grief:
If she find him not,
To England send him, or confine him where
Your wisdom best shall think.

CLAUDIUS looks to GERTRUDE, who nods.

CLAUDIUS
It shall be so:
Madness in great ones must not unwatch'd go.

Exeunt.

ACT III
SCENE II

Enter HAMLET, setting the stage.

Enter OPHELIA. A tense moment before:

HAMLET
Make you ready.

HAMLET and OPHELIA begin to put on their make up—very thick and dark eyeliner—in silence. Soon:

HAMLET
[*To the audience*] There is a play tonight before the king;
One scene of it comes near the circumstance
of my father's death:
I prithee, when thou seest that act afoot,
Observe mine uncle: Give him heedful note;
For I mine eyes will rivet to his face,
And after we will all our judgments join
In censure of his seeming.

Enter CLAUDIUS and GERTRUDE.

HAMLET
They are coming to the play; I must be idle.
[*To Ophelia*] Get you a place.

CLAUDIUS
How fares our cousin Hamlet?

HAMLET
Excellent, i' faith; of the chameleon's dish I eat
the air, promise-crammed: you cannot feed capons so.

CLAUDIUS
I have nothing with this answer, Hamlet; these words
are not mine.

HAMLET
No, nor mine now.

Enter POLONIUS.

HAMLET
My lord, you played once i' the university.

POLONIUS
That did I, my lord; and was accounted a good actor.

HAMLET
What did you enact?

POLONIUS
I did enact Julius Caesar: I was killed i' the
Capitol; Brutus killed me.[85]

HAMLET
It was a brute part of him to kill so capital a calf
there.

GERTRUDE
Come hither, my dear Hamlet.

OPHELIA has stepped forward.

HAMLET
No, good mother, here's metal more attractive.

POLONIUS
[*To CLAUDIUS*] O! do you mark that?

A planned Vaudeville between HAMLET and OPHELIA:[86]

---

[85] An old in-joke: In Shakespeare's company, the unknown older actor playing Polonius in 1601 almost certainly played Caesar in 1599, and Richard Burbage, the star of the company, stabbed that actor as Hamlet and Brutus.

[86] With no players, and Ophelia in need of more " agency," Ophelia and Hamlet perform the play-within-a-play as a vaudeville pastiche. But just how much agency does this confer upon the wronged Ophelia? Didn't Hamlet just violently berate her even as she acted according to plan? And now, doesn't he humiliate her with sexual innuendo in front of her father and the rest of the court?

87

HAMLET / Comic
Lady, shall I lie in your lap?

OPHELIA / Straight
No, my lord.

HAMLET / Comic
I mean, my head upon your lap.

OPHELIA / Straight
Ay, my lord.

HAMLET / Comic
Do you think I meant country matters?

OPHELIA / Straight
I think nothing, my lord.

HAMLET / Comic
That's a fair thought to lie between maids' legs.

OPHELIA / Straight
What is, my lord?

HAMLET / Comic
Nothing.

OPHELIA / Straight
You are merry, my lord.

HAMLET / Comic
Who, I?

OPHELIA / Straight
Ay, my lord.

HAMLET / Comic
O God, your only jig-maker. What should a man do
but be merry? for, look you, how cheerfully my
mother looks, and my father died within these two hours.

OPHELIA / Straight
Nay, 'tis twice two months, my lord.

HAMLET / Comic
So long? O heavens! died two
months ago, and not forgotten yet? Then there's
hope a great man's memory may outlive his life half
a year!

*Rim shot. Music: Dumb-show, done by HAMLET and OPHELIA:
Enter a King and Queen lovingly. He embraces her, and she him. He
lays down: she, seeing him asleep, exits. Anon comes in a fellow, takes
the King's crown, kisses it; pours poison in the King's ear, and exits. The
Queen returns; finds the King dead, and weeps. The Poisoner comes
again and woos the Queen: she seems unwilling at first, but in the end
accepts his love. Ta-Da!*

GERTRUDE
What means this, Hamlet?

HAMLET
Marry, it means mischief.

POLONIUS
Belike this show imports the argument of the play.

Re-Enter OPHELIA.

HAMLET
We shall know by this lady: a player cannot
keep counsel; she'll tell all.

GERTRUDE
Will she tell us what this show meant?

HAMLET
Ay, or any show that you'll show her: be not you
ashamed to show, she'll not shame to tell you what it means.

GERTRUDE
I'll mark the play.

OPHELIA / Prologue
For us, and for our tragedy,
Here stooping to your clemency,
We beg your hearing patiently.

HAMLET
Is this a prologue, or the posy of a ring?

OPHELIA
'Tis brief, my lord.

HAMLET
As woman's love.

HAMLET and OPHELIA play a King and Queen.

HAMLET / Player King
Full thirty times hath Phoebus' cart gone round
Neptune's salt wash and Tellus' orbed ground,
Since love our hearts and Hymen did our hands
Unite commutual in most sacred bands.

OPHELIA / Player Queen
Now, what my love is, proof hath made you know;
And as my love is sized, my fear is so:
Where love is great, the littlest doubts are fear;
Where little fears grow great, great love grows there.

HAMLET / Player King
'Faith, I must leave thee, love, and shortly too;
My operant powers their functions leave to do:
And thou shalt live in this fair world behind,
Honor'd, beloved; and haply one as kind;
For husband shalt thou–

OPHELIA / Player Queen
–O, confound the rest!

Such love must needs be treason in my breast:
In second husband let me be accurst!
None wed the second but who kill'd the first.
A second time I kill my husband dead,
When second husband kisses me in bed.

HAMLET / Player King
I do believe you think what now you speak;
But what we do determine oft we break.

OPHELIA / Player Queen
Both here and hence pursue me, lasting strife,
If, once a widow, ever I be wife!

HAMLET / Player King
'Tis deeply sworn. Sweet, leave me here awhile;
My spirits grow dull, and fain I would beguile
The tedious day with sleep.

Sleeps.

OPHELIA / Player Queen
Sleep rock thy brain,
And never come mischance between us twain!

HAMLET
Madam, how like you this play?

GERTRUDE
The lady protests too much, methinks.[92]

HAMLET
O, but she'll keep her word.

91

[92] Why this line was altered from the famous, emphatic, and iambically precise "The Lady doth protest too much" is beyond me, and I refused to say this altered version. This line would sometimes get a good chuckle. [Mark Jackson: "This alteration was actually unintentional, an unscrubbed hold-over from the online source of the text from which we worked."]

CLAUDIUS
What do you call the play?

HAMLET
The Mousetrap. This play
is the image of a murder done in Vienna:
'tis a knavish piece of work: but what o'
that? your majesty and we that have free souls, it
touches us not: let the galled jade wince, our
withers are unwrung.

Re-enter OPHELIA, already acting, but:

HAMLET
This is one Lucianus, nephew to the king.

OPHELIA
You are as good as a chorus, my lord.

HAMLET
I could interpret between you and your love, if I
could see the puppets dallying.

OPHELIA
You are keen, my lord, you are keen.

HAMLET
It would cost you a groaning to take off my edge.

OPHELIA
Still better, and worse.

HAMLET
So you must take your husbands. Begin, murderer:

OPHELIA / Lucianus
Thoughts black, hands apt, drugs fit, and time agreeing;
Confederate season, else no creature seeing;
Thou mixture rank, of midnight weeds collected,

With Hecate's ban thrice blasted, thrice infected,
Thy natural magic and dire property,
On wholesome life usurp immediately.

Pours the poison into HAMLET's ear:

HAMLET
He poisons him i' the garden for's estate. His
name's Gonzago: the story is extant and writ in
choice Italian: you shall see anon how the murderer
gets the love of Gonzago's wife!

GERTRUDE
How fares my lord?

CLAUDIUS
Give me some light: away!

Exeunt all but HAMLET, who rouses the audience to cheer CLAUDIUS out. Then:

HAMLET
[*To audience*] I'll take the ghost's word for a
thousand pound!
Didst perceive?
Upon the talk of the poisoning?
Ah, ha! Come, some music!

HAMLET pulls out a recorder.

For if the king like not the comedy,
Why then, belike, he likes it not, perdy.

HAMLET plays a short tune.

Enter ROSENCRANTZ and GUILDENSTERN.

GUILDENSTERN
Good my lord, vouchsafe us a word with you.

HAMLET
O, a whole history.

ROSENCRANTZ
The king, sir,–

HAMLET
Ay, sir, what of him?

ROSENCRANTZ
Is in his retirement marvelous distempered.

HAMLET
With drink, sir?

ROSENCRANTZ
No, my lord, rather with choler.

HAMLET
Your wisdom should show itself more richer to
signify this to his doctor; for, for me to put him
to his purgation would perhaps plunge him into far
more choler.

GUILDENSTERN
Good my lord, put your discourse into some frame and
start not so wildly from our affair.

HAMLET
I am tame, sir: pronounce.

GUILDENSTERN
The queen, your mother, in most great affliction of
spirit, hath sent us to you.

HAMLET
You are welcome.

GUILDENSTERN
Nay, good my lord;

if it shall please you to makc us a
wholesome answer, we will do your mother's
commandment: if not, your pardon and our return
shall be the end of our business.

HAMLET
Well, I cannot.

GUILDENSTERN
What, my lord?

HAMLET
Make you a wholesome answer; my wit's diseased: but,
such answer as I can make, you shall command;
or, rather, as you say, my mother: therefore no
more, but to the matter: my mother, you say,–

GUILDENSTERN
Your behavior hath struck her
into amazement and admiration.

HAMLET
O wonderful son, that can so astonish a mother! But
is there no sequel at the heels of this mother's
admiration? Impart.

GUILDENSTERN
She desires to speak with you in her closet, ere you
go to bed.

HAMLET
We shall obey, were she ten times our mother. Have
you any further trade with us?

ROSENCRANTZ
Good my lord, what is your cause of distemper? you
do, surely, bar the door upon your own liberty, if
you deny your griefs to your friends.

HAMLET
Sir, I lack advancement.

ROSENCRANTZ
How can that be, when you have the voice of the king
himself for your succession in Denmark?

HAMLET
Why do you go about to recover the wind of me,
as if you would drive me into a toil?

ROSENCRANTZ
O, my lord, if my duty be too bold, my love is too
unmannerly.

HAMLET
I do not well understand that. Will you play upon
this pipe?

ROSENCRANTZ
My lord, I cannot.

HAMLET
I pray you.

ROSENCRANTZ
Believe me, I cannot.

HAMLET
I do beseech you.

ROSENCRANTZ
I know no touch of it, my lord.

HAMLET
'Tis as easy as lying: govern these ventages with
your fingers and thumb, give it breath with your
mouth, and it will discourse most eloquent music.
Look you, these are the stops.

ROSENCRANTZ
I have not the skill.

HAMLET
Why, look you now, how unworthy a thing you make of
me! You would play upon me; you would seem to know
my stops; you would pluck out the heart of my
mystery; you would sound me from my lowest note to
the top of my compass: and there is much music,
excellent voice, in this little organ; yet cannot
you make it speak? 'Sblood, do you think I am
easier to be played on than a pipe? Call me what
instrument you will, though you can fret me, yet you
cannot play upon me!

Enter POLONIUS.

HAMLET
God bless you, sir!

POLONIUS
My lord, the queen would speak with you, and
presently.

HAMLET
Do you see yonder cloud that's almost in shape of a _____?[98]

POLONIUS
By the mass, and 'tis like a _____, indeed.

HAMLET
Methinks it is like a _____.

POLONIUS
It is backed like a _____.

---

[98] Actors were here encouraged to come up with their
own animals, much to the delight of the audience. Among
some of the sillier: teddy bear, blue-footed booby, and, my
favorite: porky-pine.
99

HAMLET
Or like a _____.

POLONIUS
Very like a _____.

HAMLET
Then I will come to my mother by and by.

POLONIUS
I will say so.

HAMLET
By and by is easily said.

Exit POLONIUS.

HAMLET
Leave me, friends!

Exeunt all but HAMLET.

HAMLET
Tis now the very witching time of night,
When churchyards yawn and hell itself breathes out
Contagion to this world: now could I drink hot blood,
And do such bitter business as the day
Would quake to look on! Soft: now to my mother.

Exit.

ACT III
SCENE III

Enter CLAUDIUS and POLONIUS.

CLAUDIUS
I like him not, nor stands it safe with us
To let his madness range.

POLONIUS
My lord, he's going to his mother's closet:
Behind the arras I'll convey myself
To hear the process;
'Tis meet that some more audience than a mother,
Since nature makes them partial, should o'erhear
The speech, of vantage. Fare you well, my liege:
I'll call upon you ere you go to bed,
And tell you what I know.

CLAUDIUS
Thanks, dear my lord.

Exit POLONIUS.

O, my offence is rank it smells to heaven;
It hath the primal eldest curse upon't,
A brother's murder. Pray can I not,
Though inclination be as sharp as will:
My stronger guilt defeats my strong intent;
What if this cursed hand
Were thicker than itself with brother's blood?
Is there not rain enough in the sweet heavens
To wash it white as snow? Then I'll look up;
My fault is past. But, O, what form of prayer
Can serve my turn? 'Forgive me my foul murder'?
That cannot be; since I am still possess'd
Of those effects for which I did the murder,
My crown, mine own ambition and my queen.
May one be pardon'd and retain the offence?
In the corrupted currents of this world
Offence's gilded hand may shove by justice,
And oft 'tis seen the wicked prize itself
Buys out the law: but 'tis not so above;
There is no shuffling, there the action lies
In his true nature;

O wretched state! O bosom black as death!
O limed soul, that, struggling to be free,
Art more engaged! Help, angels! Make assay!
Bow, stubborn knees; and, heart with strings of steel,
Be soft as sinews of the newborn babe!
All may be well.

Kneels.

Enter HAMLET.

HAMLET
Now might I do it pat, now he is praying;
And now I'll do't. And so he goes to heaven;
And so am I revenged. That would be scann'd:
A villain kills my father; and for that,
I, his sole son, do this same villain send
To heaven.[102]
O, this is hire and salary, not revenge.
He took my father grossly, full of bread;
With all his crimes broad blown, as flush as May;
And how his audit stands who knows save heaven?
But in our circumstance and course of thought,
'Tis heavy with him; and am I then revenged,
To take him in the purging of his soul,
When he is fit and season'd for his passage?
No![103]

---

[102] Two great examples of the metrical pause in this speech. Hamlet speaks his thought, and then takes a long metrical pause (three feet) to consider the ramifications. In Shakespeare's theatre, Hamlet would have spoken this directly to his visible audience and eager audience members must have responded. Even in our production, when I took the next pause of the speech, I sometimes got a verbal response.

[103] The actor has four whole feet to come up with a response! It is obvious in this case that the pause should be taken before the "No." This particular pause reminds us we must never play the end of the scene. Hamlet must believe that he will still kill Claudius until he finally utters that "No." That metrical pause is a container for a moment of Being: A decision, a choice, a course of thought, an interaction between the Actor and their Audience. Each line has that possibility embedded in it, acting like dormant DNA waiting for the act of creation.

Up, sword; and know thou a more horrid hent:
When he is drunk asleep, or in his rage,
Or in the incestuous pleasure of his bed;
At gaming, swearing, or about some act
That has no relish of salvation in't;
Then trip him, that his heels may kick at heaven,
And that his soul may be as damn'd and black
As hell, whereto it goes. My mother stays:
This prayer[105] but prolongs thy sickly days.

Exit.

CLAUDIUS
[*Rising*] My words fly up, my thoughts remain below:
Words without thoughts never to heaven go.

Exit.

ACT III
SCENE IV[106]

Enter GERTRUDE and POLONIUS.

104

[105] Both Folio and Quarto read "physic," metaphorizing Claudius' prayer as a form of medicine, and adding an internal rhyme playing off the sibilance and harsh punch of the word "sick." As I am a firm believer in an audience using context clues, I always used the mildly obscure original word.

[106] This scene is extremely condensed, and while this proved effective in performance, it is odd to cut so many of Gertrude's lines. With all of the work done to beef up Ophelia's agency, Gertrude is a woman with extreme agency: Claudius rules at her pleasure, and Hamlet's depression and subsequent psychosis derive from choices freely made by Gertrude. With Hamlet spending so much of the play haranguing everyone around him, the strong and complex Gertrude of the uncut version would have been a welcome change of pace.

POLONIUS[107]
Tell him his pranks have been too broad to bear with,
And that your grace hath screen'd and stood between
Much heat and him. I'll sconce me even here.
Pray you, be round with him.

GERTRUDE
I'll warrant you,
Fear me not.

HAMLET
[*Within*] Mother!

GERTRUDE
Withdraw, I hear him coming.

POLONIUS hides behind the arras.

Enter HAMLET.

HAMLET
Now, mother, what's the matter?

GERTRUDE
Hamlet, thou hast thy father much offended.

HAMLET
Mother, you have my father much offended.

---

[107] Polonius has a line in an earlier scene (cut in this text) in which he boasts," I will find/ Where truth is hid, though it were hid indeed/ Within the centre." Sometimes derided as a fool, Polonius is undone by his qualities as a bloodhound for the truth. He is indeed correct when he says," The origin and commencement of [Hamlet's] grief/ Sprung from neglected love." He realizes Hamlet's intense love for and jealousy over his mother drives the young Prince's moods. So when Polonius finds himself in Gertrude's locked bedroom, overhearing the final showdown between mother and son, he has indeed found where truth was hid. He pays for this knowledge with his life.
108

GERTRUDE
Come, come, you answer with an idle tongue.

HAMLET
Go, go, you question with a wicked tongue.

GERTRUDE
Why, how now, Hamlet!

HAMLET
What's the matter now?

GERTRUDE
Have you forgot me?

HAMLET
No, by the rood, not so:
You are the queen, your husband's brother's wife;
And–would it were not so!–you are my mother.

GERTRUDE
Nay, then, I'll set those to you that can speak.

HAMLET
Come, come, and sit you down;
You go not till I set you up a glass
Where you may see the inmost part of you.

GERTRUDE
What wilt thou do? thou wilt not murder me?
Help!

POLONIUS
[*Behind*] Help!

HAMLET
[*Drawing*] How now! a rat? Dead, for a ducat, dead!

Makes a stab through the arras.

109

POLONIUS
[*Behind*] O!

Falls and dies.

GERTRUDE
O me, what hast thou done?

HAMLET
Nay, I know not:
Is it the king?

GERTRUDE
O, what a rash and bloody deed is this!

HAMLET
A bloody deed! almost as bad, good mother,
As kill a king, and marry with his brother?

GERTRUDE
As kill a king!

HAMLET
Ay, lady, 'twas my word.

Lifts up the arras and discovers POLONIUS.

O!
Thou wretched, rash, intruding fool. Farewell!
I took thee for thy better: take thy fortune;
Thou find'st to be too busy is some danger.
Leave wringing of your hands: peace! sit you down,
And let me wring your heart; for so I shall,
If it be made of penetrable stuff.

GERTRUDE
What have I done, that thou dar'st wag thy tongue
In noise so rude against me?

HAMLET
Such an act
That blurs the grace and blush of modesty,
Calls virtue hypocrite, takes off the rose
From the fair forehead of an innocent love
And sets a blister there!

GERTRUDE
Ay me, what act?

HAMLET
Look here, upon this picture, and on this:
The counterfeit presentment of two brothers.
See, what a grace was seated on this brow;
Hyperion's curls; the front of Jove himself;
An eye like Mars to threaten and command;
A combination and a form indeed,
Where every god did seem to set his seal
To give the world assurance of a man:
This was your husband. Look you now, what follows:
Here is your husband; like a mildew'd ear,
Blasting his wholesome brother. Have you eyes?
Could you on this fair mountain leave to feed,
And fatten on this moor? Ha? have you eyes?
You cannot call it love; for at your age
The hey-day in the blood is tame, it's humble,
And waits upon the judgment: and what judgment
Would step from this to this?

GERTRUDE
O Hamlet, speak no more:
Thou turn'st mine eyes into my very soul.

HAMLET
Nay, but to live
In the rank sweat of an enseamed bed,
Stew'd in corruption, honeying and making love
Over the nasty sty,–

111

GERTRUDE
O, speak no more;
These words, like daggers, enter in mine ears;
No more, sweet Hamlet!

HAMLET
A murderer and a villain;
A slave that is not twentieth part the tithe
Of your precedent lord;
A cutpurse of the empire
That from a shelf the precious diadem stole
And put it in his pocket!

GERTRUDE
No more!

HAMLET
A king of shreds and patches!–

Enter GHOST. HAMLET and GERTRUDE see it; GERTRUDE denies seeing it.

HAMLET
What would your gracious figure?
Do you not come your tardy son to chide,
That, lapsed in time and passion, lets go by
The important acting of your dread command? O, say!

GHOST
Do not forget: this visitation
Is but to whet thy almost blunted purpose.
But, look, amazement on thy mother sits:
O, step between her and her fighting soul:
Speak to her, Hamlet.

HAMLET
How is it with you, lady?

GERTRUDE
Alas, how is't with you,

HAMLET
Look you, how pale he glares!
Do not look upon me;
Lest with this piteous action you convert
My stern effects! Do you see nothing there?

GERTRUDE[114]
Nothing at all; yet all that is I see.

HAMLET
Nor do you nothing hear?

GERTRUDE
No. Nothing but ourselves.

Exit GHOST.

HAMLET
Why, look you there! look, how it steals away!

GERTRUDE
This the very coinage of your brain:

HAMLET
Mother, for love of grace,
Lay not that mattering unction to your soul,
That not your trespass, but my madness speaks:

GERTRUDE
O Hamlet, thou hast cleft my heart in twain.

HAMLET
O, throw away the worser part of it,
And live the purer with the other half.
Good night.

113

[114] In this production, as in several others, Gertrude sees the Ghost, but denies it, both to Hamlet and herself.

Considers POLONIUS.

HAMLET
I must be cruel, only to be kind:
Thus bad begins and worse remains behind.

GERTRUDE
What shall I do?

HAMLET
Not this, by no means, that I bid you do:
Let the bloat king tempt you again to bed;
Pinch wanton on your cheek; call you his mouse;
And let him, for a pair of reechy kisses,
Make you to ravel all this matter out,
That I essentially am not in madness,
But mad in craft.

GERTRUDE
Be thou assured, if words be made of breath,
And breath of life, I have no life to breathe
What thou hast said to me.

HAMLET
'Twere good you let him know.
This man shall set me packing:
I'll lug the guts into the neighbor room.
Mother, good night. Indeed this counsellor
Is now most still, most secret and most grave,
Who was in life a foolish prating knave.
Come, sir, to draw toward an end with you.
Good night, mother.

Exit HAMLET dragging POLONIUS.

ACT IV
SCENE I

Scene continues.[115]

Enter CLAUDIUS.

---

[115] The following is an amalgamation of Act 4 scenes 1 and 3.

CLAUDIUS
Where is your son?

GERTRUDE
Ah, my good lord, what have I seen tonight!

CLAUDIUS
What, Gertrude? How does Hamlet?

GERTRUDE
Mad as the sea and wind, when both contend
Which is the mightier. In his lawless fit,
Behind the arras hearing something stir,
Whips out his rapier, cries, 'A rat, a rat!'
And, in this brainish apprehension, kills
The unseen good old man.[117]

116

[117] A great little speech. Look at the words Shakespeare ends his lines with: Contend, Fit, Stir, Rat, Kills, Man. These mostly monosyllabic Germanic words stress the violence of the encounter. Similarly the placement of word "Mad" in the trochaic off stress position jump starts Gertrude's disjointed utterance. The enjambment between the first and second line gives Gertrude space to coin an image: why do the two elements contend? They contend over "which is the mightier." The caesura in the middle of the line tells the actor to slow down, Gertrude is moving from her topic sentence into the actual description of the event, trying to put all the pieces together. The iambic regularity of the third line covers for the syntactical weirdness—this sentence has no subject: Gertrude cannot bring herself to connect her son to the actions that she has just witnessed. The next line, packed with information separated by a small caesura, includes a violent trochee ("Whips") mirrored by the equally strong "Cries." The enjambment of the next lines separates the verb ("Kills") from the direct object (the old man) putting extra stress onto the act of murder. The next line, shared between Gertrude and Claudius, has several spondees: ("Good Old Man"): a pounding dirge for the dead man, highlighted by Claudius' choice of adjective: "Heavy."

CLAUDIUS
O heavy deed!
It had been so with us, had we been there.
His liberty is full of threats to all;
To you yourself, to us, to every one.
Alas, how shall this bloody deed be answer'd?
This mad young man. Where is he gone?

GERTRUDE
To draw apart the body he hath kill'd.

CLAUDIUS[118]
The sun no sooner shall the mountains touch,
But we will ship him hence: and this vile deed
We must, with all our majesty and skill,
Both countenance and excuse.
How dangerous is it that this man goes loose!
Yet we must not the strong law put on him:
He's loved of the distracted multitude,
Who like not in their judgment, but their eyes;
And where tis so, the offender's scourge is weigh'd,
But never the offence. To bear all smooth and even,
This sudden sending him away must seem
Deliberate pause. Diseases desperate grown
By desperate appliance are relieved,
Or not at all.

Enter HAMLET.

CLAUDIUS
Now, Hamlet: where's Polonius?

HAMLET
At supper.

CLAUDIUS
At supper! where?

---

[118] This speech contains text from both the dialogue with Gertrude in Act 4 Scene 1 and the soliloquy at the top of Act 4 Scene 3.

119

HAMLET
Not where he eats, but where he is eaten: a certain convocation of politic worms are e'en at him. Your worm is your only emperor for diet: we fat all creatures else to fat us, and we fat ourselves for maggots.

CLAUDIUS
Alas, alas!

HAMLET
A man may fish with the worm that hath eat of a king, and eat of the fish that hath fed of that worm.

CLAUDIUS
What dost thou mean by this?

HAMLET
Nothing but to show you how a king may go a progress through the guts of a beggar.

CLAUDIUS
Where is Polonius?

HAMLET
In heaven; send hither to see: if your messenger find him not there, seek him i' the other place yourself. But indeed, if you find him not within this month, you shall nose him as you go up the stairs into the lobby. He will stay till y' come.

CLAUDIUS
Hamlet, this deed, for thine especial safety,–
Which we do tender, as we dearly grieve
For that which thou hast done,–must send thee hence
With fiery quickness: therefore prepare thyself;
The ship is ready and the wind at help,
The associates tend, and every thing is bent
For England.

HAMLET
For England!

CLAUDIUS
Ay, Hamlet.

HAMLET
Good.[122]

CLAUDIUS
So is it, if thou knew'st our purposes.

HAMLET
I see a cherub that sees them. But, come; for
England! Farewell, dear mother.

CLAUDIUS
Thy loving father, Hamlet.

HAMLET
My mother: father and mother is man and wife; man
and wife is one flesh; and so, my mother. Come, for England!

Exit HAMLET.

Exit GERTRUDE.

CLAUDIUS
I'll have him hence tonight.
And, England, if my love thou hold'st at aught–
thou mayst not disregard
Our sovereign process, which imports at full
The present death of Hamlet! Do it, England!
For like the hectic in my blood he rages,

121

[122] Ten syllables spread across four lines and two characters. Shakespeare is telling us to pick up the cue and match each other's rhythm, keep the ping-pong ball in the air.

And thou must cure me. Till I know 'tis done,
Howe'er my haps, my joys were ne'er begun.

Exit.[123]

INTERMISSION

ACT IV
SCENE V

Enter OPHELIA.

OPHELIA
Where is the beauteous majesty of Denmark?
Where is the beauteous majesty of Denmark?
Where is the beauteous majesty of Denmark?

Enter GERTRUDE.

GERTRUDE
How now, Ophelia!

OPHELIA
[*Sings*] How should I your true love know
From another one?
By his cockle hat and staff,
And his sandal shoon.

GERTRUDE
Alas, sweet lady, what imports this song?

---

[123] With Fortinbras gone, we lose one of Hamlet's best soliloquies, delivered as he watches the march of the Norwegian troops across the Danish Countryside. The Folio also cuts this scene, so we are in good company.
124

OPHELIA
Say you? nay, pray you, mark.
[*Sings*] He is dead and gone, lady,
He is dead and gone;
At his head a grass-green turf,
At his heels a stone.

GERTRUDE
Nay, but, Ophelia,–

OPHELIA
Pray you, mark.
[*Sings*] White his shroud as the mountain snow,–

Enter CLAUDIUS.

GERTRUDE
Alas, look here, my lord.

OPHELIA
[*Sings*] Larded with sweet flowers
Which bewept to the grave did go
All with true-love showers.

CLAUDIUS
How do you, pretty lady?

OPHELIA
Well, God 'ild you! They say the owl was a baker's
daughter. Lord, we know what we are, but know not
what we may be. God be at your table!

CLAUDIUS
Conceit about her father.

OPHELIA
Pray you, let's have no words of this; but when they
ask you what it means, say you this:

[*Sings*] Tomorrow is Saint Valentine's day,
All in the morning betime,
And I a maid at your window,
To be your Valentine.
Then up he rose, and donn'd his clothes,
And dupp'd the chamber-door;
Let in the maid, that out a maid
Never departed more.

CLAUDIUS
Pretty Ophelia!

OPHELIA
[*Sings*] By Gis and by Saint Charity,
Alack, and fie for shame!
Young men will do't, if they come to't;
By cock, they are to blame.
Quoth she, before you tumbled me,
You promised me to wed.
So would I ha' done, by yonder sun,
An thou hadst not come to my bed.

CLAUDIUS
How long hath she been thus?

OPHELIA
I hope all will be well. We must be patient: but I
cannot choose but weep, to think they should lay him
i' the cold ground. My brother shall know of it:
and so I thank you for your good counsel. Come, my
coach! Good night, ladies; good night, sweet ladies;
good night, good night.

Exit.

CLAUDIUS
O, this is the poison of deep grief; it springs
All from her father's death. O Gertrude, Gertrude,

When sorrows come, they come not single spies
But in battalions.

A noise within:

LAERTES
[*within*] Where is this king!

GERTRUDE
Alack, what noise is this?

CLAUDIUS
What is the matter now?

Enter LAERTES.[127]

LAERTES
O thou vile king, give me my father!

GERTRUDE
Calmly, good Laertes.

LAERTES
That drop of blood that's calm proclaims me bastard,
Cries cuckold to my father, brands the harlot
Even here between the chaste unsmirched brow
Of my true mother.

CLAUDIUS
What is the cause, Laertes,
That thy rebellion looks so giant-like?
Let him go, Gertrude; do not fear our person:
Tell me, Laertes,
Why thou art thus incensed. Let him go, Gertrude.
Speak, man.

---

[127] This highly compressed conflation of the two Laertes scenes largely works. It does lack one of my favorite lines from the Folio: as Laertes leads a rebellion into the palace, Gertrude sputters out, "O you false Danish dogs!"
[128]

LAERTES
Where is my father?

CLAUDIUS
Dead.

GERTRUDE
But not by him!

CLAUDIUS
Let him demand his fill.

LAERTES
How came he dead? I'll not be juggled with:
To hell, allegiance! vows, to the blackest devil!
Conscience and grace, to the profoundest pit;
Let come what comes! only I'll be revenged
Most thoroughly for my father.

CLAUDIUS
Good Laertes,
That I am guiltless of your father's death,
And am most sensible in grief for it,
It shall as level to your judgment pierce
As day does to your eye.

Re-enter OPHELIA.

LAERTES
How now?
Dear maid, kind sister, sweet Ophelia!

OPHELIA
[*Sings*] They bore him barefaced on the bier;
Hey non nonny, nonny, hey nonny;
And in his grave rain'd many a tear:–
Fare you well, my dove!

LAERTES
O heat, dry up my brains. O rose of May.
O heavens; is't possible a young maid's wits
Should be as mortal as an old man's life?

OPHELIA
There's rosemary, that's for remembrance; pray,
love, remember: and there is pansies. That's for thoughts.
There's fennel for you, and columbines: there's rue
for you; and here's some for me: we may call it
herb-grace o' Sundays: O you must wear your rue with
a difference. There's a daisy: I would give you
some violets, but they withered all when my father
died: they say he made a good end.

LAERTES
Thought and affliction, passion, hell itself.

OPHELIA
[*Sings*] And will he not come again?
And will he not come again?
No, no, he is dead:
Go to thy deathbed:
He never will come again.
His beard was white as snow,
All flaxen was his poll:
He is gone, he is gone,
And we cast away moan:
God have mercy on his soul!
[*Speaks*] And of all Christian souls, I pray God. God buy you.

Exit OPHELIA.

Exit GERTRUDE after.

LAERTES
Do you see this, O God?

CLAUDIUS
Laertes, I must commune with your grief,

Be you content to lend your patience to us,
And we shall jointly labor with your soul
To give it due content.

LAERTES
Let this be so.

CLAUDIUS
Now you must put me in your heart for friend,
For Hamlet hath your noble father slain.

LAERTES
Why proceed you not against this feat
So crimeful and so capital in nature?

CLAUDIUS
For two special reasons; The queen his mother
Lives almost by his looks; and for myself:
She's so conjunctive to my life and soul,
That, as the star moves not but in his sphere,
I could not but by her. The other motive,
Is the great love the general public bear him;
Who, dipping all his faults in their affection,
Convert his gyves to graces; so that my arrows,
Too slightly timber'd for so loud a wind,
Would have reverted to my bow again,
And not where I had aim'd them.

LAERTES
And so have I a noble father lost;
A sister driven into desperate terms.

CLAUDIUS
Break not your sleeps for that:
I loved your father, and we love ourself;
And this, I hope, will teach you to imagine:
A letter from Hamlet:
Laertes, you shall hear it:

[*Reads*] 'High and mighty, You shall know I am set naked on
your kingdom. Tomorrow shall I beg leave to see
your kingly eyes: when I shall, first asking your
pardon thereunto, recount the occasion of my sudden
and more strange return. Hamlet.'
What should this mean?
Can you advise me?

LAERTES
It warms the very sickness in my heart,
That I shall live and tell him to his teeth,
'Thus dids't thou.'

CLAUDIUS
If it be so, Laertes.
Will you be ruled by me?

LAERTES
Ay, my lord;
So you will not o'errule me to a peace.

CLAUDIUS
To thine own peace. I will work him
To an exploit, now ripe in my device,
Under the which he shall not choose but fall:
And for his death no wind of blame shall breathe,
But even his mother shall uncharge the practice
And call it accident.

LAERTES
My lord, I will be ruled;
The rather, if you could devise it so
That I might be the organ.

CLAUDIUS
Laertes, was your father dear to you?

LAERTES
Why ask you this?

CLAUDIUS
Hamlet comes back: What would you undertake
To show yourself your father's son in deed
More than in words?

LAERTES
To cut his throat i' the church.

CLAUDIUS
Revenge should have no bounds. So, good Laertes,
You will do this. Keep close within your chamber;
Hamlet return'd shall know you are come home:
We'll put on those shall praise your excellence,
bring you together in a match,
And wager on your heads: he, being remiss,
Will not peruse the foils; so that, with ease,
Or with a little shuffling, you may choose
A sword unbated, and in a pass of practice
Requite him for your father.

LAERTES
I will do't:
And, for that purpose, I'll anoint my sword
With a contagion, that, if I gall him slightly,
It may be death.

CLAUDIUS
If this should fail, this project
Should have a back or second.
We'll make a solemn wager on your cunnings:
When in your motion you are hot and dry–
As make your bouts more violent to that end–
And that he calls for drink, I'll have prepared him
A chalice whereon but sipping,
If he by chance escape your venom'd point,
Our purpose may hold there.–

Enter GERTRUDE.

CLAUDIUS
How now, sweet queen!

GERTRUDE
One woe doth tread upon another's heel,
So fast they follow; your sister's drown'd, Laertes.

LAERTES
Drown'd! O, how?

Brief tableaux: OPHELIA aims a gun to her temple and pulls the trigger.

GERTRUDE
There is a willow grows aslant a brook,[134]
That shows his hoar leaves in the glassy stream;
There with fantastic garlands did she come
Of crow-flowers, nettles, daisies, and long purples.[136]
There, on the pendent boughs her coronet weeds
Clambering to hang, an envious sliver broke;
When down her weedy trophies and herself
Fell in the weeping brook. Her clothes spread wide;
And, mermaid-like, awhile they bore her up:
Which time she chanted snatches of old songs;[137]
As one incapable of her own distress.
But long it could not be
Till that her garments, heavy with their drink,

---

[134] Gertrude's speech has been interpreted in many ways, and we went the route of suicide cover up. In some productions Gertrude is truly the innocent bystander. In others Gertrude has been seen smothering Ophelia, either to put her out of her misery or restore order to the court.
135

[136] Like Ophelia's mad songs, Gertrude's original complete description of the long purples ("That liberal shepherds give a grosser name,/ But our cold maids do dead men's fingers call them") mixes bawdiness with death in a grotesque mélange.
[137] Folio reads "tunes" while Quarto reads "lauds." I do not know where "songs" came from, and I consequently refused to say it. [Mark Jackson: "I believe 'songs' was yet another holdover from the corrupted and corruptible downloaded text from which we originally worked."]

Pull'd the poor wretch from her melodious lay
To muddy death.

LAERTES
Alas, then, she is drown'd?

GERTRUDE
Drown'd. Drown'd.

LAERTES
Too much of water hast thou, poor Ophelia,
And therefore I forbid my tears. Adieu.
I have a speech of fire, that fain would blaze,
But that this folly drowns it.

Exit.

CLAUDIUS
Let's follow, Gertrude:
How much I had to do to calm his rage!
Now fear I this will give it start again;
Therefore let's follow.

Exeunt.

ACT V
SCENE I

Enter a GRAVEDIGGER[139] *who digs and sings.*

Enter HAMLET and HORATIO at a distance.

HAMLET
Has this fellow no feeling of his business, that he
sings at grave-making?

138

[139] In the original text, the Gravedigger quibbles with another clown over Ophelia's death and the validity of her burial in Christian ground.

HORATIO
Custom hath made it in him a property of easiness.

HAMLET picks up a skull.

HAMLET
This skull had a tongue in it and could sing once;
how the knave jowls it to the ground, as if it were
Cain's jaw-bone that did the first murder! It
might be the pate of a politician, might it not?

HORATIO
It might, my lord.

HAMLET
Or of a courtier; which could say 'Good morrow,
sweet lord! How dost thou, good lord?'

HORATIO
Ay, my lord.

HAMLET
Why may not this be the skull of a lawyer? Where be
his cases now, his tenures, and his tricks? why does he
suffer this rude knave now to knock him about the
sconce with a dirty shovel and will not tell him of
his action of battery? This fellow might be
in's time a great buyer of land, with his fines
and his recoveries: is this the fine of his fines, and
the recovery of his recoveries, to have his fine
pate full of fine dirt?
I will speak to this fellow. Whose
grave's this, sirrah?

GRAVEDIGGER
Mine, sir.

HAMLET
I think it be thine, indeed; for thou liest in't.

GRAVEDIGGER
You lie out on't, sir, and therefore it is not
yours: for my part, I do not lie in't, and yet it is mine.

HAMLET
Thou dost lie in't, to be in't and say it is thine:
'tis for the dead, not for the quick; therefore thou liest.

GRAVEDIGGER
'Tis a quick lie, sir; 'twill away gain, from me to
you.

HAMLET
What man dost thou dig it for?

GRAVEDIGGER
For no man, sir.

HAMLET
What woman, then?

GRAVEDIGGER
For none, neither.

HAMLET
Who is to be buried in't?

GRAVEDIGGER
One that was a woman, sir; but, rest her soul, she's dead.

HAMLET
How absolute the knave is! we must speak by the
card, or equivocation will undo us.
How long hast thou been a grave-maker?

GRAVEDIGGER
I came to't the very day that young Hamlet was born;
he that is mad, and sent into England.

HAMLET
Ay, marry, why was he sent into England?

GRAVEDIGGER
Why, because he was mad: he shall recover his wits
there; or, if he do not, it's no great matter there.

HAMLET
Why?

GRAVEDIGGER
'Twill not be seen in him; there the men
are as mad as he!

HAMLET
How long will a man lie i' the earth ere he rot?

GRAVEDIGGER
I' faith, if he be not rotten before he die
he will last you some eight year
or nine year: a tanner will last you nine year.
That skull has lain in the earth
three and twenty years.

HAMLET
Whose was it?

GRAVEDIGGER
A pestilence on him for a mad rogue! He poured a
flagon of Rhenish on my head once. This same skull,
sir, was Yorick's skull, the king's jester.

HAMLET
This?

GRAVEDIGGER
E'en that.

HAMLET
Alas, poor Yorick! I knew him, Horatio: a fellow
of infinite jest, of most excellent fancy: he hath
borne me on his back a thousand times; and now,
how my gorge rises at it.
Here hung those lips that I have kissed I know
not how oft. Where be your gibes now? your
gambols? your songs? your flashes of merriment,
that were wont to set the table on a roar? Not one
now, to mock your own grinning?
Now get you to my lady's chamber, and tell her: let
her paint an inch thick, to this favor she must
come; make her laugh at that. Prithee, Horatio, tell
me one thing.

HORATIO
What's that, my lord?

HAMLET
Dost thou think Alexander looked o' this fashion i'
the earth?

HORATIO
E'en so.

HAMLET
And smelt so?

HORATIO
E'en so.

HAMLET
Alexander died, Alexander was buried,
Alexander returneth to dust; the dust is earth; of
earth we make clay; and why of that clay, whereto he
was converted, might we not
Stop a hole to keep the wind away?
O, that that earth, which kept the world in awe,
Should patch a wall to expel the winter's flaw!

143

Enter in procession: the PRIEST, the corpse of OPHELIA carried by LAERTES, followed by GERTRUDE and CLAUDIUS.

HAMLET
But soft! here comes the king
And queen; who is this they carry?
And with such maimed rites? This doth betoken
The corpse did with desperate hand
Fordo its own life:
Couch we awhile, and mark.

Retiring with HORATIO.

LAERTES
What ceremony else?

HAMLET
That is Laertes,
A very noble man: mark.

LAERTES
What ceremony else?

PRIEST
Her death was doubtful;
And, but that great command o'ersways the order,
She should in ground unsanctified have lodged
Till the last trumpet;
Shards, flints and pebbles should be thrown on her;
Yet here she is allow'd her virgin rites
and maiden strewments.

LAERTES
Must there no more be done?

PRIEST
We should profane the service of the dead
To sing a requiem and give rest to her
As to peace-parted souls.

LAERTES
Lay her i' the earth:
And from her fair and unpolluted flesh
May violets spring! I tell thee, churlish priest,
A ministering angel shall my sister be
When thou liest howling.

HAMLET
What, the fair Ophelia!

GERTRUDE
Sweets to the sweet: farewell!
Scattering flowers
I hoped thou shouldst have been my Hamlet's wife;
I thought thy bride-bed to have deck'd, sweet maid,
And not have strew'd thy grave.

LAERTES
O, treble woe
Fall ten times treble on that cursed head
Whose wicked deed thy most ingenious sense
Deprived thee of! Hold off the earth awhile,
Till I have caught her once more in mine arms:
Now pile your dust upon the quick and dead,
Till of this flat a mountain you have made.

HAMLET
[*Advancing*] What is he whose grief
Bears such an emphasis? This is I,
Hamlet the Dane.

LAERTES
The devil take thy soul!

HAMLET[145]
I prithee, take thy fingers from my throat;
For I have something in me dangerous,
Which let thy wiseness fear! Hold off thy hand.

---

[145] The metrical irregularities of this sequence suggest
Shakespeare composed this scene with naturalistic
overlapping in mind.
146

CLAUDIUS
Pluck them asunder.

GERTRUDE
Hamlet, Hamlet!

HORATIO
Good my lord, be quiet.

HAMLET
Why I will fight with him upon this theme
Until my eyelids will no longer wag.

GERTRUDE
O my son, what theme?

HAMLET
I loved Ophelia! Forty thousand brothers
Could not, with all their quantity of love,
Make up my sum. What wilt thou do for her?

CLAUDIUS
He is mad, Laertes.

GERTRUDE
For love of God, forbear him.

HAMLET
'Show me what thou'lt do:
Woo't weep? woo't fight? woo't fast? woo't tear thyself?
Eat a crocodile?
I'll do't. Dost thou come here to
outface me with leaping in her grave?
I'll rant as well as thou.

GERTRUDE
This is mere madness!

HAMLET
What is the reason that you use me thus?
I loved you ever: but it is no matter;
Let Hercules himself do what he may,
The cat will mew and dog will have his day.

Exit HAMLET.

CLAUDIUS
I pray you, good Horatio, wait upon him.

Exit HORATIO.

CLAUDIUS
[*To LAERTES*] Strengthen your patience in our last night's speech;
We'll put the matter to the present push.

Exit LAERTES.

CLAUDIUS
Good Gertrude, set some watch over your son.

Exeunt.

ACT V
SCENE II

Enter HAMLET and HORATIO.

HAMLET
Now shall you see:
There's a divinity that shapes our ends,
Rough-hew them how we will.

HORATIO
That is most certain.

HAMLET
Up from my cabin,

My sea-gown scarf'd about me, in the dark
Groped I to find it out; I found, Horatio,
His grand commission; an exact command–
Larded with many several sorts of reasons
Importing Denmark's health and England's too–
That my head should be struck off.[149]

HORATIO
Is't possible?

HAMLET
Here's the commission: read it at more leisure.

HORATIO
Why, what a king is this!

HAMLET
But I am very sorry, good Horatio,
That to Laertes I forgot myself.
For sure, the bravery of his grief did put me
Into a towering passion.
Yet, by the image of my cause, I see
The portraiture of his; I'll court his favors.

Enter OSRIC.[150]

OSRIC
Your lordship is right welcome back to Denmark.

HAMLET
I humbly thank you, sir. Dost know this water-fly?

---

[149] In the original text, Hamlet also recounts the devious means by which he dispatches R&G to their deaths.
[150] As we approach the last turn of the play, Shakespeare introduces the very odd character, Osric. In the much longer original scene, Hamlet runs circles around the pompous courtier. Despite the loss of an extended gag involving Osric's hat, our cut maintains the oddball humor, and quickly gets us to the final set piece. Another lord follows Osric in with more messages from the royals, but we lose nothing but more formality in the excision.
151

HORATIO
No, my good lord.

HAMLET
Thy state is the more gracious; for 'tis a vice to
know him.

OSRIC
Sweet lord, if your lordship were at leisure, I
should impart a thing to you from his majesty.

HAMLET
I will receive it, sir, with all diligence of
spirit.

OSRIC
My lord, his
majesty bade me signify to you that he has laid a
great wager on your head: sir, this is the matter,–
Sir, here is newly come to court Laertes; believe
me, an absolute gentleman, full of most excellent
differences, of very soft society and great showing:
indeed, to speak feelingly of him, he is the card or
calendar of gentry, for you shall find in him the
continent of what part a gentleman would see.

HAMLET
I take him to be a soul of great article;
What imports the nomination of this gentleman?

OSRIC
Of Laertes?

HAMLET
Of him, sir.

OSRIC
You are not ignorant of what excellence Laertes is.

HAMLET
I dare not confess that, lest I should compare with
him in excellence; but, to know a man well, were to
know himself.

OSRIC
I mean, sir, for his weapon;
he's unfellowed.

HAMLET
What's his weapon?

OSRIC
Rapier and dagger.

HAMLET
That's two of his weapons: but, well.

OSRIC
The king, sir, hath wagered with him six Barbary
horses: against the which he has imponed, as I take
it, six French rapiers.

HAMLET
Why is this 'imponed,' as you call it?

OSRIC
The king, sir, hath laid, that in a dozen passes
between yourself and him, he shall not exceed you
three hits: and it would come to immediate trial, if your lordship
would vouchsafe the answer.

HAMLET
How if I answer 'no'?

OSRIC
I mean, my lord–

HAMLET
–Sir, if it please his majesty, let the foils be brought;
the gentleman willing and the king hold his purpose,
I will win for him an I can;
if not, I will gain nothing but my shame and the odd hits.

OSRIC
Shall I re-deliver you e'en so?

HAMLET
I am constant to my purpose; they follow the king's
Pleasure.

OSRIC
The queen desires you to use some gentle
entertainment to Laertes before you fall to play.

HAMLET
She well instructs me.

OSRIC
I commend my duty to your lordship.

Exit OSRIC.

HORATIO
You will lose this wager, my lord.

HAMLET
I do not think so: since he went into France, I
have been in continual practice: I shall win at the
odds. But thou wouldst not think how ill all's here
about my heart; but it is no matter.

HORATIO
Nay, good my lord–

HAMLET
It is but foolery.

HORATIO
If your mind dislike any thing, obey it. I will
forestall their repair hither, and say you are not
fit.

HAMLET
Not a whit, we defy augury: there's a special
providence in the fall of a sparrow. If it be now,
'tis not to come; if it be not to come, it will be
now; if it be not now, yet it will come: the
readiness is all. Since no man has aught of what he
leaves, what is't to leave betimes? Let be.

Enter CLAUDIUS, GERTRUDE, LAERTES, and OSRIC.

CLAUDIUS
Come, Hamlet, come, and take this hand from me.

CLAUDIUS puts LAERTES' hand into HAMLET's.

HAMLET
Give me your pardon, sir: I've done you wrong;
But pardon't, as you are a gentleman.
What I have done,
I here proclaim was madness.
If Hamlet from himself be ta'en away,
Then Hamlet does it not, Hamlet denies it.
His madness is poor Hamlet's enemy.
Sir, in this audience,
Let my disclaiming from a purposed evil
Free me in your most generous thoughts.

LAERTES
I do receive your offer'd love like love,
And will not wrong it.

HAMLET
I embrace it freely;
Give us the foils.

LAERTES
Come, one for me.

HAMLET
I'll be your foil, Laertes: in mine ignorance
Your skill shall, like a star i' the darkest night,
Stick fiery off indeed.

LAERTES
You mock me, sir.

HAMLET
No, by this hand.

CLAUDIUS
Cousin Hamlet,
You know the wager?

HAMLET
Very well, my lord
Your grace hath laid the odds o' the weaker side.

CLAUDIUS
I do not fear it; I have seen you both.

LAERTES
This is too heavy, let me see another.

HAMLET
This likes me well.

CLAUDIUS
If Hamlet give the first or second hit,
The king shall drink to Hamlet's better breath;
And in the cup a union shall he throw,
Richer than that which four successive kings
In Denmark's crown have worn.
Come, begin:

HAMLET
Come, sir.

LAERTES
Come, my lord.

They play.

HAMLET
One!

LAERTES
No!

HAMLET
Judgment.

OSRIC
A hit, a very palpable hit.

LAERTES
Well; again.

CLAUDIUS
Stay! Hamlet, this pearl is thine;
Here's to thy health.
[*Drinks, then drops the pearl in the cup*]
Give him the cup.

HAMLET
I'll play this bout first; set it by awhile. Come.
They play.

HAMLET
Another hit; what say you?

LAERTES
A touch, a touch, I do confess.

CLAUDIUS
Our son shall win.

GERTRUDE
The queen carouses to thy fortune, Hamlet.

CLAUDIUS
Gertrude! Do not drink.

GERTRUDE
I will, my lord; I pray you, pardon me.[158]

LAERTES
My lord, I'll hit him now.

CLAUDIUS
I do not think't.

HAMLET
Come, for the third, Laertes: you but dally;
I pray you, pass with your best violence;
I am afeard you make a wanton of me–

LAERTES wounds HAMLET; then in scuffling, they change rapiers...

CLAUDIUS
Part them; they are incensed.

...and HAMLET wounds LAERTES. GERTRUDE falls.

OSRIC
Look to the queen there, ho!

HORATIO
They bleed on both sides. How is it, my lord?

---

[158] Audiences invariably gasped when Gertrude drank the poison. Her playful public defiance, a reassertion of control paired with the tragic irony of committing the poisoned chalice to her own lips, made this a fun line to play.
159

OSRIC
How is't, Laertes?

LAERTES
I am justly kill'd with mine own treachery.

HAMLET
How does the queen?

CLAUDIUS
She swoons to see them bleed.

GERTRUDE
No, no, the drink, the drink,–O my dear Hamlet,–
The drink, the drink! I am poison'd.

Dies.

HAMLET
O villany! Ho! let the door be lock'd:
Treachery! Seek it out.

Exit OSRIC.

LAERTES
It is here, Hamlet: Hamlet, thou art slain;
The treacherous instrument is in thy hand,
Unbated and envenom'd: the foul practise
Hath turn'd itself on me.
It is the king, the king's to blame.

HAMLET
Then, venom, to thy work.

HAMLET stabs CLAUDIUS.[160]

---

[160] In a reversal of our staging of the opening scene, Hamlet stands on the upper platform, as Claudius looks up in horror. In our production Hamlet now takes his mimed sword and hurls it—javelin like—at Claudius who, skewered, falls to his knees.

161

CLAUDIUS
O, yet defend me, friends![162]

HAMLET
Here, thou incestuous, murderous, damned Dane,[163]
Drink off this poison. Is thy union here?
Follow my mother![164]

CLAUDIUS dies.

LAERTES
Exchange forgiveness with me, noble Hamlet:
Mine and my father's death come not on thee,
Nor thine on me.

Dies.

HAMLET
Heaven make thee free of it. I follow thee.
I am dead, Horatio. Wretched queen, adieu!
Had I but time–as this fell sergeant, death,[165]
Is strict in his arrest–O, I could tell you—
But let it be. Horatio, I am dead;[166]

---

[162] In the original text Claudius also cries out "I am but hurt." I lobbied hard for its inclusion, but with the damage done him by the sword through the heart, it would have been too crude of a punch line.
[163] Hamlet picks up our production's mimed cup, and pours it down Claudius' throat.
[164] Hamlet throws the mimed glass at the stage left wall, causing the Gravedigger seated near there to turn out of the way.
[165] In the original text, Hamlet addresses the audience during this death speech as his "wonder wounded hearers."
[166] Shakespeare's text has a realistic messiness: note the frequent enjambment and asides in this speech. We then mixed Hamlet's dying lines with Horatio's famous responses to continue this effect.
167

Thou livest;
O good Horatio, what a wounded name,
shall live behind me!
If thou didst ever hold me in thy heart
Then in this harsh world draw thy breath in pain
To tell my story.

HORATIO
Now cracks a noble heart.

HAMLET
O, I die, Horatio;
The potent poison–

HORATIO
Good night sweet prince;

HAMLET
–quite o'er-crows my spirit.

HORATIO
And flights of angels sing thee to thy rest![168]

HAMLET
So tell.

HORATIO
I will speak:
Of carnal, bloody, and unnatural acts,
Of accidental judgments, casual slaughters,
Of deaths put on by cunning and forced cause,
And, in this upshot, purposes mistook
Fall'n on the inventors' heads! All this can I
Truly deliver!

---

[168] Hamlet's dying lines and Horatio's famous responses have been interspersed to further add to the realistic messiness.
169

HAMLET
The rest is silence.

Dies.[170]

FIN[171]

---

[170] In our production a lengthy silence followed Hamlet's death, punctuated only by Horatio's shock and awe at the carnage all around.

[171] All in all, we doled out a faithful and crisp production of Hamlet. The whole evening, including the role drawing and intermission, usually lasted only two and a half hours. Forward driven, the show kept to the meat of the narrative while jettisoning the political and philosophical to create a funny and action-packed edition of this famous tragedy.

172

Bibliography

Adler, S. E. "At Shotgun Players, a Game of 'Hamlet' Roulette." *East Bay Express* (online as *Eastbayexpress.com*), 4 May 2016. http://www.eastbayexpress.com/oakland/at-shotgun-players-a-game-of-hamlet-roulette/Content?oid=4774076. Accessed 30 December 2016.

Bailes, S.J. *Performance Theatre and the Poetics of Failure.* Abingdon: Routledge, 2011.

Barmann, J. "Shotgun Players' *Hamlet* (With Roulette Casting) Is A Meta Dive Into Shakespeare's Most Lyrical Tragedy." *SFist.com*, 22 April 2016. http://sfist.com/2016/04/22/shotgun_players_hamlet_with_roulett.php. Accessed 30 December 2016.

Barthes, R. *The Pleasure of the Text.* Trans. Richard Miller. New York: Hill and Wang, 1975.

Bauer, C. "Hamlet cast scrambles, with mostly amazing results." *San Francisco Chronicle* (online as *Sfgate.com*), 25 April 2016. http://www.sfgate.com/performance/article/Shotgun-Players-mostly-win-at-Hamlet-7287992.php. Accessed 30 December 2016.

Bell, B. "Repertory Is The Answer." *Howlround.com*, 25 May 2014. http://howlround.com/repertory-is-the-answer. Accessed 3 March 2017.

Berkoff, S. *I Am Hamlet.* New York: Grove Weidenfeld, 1989.

Bieshke, M. "Madness, yet with method in't." *48Hills.com*, 2 May 2016. http://48hills.org/2016/05/02/madness-yet-method-ont/. Accessed 30 December 2017.

Boenisch, P. "Exposing The Classics: Michael Thalheimer's *Regie* Beyond the Text." *Contemporary Theatre Review*, Vol. 18, No. 1 (2008): 30-43.

Boenisch, P. & Ostermeier, T. *The Theatre of Thomas Ostermeier*. Abingdon: Routledge, 2016.

Bogart, A. & Landau, T. *The Viewpoints Book: A Practical Guide to Viewpoints and Composition*. New York: Theatre Communications Group, 2005.

Colin, N & Sachsenmaier, S. *Collaboration in Performance Practice – Premises, Workings and Failures*. Hampshire: Palgrave Macmillan, 2016.

Connema, R. "Hamlet." *Talkinbroadway.com*, April 2016. http://www.talkinbroadway.com/page/regional/sanfran/s1583.html. Accessd 30 December 2016.

Critchley, S. & Webster, J. *Stay, Illusion! The Hamlet Doctrine*. New York: Vintage Books, 2014.

Daniels, R. *D.I.Y. (Do. It. Yourself.)* Chichester: University of Chichester Theater Department, 2014.

Daniels, R. *D.I.Y. Too (Do. It. Yourself.)* Chichester: University of Chichester, 2015.

Darmon, E. & Vilpoux, C., directors. *Au Soleil meme la nuit*. Documentary video distributed by Bel Air Classiques, 2011.

Daw, K. "Long Live the Revolution: a review of HAMLET at Shotgun Players." *Shakespearestribe.com*, 30 April 2016. http://www.shakespearestribe.com/long-live-the-revolution-a-review-of-hamlet-at-shotgun-players/. Accessed 30 December 2016.

Deleuze, G. & Guattari, F. *Anti-Oedipus - Capitalism and Schizophrenia*. Trans. Robert Hurley, Helen R. Lane, and Mark Seem. Minneapolis: University of Minnesota Press, 1983.

Deleuze, G. & Guattari, F. *A Thousand Plateaus - Capitalism and Schizophrenia*. Trans. Brian Massumi. Minneapolis: University of Minnesota Press, 1987.

Dostoyevsky, F. *The Occasional Writings of Dostoyevsky*. Trans. David Magarshack. Evanston: Northwestern University Press, 1997.

Feingold, M. Untitled theatre review. *The Village Voice* (online as *villagevoice.com*) 11 October 2005. http://www.villagevoice.com/arts/theater-7137041. Accessed 19 January 2017.

Felton-Dansky, M. "Rising Director Lia Neugebauer's Adventurous Theater: 'I'm Listening for the Heartbeat of the Play'" *The Village Voice* (online as *villagevoice.com*) 11 January 2017. http://www.villagevoice.com/arts/rising-director-lila-neugebauers-adventurous-theater-im-listening-for-the-heartbeat-of-the-play-9547266. Accessed on 19 January 2017.

Fisher, M. *Capitalist Realism: Is There No Alternative?* Ropley: Zero Books, an imprint of John Hunt Publishing Ltd., 2009.

Freshwater, H. *Theatre & Audience*. Hampshire: Palgrave Macmillan, 2009.

Gilligan, C. *The Birth of Pleasure: A New Map of Love*. New York: Vintage Books Edition, 2003.

Gordon, M. & Law, A. *Meyerhold, Eisenstein and Biomechanics*. Jefferson: McFarland & Company, 1996.

Harvey, J. & A. Lavender. *Making Contemporary Theatre*, Manchester: Manchester University Press, 2010.

Hillman, M. "How We Stop Abuse In Theatre." *Bittergertrude.com*, 3 July 2016. https://bittergertrude.com/2016/07/03/how-we-stop-abuse-in-theatre/. Accessed 2 March 2017.

Hoghe, R. & Weiss, U. *Bandoneon: Working With Pina Bausch*. Trans. Penny Black. London: Oberon Books, 2016.

Kafka, F. *Letters to Friends, Family, and Editors*. Trans. Clara and Richard Winston. New York: Schocken, 1977.

Kalb, J. "Nothing To Do With Patience." *Theater*, Vol. 39, No. 1. (2009): 29-39

Kessel, M., director. *The Making of a Monologue: Robert Wilson's 'Hamlet'*. Documentary video distributed by Arts Alive!, 1995.

Kruger, C. "Hamlet at Shotgun Players." *Theatrestorm.com*, 27 April 2016. https://theatrestorm.com/2016/04/27/review-hamlet-at-shotgun-players/. Accessed 30 December 2016.

Kundera, M. *The Book of Laughter and Forgetting*. Trans. Michael Henry Heim. Harmondsworth: Penguin, 1980.

Lehmann, H. "Shakespeare's Grin. Remarks on World Theatre with Forced Entertainment". In: Judith Helmer and Florian Malzacher (Eds). *Not Even A Game Anymore*. Berlin: Alexander Verlag Berlin, 2004.

Lehmann, H. *Postdramatic Theatre*. Trans. Karen Jürs-Munby. Abingdon: Routledge, 2006.

Lessing, G. P. *Nathan The Wise, Minna von Barnheim, and Other Plays and Writings*. Trans. Anna Johanna Gode von Aesch. New York: Continuum Publishing Company, 1991.

McConachie, B. *Theatre & Mind*. Hampshire: Palgrave Macmillan, 2013.

Mendeal, E. S. "Shotgun Players' 'Hamlet' in Berkeley is ingenious." *Berkeleyside.com*, 10 May 2016. http://www.berkeleyside.com/2016/05/10/shotgun-players-hamlet-in-berkeley-is-ingenious/. Accessed 30 December 2016.

Miller, J. *Ariane Mnouchkine*. Abingdon: Routledge, 2007.

Miller, S. "Shotgun Players' *Hamlet* Plays Role Roulette." *Americantheatre. org*, 21 April 2016. https://www.americantheatre.org/2016/04/21/shotgun-players-hamlet-plays-role-roulette/ Accessed 30 December 2016.

Murray, C. "Re: HAMLET question." Message to Mark Jackson. 14 March 2017. Email.

Pennington, M. *Hamlet – A User's Guide*. New York: Proscenium Publishers, 2000.

Rancière, J. *The Emancipated Spectator*. Trans. Steve Corcoran. London: Verso, 2009.

Rancière, J. *The Hatred of Democracy*. Trans. Gregory Elliott. London: Verso, 2006.

Rancière, J. *The Ignorant Schoolmaster*. Trans. Kristin Ross. Redwood City: Stanford University Press, 1991.

Reynolds, E. "Hamlet." *Theatreeddys.blogspot.com*, 21 April 2016. http://theatreeddys.blogspot.com/2016/04/hamlet.html. Accessed 30 December 2016.

Reza, Y. *Art*. Trans. Christopher Hampton. New York: Dramatists Play Service, 1996.

Ridout, N. *Theatre & Ethics*. Hampshire: Palgrave Macmillan, 2009.

Sherman, J.F. *A Strange Proximity: stage presence, failure, and the ethics of attention*. Abingdon: Routledge, 2016.

Svich, C. *Innovation in Five Acts: Strategies for Theatre and Performance*. New York: Theatre Communications Group, 2015.

Tarkovsky, A. *Sculpting in Time*. Trans. Kitty Hunter-Blair. New York: Alfred A. Knopf, 1987.

Wilkins, J. "What Happens When You Cast *Hamlet* by Pulling Names out of Yorick's Skull?" *KQED Arts*, 28 April 2016. https://ww2.kqed.org/arts/2016/04/28/what-happens-when-you-cast-hamlet-by-pulling-names-out-of-yoricks-skull/. Accessed 13 November 2016.

Contributors

El Beh* is a San Francisco Bay Area based theatre artist, performer, musician, composer, and educator. She is a proud company member of Mugwumpin, detour dance, and Shotgun Players, and a co-host of *Drag Spectacular Spectacular.*

Kevin Clarke* is an actor, dancer, and nightlife performer who has worked in the Bay Area for twenty years. He also works as a graphic designer and visual artist.

Christine Crooke* is a costume designer and performance/installation artist based in Oakland, CA. Her work has been seen in the San Francisco Bay Area; Los Angeles; Marfa, Texas; and Berlin, Germany.

Patrick Dooley* started Shotgun Players in the basement of a pizza parlor with a few friends and a bucket of black paint in 1992. Since then he's directed over 40 plays by the likes of Jason Craig, Dave Malloy, Penelope Skinner, Caryl Churchill, and Tom Stoppard, among many others.

Mark Jackson* is a theatre maker based in the San Francisco Bay Area. His work in theatre, dance, and performance has been seen there as well as nationally, in the UK, Germany, and Japan.

Carolyn Jones is a Berkeley native and has been a theatregoer in the Bay Area, New York and London all her life. She currently serves on the Shotgun Players Board of Directors.

Nick Medina* is an actor, director, and educator located on the US West Coast. A University of California Berkeley alumnus, he started as an intern at Shotgun Players and worked his way to company member.

Clark Morgan is a playwright and embarrassment to his family. His work has been performed in Edinburgh, London, New York, San Francisco, and, curiously, Bologna, Italy. He lives in New York and drinks in San Francisco.

Chard Nelson is a software engineer, theatre enthusiast, and scuba diver who lives in Oakland, CA. He is a member of the Shotgun Players Board of Directors.

Sally Picciotto has a PhD in math and practices modern dance on a regular basis. She tends to get a little over-enthusiastic about things.

Cathleen Riddley is a Bay Area actor, singer, and ASL interpreter, who also works with incarcerated men in San Quentin.

K.M. Soehnlein is an author whose novels include *The World of Normal Boys*, *You Can Say You Knew Me When*, and *Robin and Ruby*. He teaches creative writing at the University of San Francisco.

John Wilkins is the theatre critic for KQED Arts. He was the Artistic Director of Last Planet Theatre for ten years and teaches in the Writing and Literature program at California College of the Arts.

Beth Wilmurt* is a performer, director, maker, and teacher whose work has been seen throughout the San Francisco Bay Area, in New York, and Berlin, Germany.

With thanks to Nikita Kadam*, Christine Murray, and Megan Trout* who also contributed. Special thanks to Ian Hornsby, Audrey Moyce, and Noelle Viñas for their keen eyes.

Personnel of the 2016 Shotgun Players production of *Hamlet*

The Cast
El Beh*
Kevin Clarke*
Nick Medina*
Cathleen Riddley
Megan Trout*
David Sinaiko
Beth Wilmurt*
Caleb Cabrera (understudy)

Production Team
Nina Ball*, Set Design
Heather Basarab, Lighting Design
Christine Crook*, Costume Design
Mark Jackson*, Director

Nikita Kadam*, Stage Manager
Heather Kelly-Laws*, Production Assistant
Devon LaBelle, Props Design
Alice Ruiz, Costume Assistant
Molly Stewart-Cohn, Master Electrician
Matt Stines, Sound Design

Shotgun Players Staff*

Shereen Adel, Marketing & Communications Director
Daniel Alley, Box Office Associate
Brady Brophy-Hilton, Development Associate
Patrick Dooley, Founding Artistic Director
Amy Langer, Box Office & Patron Services Manager
Liz Hitchcock Lisle, Managing Director
Joanie McBrien, Development Director & Dramaturge
Katherine McClennan & Marilyn Stanley, Accounting Associates
Trish Mulholland, Casting Director
Leigh Rondon-Davis, Make a Difference (MAD) Coordinator
Hanah Zahner-Isenberg, Production Manager

*Company member of The Shotgun Players.

More Plays From EXIT Press

The Chamber Plays of August Strindberg: translated by Paul Walsh
New translations by Yale drama professor Paul Walsh of the intimate chamber plays of August Strindberg, one of the major pioneers of naturalism in the theater: *The Ghost Sonata, Storm, Burned House, The Pelican,* and *The Black Glove.*

Three Plays by Mark Jackson
"Playwright/director Mark Jackson has made his name as a first-class theatrical provocateur. Gutsy showmanship, brainy literary instincts and laser-sharp satire mark his canon." — San Jose Mercury News
The second collection of plays by Mark Jackson includes three plays based on incredible historic events: *God's Plot, Mary Stuart,* and *Salomania.*

Songs of Hestia: Plays From the 2010 San Francisco Olympians Festival
Playwrights Nirmala Nataraj, Bennett Fisher, Stuart Eugene Bousel, Claire Rice, and Evelyn Jean Pine adapt some of Western culture's oldest stories, illuminating our present-day concerns with imagination, creativity, curiosity and passion.

Hilarity by Allison Page
A play about a girl named Cyd. She's not so nice. She's not so sober. She's not so happy. But she is funny. Cyd is a comic on the edge of destruction. Liz is the only person keeping her from pickling herself to death. Maybe she'll turn it all around, or maybe her drunken lies, hungover manipulations and impulsive violence will finally bury her. Does it matter if you're good at something, if you don't know how to be a person?

EXIT Press is the publishing division of EXIT Theatre, a San Francisco theater company founded in 1983.　　　　www.exitpress.org